The

VAN GOGH
SISTERS

Vincent van Gogh, *Parsonage Seen from the Back*, 1884. Pen, black chalk, heightened with white, 24 × 36 cm (9½ × 14⅛ in.). This drawing was owned by Lies van Gogh until 1928.

The

VAN GOGH
SISTERS

Willem-Jan Verlinden

Contents

Preface

It seems difficult to imagine now, but there was a time I did not know Vincent van Gogh had three younger sisters. I only discovered Anna, Elisabeth and Willemien van Gogh in the course of research I was undertaking for another book on Vincent and his London years. Quickly I became fascinated by these three women and their eventful lives. As I investigated them further, I was greatly rewarded, discovering hundreds of letters they had written and that were saved – letters to their parents, to each other, to uncles and aunts and to their now famous brothers. I also found dozens of other documents: school reports, certificates, diplomas, medical reports, photos, and of course drawings and paintings by Vincent, including the ones he had made for his youngest sister Willemien (Wil) and their mother.

I decided to undertake an extensive study of all this material – hidden away in archives, libraries, family photo albums and of course the collection of The Van Gogh Museum in Amsterdam – and to make the letters the backbone of a new narrative that would bring the three sisters out of their brother's shadow.

Most of these documents have survived out of the love of family and friends, and the habit of collecting letters, dated in order of receipt, with a ribbon around them. As Vincent became more and more famous over the course of the twentieth century, family members and museums were more careful to preserve everything they had on him, and started to deliberately collect things.

There is of course Vincent himself as well, who depicts his relatives in letters, drawings and paintings. He drew and painted not only his mother and Willemien, but also the houses they lived in, the churches his father preached in, the gardens and courtyards they played in and the nature surrounding them in the villages where they lived as a family, their home base in the North Brabant period of their joint history.

In 2016 my book on the Van Gogh sisters was published in Dutch. This book, and all the sisters' letters, could only be read in that language until Thames & Hudson decided to publish it in English. And now here it is, in your hands: a book in English about the lives of Vincent van Gogh's sisters, based in large part on their letters.

After the Dutch edition was published, I became acquainted with people who had known Vincent's sisters, as well as some of their descendants, all of whom were kind enough to grant me access to personal documents and photographs of their great-great-grandmothers or their relatives' acquaintances. And as a result you are holding a unique document, containing letters that have rarely, or never before, been published in English or in any other language, interspersed with photographs of the Van Goghs from family archives that have never been seen by anyone outside the immediate family circle.

I hope that Vincent's sisters become as dear to you as they have become to me – even though Vincent himself occasionally could not stand them. Because indeed, you not only get to know the sisters, but of course you also learn much more about Vincent and the rest of the Van Gogh family, through their own words.

CHAPTER 1

It Was Terrible.
I Shall Never Forget That Night

Nuenen, 1885–1886

In 1885, the Protestant Van Gogh family was living in the village of Nuenen, in the Dutch province of North Brabant. On Thursday 26 March that year, Reverend Theodorus (Dorus) van Gogh, father of Vincent van Gogh and his five siblings, arrived home after a long journey across the heathland and collapsed at the parsonage doorstep. The family's servant was just able to catch the minister as he fell, and word was sent to his youngest daughter, Willemien, who was visiting neighbours. She ran home and attempted to resuscitate her father, but it was too late: Dorus van Gogh, known as Pa to his children, had died, aged sixty-three.[1] Uncle Johannes van Gogh and Aunt Wilhelmine Stricker-Carbentus, who met coincidentally on the train to Eindhoven, were the first to come to the house and assist the family.[2]

The Protestant reverend was buried in the Tomakker general cemetery, at the foot of Nuenen's old tower, on 30 March 1885. The burial site could be located from a distance because of this tower, also visible from the garden of the parsonage. Vincent made a drawing

Dorus van Gogh. Date and photographer unknown.

8

Vincent van Gogh, *Parsonage at Nuenen*, 1885. Oil on canvas, 33.2 × 43 cm (13 × 17 in.).

of just this angle with pencil, pen and ink in March 1884 (see pl. III). In a letter to his colleague and friend Anthon van Rappard he described the woman in the composition as a black fairytale in the form of a splotch, rather than as an example of the human body worthy of imitation.[3] The date of Dorus's funeral, 30 March, held great significance for the family: not only was it the date of Vincent's birthday in 1853, but also of the family's first son, also named Vincent, who had been stillborn in 1852.[4]

Dorus's sudden passing escalated a tension that had been smouldering in the family for years. Vincent, approaching his thirty-second birthday when his father died and still living in the family home, had become more and more of a nuisance to his parents. His eccentric habits and occasional outright belligerence were an embarrassment to Dorus, whose authority over his flock depended in part on his family's comportment. Not long after the funeral, Anna, the eldest of the Van Gogh sisters, and Vincent had an explosive argument over Vincent's continued presence at the family home, which she and her siblings felt threatened not only his mother's well-being but also the family's standing in the village – just as he had their father's.[5] It was this confrontation that provoked Vincent to leave his home, and the Netherlands, for good. By the end of the year he moved to Antwerp, and from there travelled to France to pursue his dream of becoming a painter.

His sister Willemien, known as Wil, was just twenty-three years old when she found her father dead at the family home. She was a caring young woman who was close to her siblings and mother (who the children called Moe, pronounced 'moo'). While her older brothers and sisters each left home in their turn, Willemien stayed with Moe to help look after the household, and moved with her to the town of Breda after Pa's death. Dorus had grown up there; his father, Vincent, had been minister at the Grote Kerk (Main Church) and pastor at the Koninklijke Militaire Academie (Royal Military Academy). Moe and Willemien lived in Breda for only a few years before moving to the university town of Leiden, where Anna lived with her husband and daughters.

Willemien was to make very different life choices from her sisters Anna and Elisabeth (Lies): she never married or had children, and pursued independence. In Leiden she found work as a teacher of scripture and as a nurse – caring for the poor, the weak and the elderly, as she had always done. In doing so, she was exploiting the limited employment opportunities available to women. Social work – education, caring and nursing – was the only sector in the Netherlands in the second half of the nineteenth century that offered paid work to women from the upper middle class, to which the Van Gogh family belonged. Willemien became a committed participant in the first wave of Dutch feminism, travelling more and more to The Hague and Amsterdam, where as well as calling on family she visited friends, who often shared the same background and were, like her, beginning to question the position of women in society. Their discussions and initiatives were fuelled by similar movements in the United Kingdom, France and the United States. These women became increasingly organized; their activities expanded over the decades and focused on securing equal rights for women, such as female legal emancipation, women's suffrage, and access to education – including to universities – and paid work.

LEFT Vincent van Gogh, *Willemina Jacoba ('Willemien') van Gogh*, 1881.
Pencil and traces of charcoal on laid paper, 41.4 × 26.8 cm (16¼ × 10½ in.).
RIGHT Anna van Houten-van Gogh, 1878. Photographed by J.F. Rienks.

Vincent and Willemien were both 'different' – different from their sisters Anna and Lies, and from their brothers Theo and Cornelis (Cor) – in their rejection of society's prevailing norms. Their similarity to each other could be seen from an early age, in the difficulties they both experienced at school, and which continued into later life. They were both socially engaged and very creative, and shared a deep interest in religion, art and literature. They both remained unmarried and never had children, and struggled with their mental health, which they discussed openly with each other. Willemien probably also gradually discovered that she was different in her sexuality.[6] They were above all willing to fight for ideals that were perhaps a little too far ahead of their time, and refused to conform to the expectations of those around them. Pa and Moe were socially minded with strong artistic leanings, and ensured that their children received a broad education. Thus, rather than hiding their differences, Vincent and Wil each became pioneers in their own distinct way – Vincent with his progressive art, and Wil with her social causes.

Yet the course of their lives was deeply influenced by these dramatic events: the death of their father Dorus and the subsequent argument between Vincent and Anna. Willemien was haunted by the image of her dying father. She wrote to her friend Line Kruysse that Pa had left the house healthy and well in the morning, but collapsed lifeless in the doorway when he returned that evening: 'It was terrible. I shall never forget that night....I hope that you will be preserved from ever experiencing something like that.' In the same letter she reflected on her brother Vincent, commenting that she thought he had been embittered by his fight with her eldest sister, and expressing her fears of the conflict's impact on the family.[7]

Anna's anger was the outcome of a long-standing discord between Vincent and his father. In 1881, when the family was living in the village of Etten, Vincent had refused to attend church at Christmas, undermining Dorus's authority as the minister of the Dutch Reformed church.[8] Vincent frequently disregarded his father's wishes in the family home as well, often in the presence of his siblings. For his part, Vincent felt that his father did not take his ambitions – first to become a minister or an evangelist, and later a good artist – seriously. Yet Vincent was willing to stand up for himself, for a new life worth striving for.[9] Father and son quarrelled frequently; the other family members regularly wrote to each other on the subject. Yet two of the most important tenets of Dorus's upbringing of his children were unity and the desire for togetherness, so Vincent was deeply dismayed when Anna reproached him for arguing so much with Pa and alleged that he was a burden on Moe. He was also hurt that none of his other siblings had stood up for him, although Theo had also previously tried to encourage Vincent to leave home. Vincent seems to have been especially disappointed in Willemien. He had always considered her an ally, but the aftermath of the incident had abruptly put paid to that assumption. For Wil, as for the other siblings, her mother's well-being was more important than her eldest brother's ability to stay in the parsonage after Pa's sudden death. For a time, Vincent did not even want to see her.[10]

Vincent moved into the attic above the studio he had for a time been renting from the Catholic sacristan Schafrat in the centre of Nuenen. On 6 April 1885 he explained to Theo that it was not for his convenience that he lived there, but to diminish the chance of future accusations, especially from Anna: 'however absurd those reproaches were and her unfounded presumptions about things that are still in the future – she hasn't told me she takes them back. Well – you understand how I simply shrug my shoulders at such things – and anyway, I increasingly let people think of me just exactly what they will, and say and do too, if need be. But consequently I have no choice – with a beginning like that, one has to take steps to prevent all that sort of thing in the future. So I'm absolutely decided'.[11]

Vincent thought there was also a practical reason that his sisters had wanted him to leave the parsonage; Moe could take in a lodger and thus generate some extra income. Living in the parsonage was simply too expensive for her.[12] Two months later he was still very disgruntled about the events after Pa's death and the settlement of his estate, writing to Theo that he was disappointed it was settled entirely in his mother's name. He also defended himself for the little time he spent with his mother, writing that visiting 'Occasionally, from time to time, is sufficient. I find them at home (I know – contrary to your opinion, and contrary to their own opinion) very far, very far from sincere'.[13] It was not Moe, but his sisters who were on the receiving end of his criticism: 'since I foresee that the characters of the 3 sisters (all three) will get worse not better with time'.[14] Vincent wrote that they irritated him, and that he found them downright unpleasant; moreover he complained that his sisters did not understand him, and did not *want* to understand him. Almost forty years later, in 1923, Anna recalled the awkward situation she had found in the parsonage on arriving in Nuenen the summer after the death of their father, when she, her two daughters and a nanny had stayed with Moe: '[Vincent] indulged all his desires and did not spare anything or anyone. How Pa must have suffered. Even though I admire his art, I despise his person.'[15]

Vincent decided not much later to leave Nuenen – and thus Moe and Willemien – permanently. Staying in the village had become untenable for him, not only because of the awkward situation created by his quarrels with his father and with Anna, but also because of his dealings with the mostly Catholic villagers who modelled for him – often paid for with money from Theo. His family felt that such behaviour was unbecoming for a pastor's son, and the Catholic community shunned him when it became widely known that his model Dien de Groot, with whom he had been having an affair for some time, had fallen pregnant. All suspicion was directed at him, however unfairly; Vincent turned out not to be the father.[16] Nonetheless he left Nuenen on 23 November 1885 and went by train to Antwerp, the city where famous artists such as Peter Paul Rubens, Jacob Jordaens and Anthony van Dyck had made their name. He would never return to his beloved Brabant. In Antwerp he enrolled in the art academy's life drawing classes, and hoped to earn a living painting landscapes, cityscapes and portraits, selling them to tourists and day trippers.[17]

Vincent's belongings in the Nuenen studio and the works he had completed there were packed into boxes and stored in the chicken coop behind the Van Goghs' home. After Dorus's death, Moe had received permission from the Reformed congregation to stay at the parsonage for just one year, until a new minister took office.[18] Although Theo sent Vincent several letters from Paris – where he had settled as an art dealer for the firm Goupil & Co. – entreating him to return to Nuenen and help their mother with the preparations for the upcoming move to Breda, Vincent refused. Instead he travelled to Paris to join his brother.

Moe and the sisters would never see Vincent again.

CHAPTER 2

Undisturbed Married Felicity

The Hague, Breda, Zundert, 1851 and earlier

Anna Carbentus, the later Moe van Gogh, was born on 10 September 1819 in The Hague. The city, which was the monarch's residence and the seat of government, was home to 70,000 of the country's 5.5 million citizens, including the court – noblemen and dignitaries serving the king – and the civil servants who administered governmental departments. Anna's father was a royal bookbinder, as was Gerrit, one of her younger brothers. Known unofficially as the United Kingdom of the Netherlands, the kingdom included what are now the Netherlands and Belgium, and the Grand Duchy of Luxembourg in a personal union under the Dutch Crown with King William III as its reigning monarch.

The history of the Carbentus family had been chronicled by various family members since 1740, and the tradition continued well into the nineteenth century. The handwritten history was carefully passed on from generation to generation.[1] Anna's parents, Willem and Anna Cornelia Carbentus, had nine children, but their youngest daughter, Gerarda, died in 1832, aged only three-and-a-half months. This was not unusual; in the first half of the nineteenth century, almost a third of all children born in the Netherlands died in infancy. Anna Cornelia was forty years old at the time, and would not have any more children.

Anna Carbentus was Willem Gerrit Carbentus and Anna Cornelia Carbentus-van der Gaag's third daughter. Her eldest sister, Wilhelmine, married the theologian and clergyman Johannes Paulus Stricker, who served at the Amstelkerk (Amstel Church) in the centre of Amsterdam for twenty-eight years. The second oldest of the sisters, Clara, never married, because of a condition that the Carbentus family preferred to conceal. In the terminology of 1850, Clara was 'epileptic', a diagnosis that referred to a range of emotional and mental disorders. Social norms dictated that Clara was to live in isolation. Her family looked after her, in the manner that was customary for the 'neurotic' relatives of more affluent people. The asylums where psychiatric patients were detained at the time were considered very disagreeable and stigmatizing for both patients and their families. The first modern psychiatric clinic in the Netherlands only opened in 1849. Clara lived with a companion, Anna Paulina Lettow, who was employed to take care of her, at 60 Noordeinde, between the royal palace and parliament, until she died in 1866, at the age of forty-eight.

While the circumstances of Clara's death were omitted from the Carbentus chronicle, Anna van Gogh-Carbentus would learn from it that her youngest brother, Johannes, committed suicide at the age of forty-seven.[2] And her father, Willem, was explicitly referred to as 'mentally ill'. The chronicle records his death on 20 August 1845 in some detail: 'too much excitement, which was followed by spasm, he was also frothing from his mouth, this was followed by death.' The Register

Office recorded the cause of death as pasteurellosis, or 'snuffle disease', but this condition only occurs in cattle and is nowadays not thought to be transmissible to humans, so the actual cause of death remains unclear. One of Willem's three brothers wrote in the family chronicle that his dear brother died of a 'nervous disease after a period of 11 days'.[3] This succession of psychological problems in her father, brother and sister gave Anna Carbentus lifelong anxiety about her and her children's mental state.[4]

Anna van Gogh-Carbentus ('Moe').
Date and photographer unknown.

Anna had a strong bond with her younger sister Cornelia. They shared a passion for drawing and watercolours, and a friendship with the Van de Sande Bakhuyzen family in the years they both lived in The Hague. Hendrik van de Sande Bakhuyzen, a well-known landscape painter, gave them and two of own his children drawing and painting lessons. Cornelie and Anna very often chose bouquets, flower arrangements and plants as their subjects, and Anna continued to paint into adulthood.[5] Painting watercolours was mainly fashionable as a suitable indoor pastime for ladies of up-and-coming families, with plants and flowers becoming an integral part of the interior. Special furniture was even designed for them, such as plant tables and étagères.[6] It is not possible to ascertain whether Anna received any schooling that might have enabled her to support herself financially, but it is unlikely. Upper-middle-class women in the Netherlands in the middle of the nineteenth century had very limited opportunities for paid work. Like most girls of her class, Anna learnt to knit at a young age, and she later taught her daughters and other young women in sewing and knitting classes that she set up. The family chronicle remarks upon the enormous speed with which she knitted. Speed was a characteristic of Anna Carbentus's way of doing things, including letter writing. She wrote scores of letters, which also necessitated many responses. Her writing was sloppy and hurried, and her syntax jumbled – she regularly used abbreviations, even making up her own, and often pursued tangents that sometimes had nothing to do with the original subject of the letter.[7]

The Carbentus family were not the only ones to keep a written history. The Van Gogh family also had a chronicler – Vincent's Aunt Mietje. She was Dorus's youngest sister, born in 1831 in Breda. Aunt Mietje described the family's history as thoroughly as possible in three blue notebooks, arranged by date and titled *Aanteekeningen over de familie Van Gogh door tante Mietje* (Notes about the Van Gogh family by Aunt Mietje). She briefly described the lives of her parents' and grandparents' generations, giving more detailed commentary from 1850, when she went to live with her brother Dorus at the parsonage in Zundert and helped run the yet unmarried reverend's household. The chronicle continues up to 1900, when Aunt Mietje was living in Leiden. She wrote about matters

Maria Johanna van Gogh (Aunt Mietje),
before 1911. Photographed by P.W. Roemer.

of national importance: the advent of the telegraph and the postage stamp; the new Constitution of 1848; the commotion surrounding the publication of *Max Havelaar* (the controversial novel by the Dutch writer Multatuli, pseudonym of Eduard Douwes Dekker, in which the protagonist campaigns against corruption in the Dutch East Indies) in 1860; the royal family; national cholera epidemics; and various agricultural crises. She also reported significant international news stories, including the riots in Paris around 1850, the Franco–Prussian War of 1870–1871 and the Aceh War of 1873–1914. She devoted attention to small things with far-reaching personal consequences, such as the schooling, work and health of her family and acquaintances, as well as aspects of their everyday lives and life events, such as moving house. She also used a 'ladies' almanac' given to her by her elder sister Truitje in 1853 to record births, deaths and marriages. In the *Notes*, Aunt Mietje usually used the third person, referring to herself only by the initial 'M.'. She continued writing the *Notes* until she was almost seventy years old, and recorded the family history in other ways too. She composed a separate text for Sara Maria van Houten, the eldest daughter of Vincent's sister Anna, describing the family of Pa and Moe van Gogh and their children, titled *Voor Saar* (For Sara), and also wrote *Ons huis te Breda* (Our House in Breda), a document in which she described her childhood in the city of that name.

Like the Carbentus family, the Van Goghs had been living in The Hague for generations. They were part of the upper middle class – 'the second highest rank on the social ladder', as Aunt Mietje wrote almost a century and a half later.[8] Their ancestors, from the German border town of Goch, settled in the Dutch Republic in the seventeenth century. The name, spelt Van Goch, is even mentioned in the sixteenth century. A long period of peace and security made the Low Countries, as the Netherlands and Belgium were also known, attractive to many Germans and other Europeans, and large numbers of Protestants from surrounding countries migrated to Dutch cities between 1600 and 1900. A gold-threadmaker named David van Gogh settled in The Hague at the beginning of the eighteenth century. He was the start of the branch of the family that would stay in The Hague for more than 250 years.

Dorus van Gogh, however, was not born in The Hague, but in Benschop in the Lopikerwaard – a drained polder containing several small villages to the west of the city of Utrecht – on 8 February 1822. His father, Vincent, had a parish there after studying theology in Leiden and starting his career as a minister in the village of Ochten, on the Waal river in the Betuwe, where fruit trees dominate the landscape. Dorus did not grow up in Benschop, but moved as an infant to Breda, a fortress and garrison city in the predominantly Catholic province of North Brabant, when his father accepted a new appointment as a minister there, after failing to get a position in his native city of The Hague because of his poor health. The provinces of North Brabant and Limburg, located below the great rivers Rhine, Meuse and Waal, were predominantly Roman Catholic, in contrast to the territories above these rivers, which were predominantly Protestant or secular. Reverend Vincent van Gogh was confirmed in his office at the Grote Kerk (Main Church) in Breda on

Sara Maria van Houten, 5 December 1880. Photographed by J. Goedeljee.

3 November 1822. This imposing church has an enormous tower and has been Protestant since 1637. Built as a Catholic place of worship, it is also the final resting place of the counts of Nassau, the ancestors of the Dutch royal family. Despite the church's magnitude and historical significance, it had only a small congregation – more than 90 per cent of Breda's population of 10,000 was Catholic.

Reverend Vincent van Gogh was thus the first Van Gogh to live in the province of North Brabant. With five daughters and six sons to feed, he was not a wealthy man. In addition, the spectre of the Belgian Revolt – the bourgeois revolution in 1830 against the authoritarian Dutch King Willem I, which led to the creation of Belgium in what had been the south of the United Kingdom of the Netherlands – was a constant concern for this Protestant family in Catholic Breda. The Protestants feared that Brabant would join the new kingdom of Belgium. The Catholic population was well prepared for any struggle, keeping lists of Protestant targets, such as preachers' homes and prominent Protestants, who could be attacked first in the event of any conflict. As a precaution, Reverend Vincent van Gogh temporarily sent his wife and children to stay with family in the large port city of Rotterdam, located in Protestant Holland, above the rivers Rhine, Meuse and Waal, and far from the Belgians. Some travelled on to family in The Hague, even further north, and further from the turmoil. The pastor stayed behind in Breda with his eldest son Hendrik, who had a bookshop

Reverend Vincent van Gogh, before 1874. Photographed by Dirk Le Grand.

in Rotterdam. The other family members only returned to Breda when Brabant was definitively seceded to the Netherlands.[9]

Dorus van Gogh, the seventh child, went to Latin school, a type of grammar school found throughout Europe where boys were prepared for religious office or university study. At that time Latin was the language of science, and all lectures were given in this language. Dorus rose at five o'clock every morning to study, and his diligence reaped rewards; at the end of his schooling he was the best student of his year. He moved to Utrecht in 1840 to study theology with a scholarship from the university. Dorus soon grew accustomed to his new circumstances; he enjoyed his studies, found his student corps hazing tolerable – it was the oldest student association in Utrecht, of which more than half of all young men studying in the city were members – and enjoyed having his own room. He followed his lectures in Latin. In addition to compulsory theology courses, both law and religious studies students were required to pass a first-year examination in philosophy and literature. In this way the university impressed on students the importance of developing broad erudition.

Dorus built a network of high-level friends while in Utrecht, to which he would repeatedly have recourse later in life. He developed an intense friendship with fellow theologian Theodorus van Baumhoven. The men frequently studied together, and Dorus often visited the Van Baumhoven family; Aunt Mietje thought that her brother's 'cleanliness and decency' made a good impression.[10] Dorus was the only son to follow in his father's footsteps and become a reverend. His brothers became art dealers and booksellers, or joined the navy. None of them remained in North Brabant, instead moving above the great rivers, to the cities of Rotterdam, The Hague, Dordrecht and Amsterdam. Some of them would, however, return to the south of the country at the end of their working lives.[11]

Dorus struggled to find a permanent appointment as a minister after graduating. He was known as 'the handsome reverend' for his noble face and fine features, yet he did not possess great talent as a preacher. He stumbled over his words, and lacked charisma. Aunt Mietje wrote that the presence of too many other, more capable graduate theology students impeded his quest for a permanent appointment.[12] Dorus's prospects were not improved by the conflict that arose in the Maatschappij van Welstand (Society of Well-Being) in these years. The organization, founded in 1822, sought to offer Protestant families a new livelihood in predominantly Catholic regions of the Netherlands by purchasing farms and surrounding farmland, which were then leased to these families for a below-market sum. The Society's efforts stemmed the decline in the number of Protestants in these areas, and sometimes even succeeded in increasing them. But several members of the Society rebelled against the board, in part because they deemed the policy results to be opaque and in part because they wanted to focus on sectors beyond agriculture, and help people on a more individual level.[13] The conflict was especially fierce in the district of Breda, where Dorus's father was a member of the board.[14]

Dorus's rather unenviable situation changed in 1848, when the twenty-six-year-old accepted a temporary position as auxiliary vicar under Reverend Aarnout Marinus Snouck Hurgronje in Middelburg, the capital of the province of Zeeland.[15] In 1849 he took up a permanent position in Zundert, a small rural municipality 14 km (8½ miles) from Breda, in North Brabant. The village had about 600 homes and 3,000 inhabitants, whose main livelihood was tree cultivation. Dorus's predecessor, Reverend Van der Burg, had been forced to resign due to long-term health problems. In accepting the post, Dorus followed in his father's footsteps as a Protestant minister in Catholic North Brabant. There had been Protestants in Zundert since the seventeenth century and the village had its first preacher in 1615; Dorus was the twenty-fifth minister in a line of Protestant pastors. They did not initially have their own church, but the States General – the parliament of the Dutch Republic in The Hague – allocated the village's Roman Catholic Church to the Protestants after the Peace of Munster in 1648.

Just over two centuries later, on 1 April 1849, Dorus van Gogh was confirmed as the Protestant church in Zundert's twenty-fifth minister by his father, who was still a minister in Breda. The ceremony took place in this small, sober, brick building without a tower. It was naturally a religious and ceremonial affair, but the father–son relationship gave it a familial and intimate aspect too. There were sixty-one guests in attendance, including family members, fellow ministers from the region, Protestant notables and Dorus's university friend Van Baumhoven, as well as the Catholic town mayor Van Beckhoven and other Catholics from the village (the latter were consistently denoted by Aunt Mietje in the *Notes* with 'rc' for 'Roman Catholic'). After the confirmation, there was coffee with bread, and later meat, Bundt cake, wine and tea in the parsonage. The local brass band, named *Nut en Vermaak* (Utility and Amusement), played a serenade in the afternoon 'as a signal of the rc population's

Dorus van Gogh, *c.* 1852. Photographer unknown.

good disposition'.[16] Aunt Mietje, who was, like Dorus, unmarried, moved in with him after his confirmation. She helped him run his household until his marriage. It was not uncommon at the time for unmarried sisters to live with their unmarried brothers.[17]

Marriage was the only way that women could move up in the social strata, and not end up depending on their families. Anna Carbentus and Reverend Dorus van Gogh became acquainted through Anna's youngest sister Cornelie, who was ten years Anna's junior. In March 1850 Cornelie announced her engagement to the art dealer Vincent van Gogh, known by family and friends as Cent. Cornelie's fiancé had a younger brother, Dorus, a good-looking minister in Zundert – a highly respectable vocation. More importantly, he was an eligible bachelor. A meeting was set up three months later. The Reverend Dorus van Gogh showed as much eagerness to come to an engagement as Anna Carbentus. They agreed to marry after several meetings, and the announcement was made shortly

Kloosterkerk and Lange Voorhout, The Hague, *c.* 1870. Photographer unknown.

afterwards. Anna was already thirty-two years old when she became engaged to Dorus, who was three years her junior, in The Hague on 5 July 1850.[18] People generally married later in life in the eighteenth and nineteenth centuries than in earlier times, and a relatively large proportion of people never even married at all. Typically, women married at the average age of twenty-seven; for men it was twenty-nine. The fear of becoming an old spinster would certainly have expedited Anna's decision.[19]

On 21 May 1851, Anna married the young Reverend Dorus Van Gogh in the Kloosterkerk, a former Augustinian church on Lange Voorhout. The Hague was the royal heart of the nation, and its large city villas exuded eminence and cleanliness: outsiders and particularly foreigners regularly noted in their observations how tremendously clean and shiny everything was. The ceremony was performed by the groom's father. A carriage was rented for the big day. The ride to church along the avenue, lined with linden trees, must have been crisp; Moe recorded that the maximum temperature was just thirteen degrees that day.[20] It was dry, but very humid. The route to the Kloosterkerk church was decorated with garlands of leafy branches and blossom, and the young couple's path was strewn with petals. The procession probably went from Anna's parental home to the distinguished Prinsegracht (Canal of the Princes) via the Grote Marktstraat and the Spuistraat, on which her father Willem Carbentus's bookbindery was located. He had died in 1845, and the shop had since been taken over by her brother Gerrit. Her new brother-in-law Cent's art gallery was on the same street. The route continued from the Spuistraat past the Binnenhof – the seat of both houses of Parliament – and the Hofvijver alongside Gevangenpoort on the Buitenhof, then on to the Kneuterdijk, which was graced by the elegant city palace where King Willem II had lived, and the route continued to the Kloosterkerk on the Lange Voorhout. After the ceremony they went for a carriage ride through the Haagse Bos (Wood).[21]

Anna wrote about her wedding day in a document dated 20 March 1852. The occasion for recording her recollections was the imminent birth of their first child, and that the marriage had thus far been a happy one was clear: 'If we consider how much joy we have had together for over 1.5 years, we have so much to be thankful for, as we constantly looked into a clear sky, so that the days we wanted to keep in mind are almost entirely happy.'[22] The document contains a detailed account of the prelude to her marriage, the wedding day itself and the start of the couple's honeymoon. Though Anna devoted special attention to the flower arrangements, she did not reveal anything about her wedding dress. Considering contemporary fashion, she probably did not wear a veil and was (presumably) dressed in black. This was common attire for brides: most women married in a home-made black dress with a scarf that could later be reworn at other rituals and ceremonies. A black dress was also useful as it could be used to clothe the woman when she died; a white dress that was only worn once was simply too expensive. Dorus, like most urban Dutch grooms at the time, probably wore a suit: the fashion was black, with dark trousers, a formal black coat, a black top hat, a collar or bow, and gloves.[23]

Despite the festive nature of the day, it was not a solely happy occasion for the bride and groom. This was partly because of the absence of some family members, including Dorus's three unmarried sisters Antje, Truitje and Doortje van Gogh. Antje and Truitje had stayed in Breda to take care of Doortje, who had been taken ill. And a certain uncle Van Bemmel died just before the wedding day. Dorus had in fact been staying with him in the Hague when he fell suddenly and seriously ill, and had watched over his deathbed. Due to this unhappy coincidence of marriage and death, Anna's parental home on the Prinsegracht canal was decorated with festive foliage inside, but the shutters were closed as a sign of mourning. It made it difficult for the bride-to-be to enjoy all the attention, although the couple's family and friends tried to give them a complete wedding celebration, which traditionally lasted several days. In addition to the carriage ride to the church, the bridal couple was also given a reception prior to their wedding, probably at the bride's house, to which many family members and friends came. After the wedding ceremony, the young couple would have once more mounted a carriage and gone to the Haarlemmerhout, the wood in the city of Haarlem, popular as a retreat among the wealthy since the Dutch Golden Age in the seventeenth century. There Anna and Dorus spent 'unforgettable days in the gorgeous surroundings'.[24] The honeymoon gave them an opportunity to recover from the sadness and the festive commotion and realize that they had been 'reserved a happy fate'.[25] On Monday 26 May, the newlyweds started a journey across the whole country; they visited Dorus's brother Cor van Gogh, a bookseller in Amsterdam, as well as friends and colleagues of Dorus, and explored Utrecht, the city where he had studied. After their trip they travelled to Breda, where Reverend Vincent van Gogh and his eldest daughter Antje joined them in the carriage, accompanying them part of the way home. They parted company at Het Haagje (The Little Hedge; most likely Princenhage, a village near Breda).[26]

On arrival at the parsonage in Zundert, Anna and Dorus were welcomed warmly by members of the congregation, who had strewn flowers around the church and handed out pretty bouquets. The parsonage anteroom was decorated with greenery, and the text 'Peace be upon Your Arrival, your House and your Congregation' adorned the mantelpiece in beautiful letters.[27] Dorus did not come from a wealthy family, but Anna did not care about money: their mission to strengthen the congregation and increase the number of Protestants in Zundert was compensation enough. Yet the move from the grandeur of The Hague to a rustic village in deeply Catholic Brabant was a dramatic transition for her, even though she and her husband were, after all, village notables, along with the doctor, the mayor, the Catholic priest and the notary. For Anna, North Brabant felt strange and unfamiliar – she did not speak the dialect, nor readily understand local customs. Shrove Tuesday, the night marking the end of the carnival and introducing Lent, was celebrated exuberantly in the south of the Netherlands, and the annual fair on the village square must have appeared to her a spectacle of Brueghelian barbarism.

Although Anna enthusiastically followed her husband to his post, it must initially have felt as though she had travelled to a foreign land. However, both the marriage and the village proved to be propitious choices. Years later, their middle daughter, Lies, described her parents in her book *Vincent van Gogh: Persoonlijke herinneringen aangaande een kun-stenaar* (Vincent van Gogh: Personal Recollections Regarding an Artist), published in 1910: '[he] with finely chiselled features, set in silver locks, not suited to his age; she with less regular features and the wide-awake, alert look of deep-seeing eyes which her eldest son had inherited'.[28] She paints a picture of two dark figures in the lonely landscape around Zundert, occasionally pausing to continue a conversation that they had been having while walking, or to point out some or other natural beauty to one another. Neither of them was tall, according to Lies, but they walked upright and with purpose. The couple were still part of Zundert's collective memory years later: 'They are not forgotten, this honoured couple, in the small world in which they lived in undisturbed married felicity'.[29]

CHAPTER 3

Land of Desire

Zundert, 1851–1871

Anna fell pregnant soon after her arrival in Zundert, and gave birth to a son on 30 March 1852, whom she and her husband named Vincent. The child was stillborn. He was buried in the cemetery next to the Dutch Reformed church, and his grave marked with a stone inscribed with his name and a passage from the Gospel of Saint Luke: 'Suffer little children to come unto me, and forbid them not: for of such is the kingdom of God' (Luke 18:16).[1] Giving the baby a name and burying him set the Van Goghs apart from their Catholic neighbours, for well into the twentieth century Catholic doctrine proscribed the burial of unbaptized children on consecrated ground. For Dutch Protestants, conversely, burial was primarily a family affair and not dictated by the church. The minister was present at the home and in the cemetery, but primarily to assist the deceased and their family, not to represent the church. Anna seemed to recover relatively soon after the death of their first son, but Dorus became 'nursing ill'[2] and went to recuperate at his mother-in-law's home in The Hague.

Exactly one year later, on 30 March 1853, the second Vincent van Gogh was born. He was named Vincent Willem, after both of his grandfathers. Dorus van Gogh baptized his first surviving son on 24 April 1853 in the church's copper baptismal font, where his other five children would also subsequently be baptized – Anna in 1855, Theo in 1857, Lies in 1859, Wil in 1862 and Cor in 1867.[3] Moe might not have foreseen such a large family, considering her late marriage and stillborn first child, but throughout her letters it is clear that she saw her children as a great blessing.

As an adult Vincent mentioned his stillborn elder brother only once: in a letter of condolence to Hermanus Tersteeg, his former boss at Goupil & Co., the gallery in The Hague where he trained as an art dealer. Tersteeg had recently lost his daughter Marie. Vincent wrote how his father had found comfort in Laurence Louis Félix Bungener's *Trois jours de la vie d'un père: quelques pages intimes* (Three Days in the Life of a Father: A Few Intimate Pages). While he must have visited his deceased brother's grave on occasion, he never revealed his feelings for the brother he never knew in his letters.[4]

The old parsonage in which the Van Gogh children grew up was on a square in the centre of the village of Zundert, only a few dozen metres from the church where their father preached. It faced the neoclassical village hall designed by the architect Pierre Huijsers, which also served as a gendarmerie and prison. Nearby was the larger Saint Trudo Catholic church, named in honour of the seventh-century preacher from what is now Belgian Limburg, where he founded the town of Sint-Truiden. An inn called Het Wapen van Nassau (The Nassau Arms) attracted coaches from the Van Gend & Loos delivery company, which operated the Rotterdam–Antwerp–Brussels route. These stage coaches transported not only goods, but also travellers, including family and friends visiting the parsonage. The parsonage itself, an imposing house with an elegant entrance, was built at the beginning of the seventeenth century, when it was also used as a church. On the ground floor three rooms, all wallpapered and with pine floors, opened off a long corridor. The front room, facing the street, was the parlour and minister's office, but was also used for meetings, catechism, and coffee after the Sunday service. Reverend Van Gogh hung a reproduction of Jacob Jan van der Maaten's *Begrafenisstoet in het koren* (Funeral Procession in the Wheat Field) in his office. Van der Maaten, a famous landscape painter and forerunner of the The Hague School, was a pupil of Hendrik van de Sande Bakhuyzen, who had given Anna and the other Carbentus girls drawing lessons as children in The Hague.[5] Dorus referred to this image in a sermon at the funeral of his old friend Jacobus Lips on 16 August 1877, and talked about the resemblance of spiritual growth and human life as a cycle of sowing and harvesting (Mark 4: 26–29). Later Vincent would add other passages of the Bible and inscribe them in the passepartout of the lithograph, as well as some lines from a poem by H.W. Longfellow.[6]

The middle room was Dorus and Anna's bedroom, and the back room, looking onto the grounds and garden, was used as a dining and living room. This is where the children read and played. The kitchen, which was principally the housemaids' domain, was in an annex at the back of the house. The Van Gogh family almost always employed two staff: a maidservant for the housekeeping and a governess to take care of the children. Anna herself apparently did not spend much of her time cooking or washing; she mostly talked about other pursuits in her letters, such as gardening, the spring clean, sewing, and knitting. The family regularly employed Catholic girls in their years there, which was unlikely to have been appreciated in their own milieu. Yet there were few Protestant families in Zundert, so they were generally dependent on girls from Catholic homes. Behind the kitchen, next to a laundry room, was a shed that was used as a stable and to store fuel, among other things. The children slept in the attic, which also accommodated Dorus's study, the maidservant's room and, from 1862, the governess's room.[7]

Jacob Jan van der Maaten, *Funeral Procession in the Wheat Field* (detail), 1863. Lithograph, 26.1 × 33.6 cm (10¼ × 13¼ in.). Vincent van Gogh inscribed the print with quotes from the Bible and a poem by H.W. Longfellow.

Jac. van Faassen, after Ferdinand Reissig,
Parsonage of Zundert (detail), after 9 May 1900.

The garden behind the parsonage was maintained with great care by Moe, who adored nature and had a keen interest in botany. She consulted the famous gardening manual of the period, Jean-Baptiste Alphonse Karr's *Voyage autour de mon jardin* (Travel around my Garden; see pl. 11), published in 1845 and illustrated by various artists in its 1851 edition. She drew the garden she so loved in watercolours and sketches. A family album contains several sketches by her. One of the watercolours that has survived portrays violets, forget-me-nots, sweet peas and lilies of the valley in a basket.[8] The back garden was partly an ornamental flower garden and partly a kitchen garden, with fruit trees and vines. The Van Goghs kept three goats and a big black dog, Fedor. He was a gift from Uncle Jan van Gogh, who had brought him back from a trip to the Dutch East Indies for his nephews and nieces.[9] The animals gave the home the feel of a small farm; it was not uncommon in the first half of the nineteenth century for a parsonage not only to function as a home and a place for a minister to undertake pastoral duties, but also to provide part of the family's food, keeping costs down.

The Van Gogh children grew up protected and carefree. The hedge that enclosed the garden delineated where they played outdoors under supervision. But it also marked the transition to a place where they could run and explore unchecked, and thus symbolized the unknown. Lies called the world beyond the hedge a 'land of desire' in her later work.[10]

The family made lifelong friends in Zundert, including the Hamming family and the unmarried daughters of Dorus's predecessor, Reverend Van der Burg. The Van Gogh children regarded the Van der Burg daughters as aunts; the women always called themselves 'your old Zundert aunts' in their letters, and continued writing to the children until an advanced age. One of them, Aunt Louisa, sent a pair of baby socks when Theo's son was born in 1890. Aunt Elisabeth reminisced in a letter to Theo about her friendship with his parents and recalled the love she had felt for the Van Gogh children from their earliest years.[11] The Van Gogh family and the Van der Burg sisters also shared a gardener: Jan Doomen tended to the parsonage garden and the sisters' vegetable garden. Likewise, they corresponded with Aunt Mietje van Gogh, who of course did the housekeeping in the first two years of Dorus's ministry.[12]

The Reverend Van Gogh and his wife's customs and habits were rather unlike those of the average inhabitant of Zundert in the mid-nineteenth century. Wherever the family lived in North Brabant, it was always as part of a Protestant minority amid a Catholic majority. At the time Zundert was a small municipality with about 100 Protestants, in a sizeable village of around 3,000 people. Dorus was rather strict, 'a real Protestant Pope', as mayor Gaspar van Beckhoven called him.[13] The people of Zundert would have agreed with this description. Yet Dorus was well liked and appeared to grow in his role. He saw himself not only as a servant of the Word, but also as the guardian of the community and champion for its continued existence; his post had at least as much social as spiritual significance. He was devoted to his Protestant flock, but did not disregard less fortunate Catholics. It was Reverend Van Gogh's duty to increase the number of Protestants in the village – not by proselytizing locals, but by importing fellow believers.

He, like his father, was a member of the Society of Well-Being for this reason, but offering Protestants from other parts of the Netherlands agricultural land in and around Zundert to attract them to North Brabant was not without problems. The minister often worried about the soil's lack of fertility – the area around Zundert consisted partly of heathland, which was attractive to look at but difficult to farm. Dorus van Gogh concerned himself with the newcomers' fate, and rightly so, as those who failed to farm the soil successfully would eventually find their land expropriated. The minister considered this inhuman and unchristian. He was keen to show that the new tenants and their families were beneficial to the community, and his emphasis on their importance, rather than the importance of their rents, earned him much admiration from the local population, Protestant and Catholic alike. Dorus expended much energy directly supporting his newcomers and utilizing the Society of Well-Being's capacity to increase the number of new members of the congregation. He knew his congregation's needs and the local investments needed for his people to flourish, and utilized his extensive network to channel the Society's financial resources to this end, bringing his influence to bear when new farms were being purchased or when there were job appointments in and around Zundert.

The Dutch Reformed congregation of Greater Zundert included Protestants living in the villages of Rijsbergen and Wernhout, on the new border with Belgium. Zundert, located on a major trade route between Rotterdam and Antwerp, had been a border town since the Belgian Revolution, which had resulted in an influx of military and customs personnel. There was a staging post where horses could be changed, and several postal and courier companies had offices in the village, greatly increasing traffic. The railway line from Rotterdam to Roosendaal and Antwerp, which passed Zundert, was completed in 1854. The first railway line in the Netherlands, running from Amsterdam to Haarlem, had been completed in 1839. It was extended to Leiden, The Hague and then to Rotterdam between 1842 and 1847. Lines in the south of the Netherlands and Belgium and Germany were built in the 1850s, when it became possible to build rail bridges over the great Rhine, Meuse and Waal rivers. All these developments in transport, distribution and border control created new jobs in Zundert, Rijsbergen and Wernhout. Compared to Britain, where the steam engine and steam locomotive were invented, the development of a national railway system in the Netherlands came rather late. Trains had been running in the United Kingdom between Stockton and Darlington as early as 1825.

Those jobs were often awarded to people from other parts of the country, including a relatively large number of Protestants.[14] The newcomers gave Dorus the opportunity to establish a more resilient congregation in Zundert than the one he had found in 1849. The congregation's administration was better organized, parishioners' contributions were collected more systematically, and the congregation required less financial aid from the diaconate. The farmers' earnings from their farms and large families were a positive contribution to the congregation, the village's economy and therefore to society as a whole.

Like Pa, Moe had a pure conviction to help fellow human beings in distress, combined with a particular form of class consciousness. She regarded it as her duty as a minister's wife to support her husband, and joined him on home visits, whether they be to the indigent or well-off parishioners from their own Protestant milieu, or Catholics who were not so fortunate. She prepared the food that was distributed among poor families – their denomination appears to have been less important than alleviating the suffering of the needy. As befitted good, socially minded Christians, the Van Gogh children were taught from a young age concepts such as servitude, compassion and caring, and awareness of the needs of others. Dorus also dealt with other village notables, such

Staging post, Zundert. Date and photographer unknown.

as count Van Hogendorp, mayor Gaspar van Beckhoven and notary Franciscus van Mens. Their doctor, Cornelis van Ginneken, and his family would remain good friends for many years and they paid each other regular visits. Van Ginneken was even witness to the declaration of Vincent's birth.[15]

While Dorus and Anna's pastoral activities made them mindful of the Catholics in the community, Protestant mores prevailed in their home. The Van Gogh children occasionally kept company with the small group of Protestant children in Zundert, but were not allowed to play in the street, as the family lived on a busy road, and in any case most of the Protestant families lived on outlying farms rather than in the centre of the village. The siblings therefore tended to spend much time with each other. As a result, they were a close-knit family. The children were often indoors or in the garden, or walking in the surrounding countryside accompanied by their parents or a governess, or reading books. Like many Dutch Reformed children, they read volumes of poetry known as 'caption poetry'. These books were written by minister-poets and were intended for children and adults. They mainly consisted of pictures and often contained moralistic texts. Reverend Jan Jakob Lodewijk ten Kate's poetry was particularly popular, and his poem *De Schepping* (The Creation), composed in 1866, could be found in virtually all Dutch Reformed homes. They also read the minister-poet Eliza Laurillard's books, which contained photographs and reproductions of the works of both contemporary artists and old masters. It is highly likely that his book *Kunstjuweeltjes voor de salontafel* (Art Gems for the Coffee Table) was among the young Van Gogh children's first introductions to poetry and art.[16]

Dorus and Anna wanted their offspring to have a good position in society, high moral standards and a broad general development. They also undoubtedly wanted to ensure their daughters' financial independence, preparing them for life with or without a suitable husband, and so they were intent on securing a good education for all of their children. Although Dorus, like his father, had attended Latin school – which had been the most important type of education for boys from the upper classes for centuries – his sons Vincent, Theo and Cor did not. Latin schools around the country were already in decline when Vincent and

Theo and later Cor started secondary school. A new kind of school was on the rise at the time, the HBS or Hogere Burgerschool (Higher Civic School). Vincent was one of the first students at the new 'King William II' Higher Civic School, which opened in the former royal palace in Tilburg.[17]

Dorus and Anna had difficulty finding suitable schooling for their children. Education did not become compulsory until mandated by the Dutch parliament in 1900, so at this time most children were educated by their parents or neighbours at home. This did not amount to much: they were taught some reading and writing, and, if Catholic, were prepared for their Holy Communion. There was, however, a public school in Zundert, opposite the Van Goghs' house on the corner of the marketplace. This kind of public education was made possible by what is called the 'school struggle', which arose in response to the French-inspired Education law of 1806. This legislation was enacted during the French occupation of the Low Countries and would remain in force until the fall of Napoleon and the establishment of the Kingdom of the Netherlands in 1813. It would take more than a century to settle the school struggle; its most important legacy was that parents were free to set up a school for the education of their children, and that all schools would receive equal finance from the government, regardless of their denomination. These innovative developments were the result of Prime Minister Thorbecke's constitutional reforms, which were adopted by parliament in 1848. Although the school was a public institution, run by Catholics – there were very few Protestant schools at that time in North Brabant, and indeed this was the only school in Zundert – the Van Goghs decided to send their two eldest children there when Vincent was eight years old and Anna was six.[18]

A very old school building had once stood in the cemetery near the municipal council office. It had been used by Dutch troops as a guard post at the outbreak of the Belgian Revolution in 1830, but it was demolished because it was in such deplorable condition. The new school, founded in 1850, followed the Catholic calendar for holidays and days off. Fees were modest: 30 cents a month for the youngest children, and 40 cents a month for older children who could already write and were taught subjects such as geography, history and natural history.[19] An additional guilder had to be paid directly to the new headteacher, Jan Nicolaas Dirks, each month. He was responsible for the new school building and for extending the curriculum to include English, French and German lessons. This policy attracted more children from wealthy milieus; when Anna and Vincent attended the school, the class size could vary from 132 to as many as 243 children. The school had only one classroom, with three blackboards, several maps, abacuses and type cases, as well as twenty-one desks equipped with inkwells and drawers for notebooks and books, and nine benches. School was hard going for Anna and Vincent: the days were long, from half past eight in the morning to four in the afternoon without a break, supplemented with additional religious lessons at the parsonage. Many children stayed at home to help their parents on the land in summer or during the harvest, or might be taken out of school for extended periods to care for younger siblings, but most attended school for the rest of the year.[20]

Anna and Vincent did not attend the village school for long: their parents decided to withdraw them in the autumn of 1861. There were several reasons for this. Dirks's behaviour had changed in a very short period: he had lost four of his children within just a few years, was often

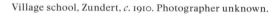

Village school, Zundert, *c.* 1910. Photographer unknown.

Anna Philipina Carolina Birnie, between 1870 and 1880. Photographed by J.C. Reesink.

absent from school and had taken to drink. Pa and Moe also felt that the crude behaviour of the farmers' children was a bad influence on their two eldest. Their solution was home schooling, and not only for Anna and Vincent; Theo, Lies and Wil were taught at home, too, until they went to secondary or boarding school. Home schooling was a female affair. The Van Gogh children had several governesses over the years, whose departure was often because they were getting married and were thus no longer permitted to work. Their first governess, Anna Philipina Carolina Birnie, arrived in February 1862, when Vincent was almost nine years old, Anna seven and Theo five. Lies and Wil would only join their classes later. The governesses were assisted by Dorus in a specially furnished teaching room in the parsonage.[21] In addition to arranging for home schooling, Dorus and Anna devoted much attention to their children, teaching them about art, music, literature and even dancing and fencing. The girls were given knitting and sewing lessons. They learned to play the piano and often read literature when they were older, sometimes translated from French or English.

The six Van Gogh children were instilled with a great patriotism and love for their locality, and a deep sense of awe for God's creation and the expansive nature around them. Zundert was hedgerow country, with forests, fields, estates, moors, streams and tree nurseries. In later years Vincent and Theo often reminisced about wandering in the woods, vast heathland and wheat fields for days on end as children: it was a time of happiness and paradisiacal unity with nature, and laid the foundation for a lifelong love of North Brabant. In their letters the brothers warmly recalled the parsonage and the village where they grew up with their sisters and younger brother. 'Oh that Zundert, the thought of it's almost too much at times', Vincent bemoaned in a letter to Theo from 3 October 1876.[22] On being discharged from hospital in Arles in January 1889, he wrote to Theo: 'During my illness I again saw each room in the house at Zundert, each path, each plant in the garden, the views round about, the fields, the neighbours, the cemetery, the church, our kitchen garden behind — right up to the magpies' nest in a tall acacia in the cemetery.'[23] Lies described her own fond memories of the Zundert of her youth in her memoir, writing how, after forty years, Vincent's childhood experiences were still 'sharply etched in her memory'.[24] She recalled Vincent's solitary nature, his predilection for nature and how he liked collecting beetles and insects, his funny ideas for plays, and his first drawings.

The young Van Gogh children found much warmth and protection in and around the parsonage, but it was a sheltered upbringing. The sisters faced the same limitations in their youth as the boys: they were not allowed to play with the other children from the village, and they were in principle only allowed to leave the parsonage garden under supervision. Their parents' strict selection of their playmates fostered a blinkered attitude towards the outside world, and the siblings were dependent on each other for company. Yet the harsh struggle of life was postponed for the sisters a little longer than for the brothers. After their home education they were sent to boarding school, where they followed the traditional path deemed necessary for a young lady's development.

CHAPTER 4

Young Mistresses

Helvoirt, Leeuwarden, Tiel, 1871–1875

In 1870 Dorus van Gogh accepted the post of minister at the village of Helvoirt, some 50 kilometres (30 miles) to the east of Zundert. He gave his final sermon to the Zundert congregation on 29 January 1871 after more than twenty years of service. Two days later the family moved to Helvoirt.[1] Vincent had already left Zundert by that time; a little more than a year earlier, at the age of sixteen, he had moved to The Hague. There he worked a stone's throw from the Binnenhof, the centre of parliament and government, for the art dealership Goupil & Co. The Parisian Adolphe Goupil had bought Uncle Cent's art gallery in 1861, and built an international network of dealerships.[2]

Uncle Cent continued to work for the company until 1878, a useful connection for his culturally minded nephews. It was customary for upper-middle-class boys who were not going on to further study to learn a trade straight after boarding or secondary school. Theo followed his brother into the profession, leaving home in 1873, also aged sixteen, to work at Goupil's Brussels branch.[3] He had never attended the public primary school in Zundert,

Vincent van Gogh (Uncle Cent).
Date and photographer unknown.

Theo van Gogh, between 1869 and 1871. Photographed by H.J. Weesing.

as Vincent and Anna had, but from 1872 he walked every day from Helvoirt to the Protestant school in Oisterwijk, 8 kilometres (5 miles) to the south.[4] Theo was unhappy at school, but could only start his career at Goupil after he had obtained his father's permission to end his education. The eldest sisters, Anna and Lies, were sent to boarding school while the family lived in Helvoirt; Willemien would subsequently also leave the parsonage for an extended period. Only the youngest brother, Cor, stayed with his parents throughout Dorus's posting.

The move to Helvoirt had several advantages for Pa and Moe. For a start, the new parsonage was bigger and more beautiful than the one in Zundert. Furthermore, the village presented a new challenge for Reverend Van Gogh. There were only sixty-six members of the Dutch Reformed community when he arrived, and he was tasked with the same kind of community development to which he had devoted himself in Zundert. Although Helvoirt did not have a large Protestant community in the 1870s, the congregation did have a strong social infrastructure, with a deep-rooted tradition of coexistence and cooperation with the Catholic majority. Dorus was used to visiting parishioners' homes with his wife from their years in Zundert and continued to do so in Helvoirt. The Van Goghs lived among many like-minded people: the parsonage was in a well-heeled part of the village, adjacent to the Jagtlust country estate, inhabited by squire De Jonge van Zwijnsbergen, his wife and children. The Van Gogh family often took walks in the estate's enormous grounds. The De Jonge van Zwijnsbergen family was also Protestant, as were several other neighbours. The squire was himself a member of the church council. His elder brother lived in Zwijnsbergen Castle on the

Zwijnsbergen Castle, Helvoirt. Date and photographer unknown.

Geertruida (Truitje) Johanna 's Graeuwen-van Gogh with her
daughters Fanny and Betje, *c.* 1864. Photographer unknown.
From the family album of Theo van Gogh.

north side of the village, and another brother would subsequently take up
residence in Huize Mariënhof, an estate on the south side of the village.[5]
Reverend Van Gogh made good use of this small but strong Protestant
presence over the course of his four years in Helvoirt. Protestants had
held extensive landholdings – houses, farms, fields and forests – in the
area for centuries, which were now managed by the Society of Well-Being.

The presence of family in Helvoirt gave the Van Goghs a sense of
coming home. Dorus's sister, Truitje van Gogh, had been living there
with her husband, Abraham 's Graeuwen, since 1872. Their son, Bram,
and two daughters, Fanny and Betje, were almost exactly the same

age as the Van Goghs' children. Fanny and Lies attended the same
boarding school in Tiel for a time, and Willemien attended school in
's-Hertogenbosch, the capital of North Brabant, with Betje. They also
saw each other in their leisure time: in the summer of 1874, Wil joined
the whole 's Graeuwen family for a visit to Uncle Cent and Aunt Cornelie
in Princenhage, near Breda. Years later, from 1883 to 1885, Johannes
(Jan) van Gogh, a vice-admiral and the minister's brother, also lived
in Helvoirt. He spent this period at his sister Trui's home in Villa
Molenhuize, later called Huize Rozen-Haeghe on the Molenstraat.[6] It
was Uncle Jan with whom Vincent stayed in 1877 when he was preparing to study theology in Amsterdam. But Vincent had not finished his
HBS education and did not master Latin and Greek, subjects that were
required in order to study theology and eventually become a minster.

The parsonage in Helvoirt was a stately whitewashed house on the
Kerkstraat, one of only two paved roads in the village. It resembled an
eighteenth-century townhouse in the Empire style, with louvre shutters and six-sided windows, but was in fact a rectangular, oak-framed

house built in 1657 with a pitched
roof and gables. The parsonage had
an exceptional history. Its construction was a compromise after the
religious strife of the Eighty Years
War (1568–1648); in exchange for the
building of the Protestant parsonage and provision of a salary for
their minister, the Catholics were
granted back a great amount of the
land that they had lost during the
war. A wall to the left of the house
concealed the deep garden, with its
vegetable patch and fruit trees, from
view of the street. A wide corridor

Parsonage and choir of the Dutch
Reformed Church, Helvoirt, *c.* 1950.
Photographer unknown.

led from the front door to a spacious kitchen; the sitting room was to the left of the corridor, and behind that was the dining room, which overlooked the garden. On the other side of the central corridor was Reverend Van Gogh's study and consulting room. It had a library and an upstairs room above a cellar with a vaulted ceiling. The bedrooms were situated on the upper floor; Pa and Moe's bedroom above the study, the servants' quarters above the kitchen, with a view onto the garden, and the children's rooms at the front of the house. One of the children's rooms had a dormer window, clearly visible from the street, that looked onto a row of chestnut trees and the church where Pa delivered his sermons. Moe wrote on 10 July 1874 that Vincent, who had by then moved from The Hague to London to become an art dealer at Goupil, was in Helvoirt for his summer leave. He had been sitting outside the house drawing 'in front of Lies, the bedroom window and part of the front door – that part of the house. He stood to the side of Jans's house, it turned out nicely'.[7] The drawing, which Vincent gave to his sisters Lies and Wil, has not survived.

Pa simply had to cross the road to reach his pulpit in Helvoirt. He entered what was called the Oude Kerk (Old Church) or the Oude Nicolaaskerk (Old Nicholas Church) through the narthex. The site of Helvoirt's Oude Kerk had been a place of worship since 1192, when a wooden chapel dedicated to Saint Nicholas – as was the later brick church – was established. Nicholas, the patron saint of itinerant traders, was a suitable patron for the village, which was located on several trade routes and a popular rest stop for travellers. The beauty of the Gothic cruciform church could be admired far beyond the village limits, with its awe-inspiring tower housing four bells. This was in sharp contrast to the modest church the minister had left behind in Zundert.

Yet the building was in a pitiable state when Reverend Van Gogh assumed responsibility for it. The roof leaked, the exterior needed to be painted, and the organ required urgent repairs – none of which could be done until the necessary funds had been found. This much-needed restoration project aligned closely with Dorus's goal of expanding Helvoirt's Dutch Reformed congregation.[8] More parishioners would generate revenue and support for the restoration, and a larger Reformed

Vincent van Gogh, *The Church of Helvoirt*, 1874.
Black chalk on paper, 21 × 32 cm (8¼ × 12⅝ in.)

community would deserve a beautiful church. A drastic decision was inevitable: the fifteenth-century Gothic rood screen – an oak partition separating the nave from the chancel that had dominated the church's interior for centuries – was sold to Donatus Alberic van den Bogaerde van Terbrugge from the nearby De Nemelaer Castle. While the choir screen was the only one of its size and age in the Netherlands, Dorus's decision to sell it was understandable, for it had lost its Catholic function after the Reformation. The squire paid 400 guilders for it, not an astronomical sum (the minister himself earned about 800 guilders a year), but sufficient to finance the requisite maintenance and restoration works.[9] The funds were used to draught-proof and damp-proof the church. It was painted, and a wall was erected between the chancel and the nave, where the rood screen had formerly stood. The chancel was converted into a sexton's residence.

When the restoration was completed, Reverend Van Gogh gifted his congregation a Dutch States Bible that had been published in 1704. The

Bible, which he had been given by his younger brother Cornelis, contained the inscription: 'This Bible, being a gift from Mr. C.M. van Gogh, bookseller in Amsterdam, to his brother, Rev. Th. van Gogh; is for the benefit of the Reformed congregation at Helvoirt, on 17 November 1872, on the day of the inauguration of the renovated church building, and thus in the year 1872.'[10] So Dorus managed to achieve both of his goals: not only had the church been renovated by the end of his time in Helvoirt, but also the number of parishioners had increased.

When Anna van Gogh turned seventeen in February 1872, her parents sent her to Leeuwarden, the capital of the province of Friesland, more than 200 kilometres (125 miles) to the north of Helvoirt, to attend the French Day and Boarding School for Young Mistresses.[11] From the end of the eighteenth century onwards, the French language had gained immense popularity in Europe, partly because of France's territorial expansion under Napoleon, who had added the whole of Western Europe to his empire and reduced several surrounding countries to vassal states between 1804 and 1812, the Netherlands being one of them. French deposed Latin as Europe's lingua franca, and the Netherlands' participation in the burgeoning international trade of the industrial era created the need for formal education in subjects such as accounting and commercial arithmetic in the Gallic language. This resulted in the emergence of what were referred to as 'French schools'.[12] Most were for boys, but several trained girls to be good wives and mothers, or teachers, ladies' companions or governesses. One of the Van Goghs' former governesses, Annemie Schuil, had attended the Leeuwarden French School, no doubt influencing the decision to enrol Anna there. It was customary for a picture to be taken of all students of the French Day and Boarding School for Young Mistresses. This was done nearby by local photographer H.A.K. Ringler. Anna sent one of her photographs to Theo, asking him for a photograph in return with which to remember him: 'When you have a portrait or a little picture you like very much, you must send it me if you like and I shall make a lijstje [frame] from *bathren* flowers for it.'[13]

The school was housed in a large neoclassical building in the centre of Leeuwarden, built around 1860 by the town architect Thomas Romein.

Anna van Gogh, *c.* 1872–73. Photographed by H.A.K. Ringler.

It had a spacious courtyard and large beeches, shrubs and flowers in the grounds; the girls were allowed ten-minute walks in the garden between lessons. Anna's enrolment states that her father was a minister, that she had hitherto had private education, and that Dr Landman from Helvoirt had vaccinated her against cowpox,[14] a highly contagious bovine disease related to smallpox in humans. This 'pox note' was important; girls were not admitted to the school without proof of vaccination.[15] The school was run by Miss Plaat, who was very strict, but well-liked by many – especially parents. School fees were 13 guilders quarterly, and were paid directly to Miss Plaat.[16] Girls who did not come from Leeuwarden were housed in the school building; board and lodging, laundry, clothing, school supplies, and travel all incurred additional expenses. Pa found the boarding school 'surprisingly dear',[17] but in spite of the high costs Anna remained there until the summer of 1874.

I ABOVE
Anna van Gogh-Carbentus,
Bouquet of Flowers, 1844
Watercolour on paper,
12.3 × 7.8 cm (4⅞ × 3⅛ in.)

II RIGHT
Alphonse Karr, *Voyage autour
de mon jardin* (Travel around
my Garden), Paris, 1851

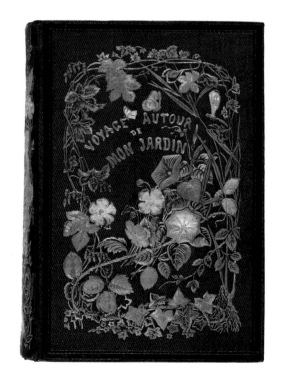

III
Vincent van Gogh,
Wintertuin (Winter Garden), 1884
Pencil, pen and ink on paper,
40.3 × 54.6 cm (15⅞ × 21¼ in.)

IV ABOVE
Vincent van Gogh,
Vicarage and Church at Etten, 1876
Pencil and pen on paper,
9.5 × 17.8 cm (3¾ × 7 in.)

V BELOW
Willemien van Gogh,
Vicarage and Church at Etten, 1876
Pencil, pen and ink on paper,
9.1 × 17.5 cm (3½ × 6⅞ in.)

VI
Vincent van Gogh,
Memory of the Garden at Etten, 1888
Oil on canvas,
73 × 92 cm (28¾ × 36¼ in.)

VII
Vincent van Gogh,
Letter to Willemien van Gogh with sketch
of *Memory of the Garden at Etten* (detail),
c. 12 November 1888
Pen and ink on paper,
21.1 × 26.9 cm (8¼ × 10⅝ in.)

VIII ABOVE
Vincent van Gogh,
Leaving the Church in Nuenen, 1884–85
Oil on canvas,
41.5 × 32.2 cm (16⅜ × 12⅝ in.)

IX OPPOSITE, ABOVE
Vincent van Gogh,
Watermill at Kollen near Nuenen, 1884
Oil on canvas on cardboard,
58 × 78 cm (22⅞ × 30¾ in.)

X OPPOSITE, BELOW
Vincent van Gogh,
The Potato Eaters, 1885
Oil on canvas,
82 × 114 cm (32¼ × 44⅞ in.)

XI ABOVE
Vincent van Gogh,
Detail from a letter to Willemien
van Gogh with sketch of *The Novel
Reader*, *c.* 12 November 1888
Pen and ink on paper,
21.1 × 26.9 cm (8¼ × 10⅝ in.)

XII BELOW
Vincent van Gogh,
The Novel Reader, 1888
Oil on canvas,
73 × 92 cm (28¾ × 36¼ in.)

The French Day and Boarding School for Young Mistresses endeavoured to instil virtue, decency and good manners in its pupils. The girls learned to dress appropriately, were taught singing, music and handicrafts, and devoted much time to learning foreign languages. The students in the senior classes were not allowed to speak any Dutch at all; they risked being barred from leaving the school grounds on days off if they failed to converse in French or English.[18] Anna did not feel at home there; even a year after she arrived at the school she wrote to her brother Theo, who had recently moved far from home to Brussels, that she felt sorry for him because she knew how it felt. But she realized that leaving home, for him too, was the only way of becoming independent. She wrote to Theo in poor English, as the girls were obliged not only to converse in a foreign language but also to conduct their correspondence in either English or French. Anna explained this obligation in English: 'I do not write you in Dutch, but it is not permitted at all.'[19] Perhaps newly mindful of her family's social standing owing to her recently gained independence, she also offered her brother some advice: 'Oh Theo, pray and follow Vincent's example; remain a gentleman and settle with those

The French School for Young Mistresses, 12 Grote Kerkstraat, Leeuwarden, *c.* 1905. Artist unknown.

who want to tempt you to do things which you know are bad. We have no money, but we still have a good name.'[20]

Anna initially sent few letters to her family, but this changed towards the end of her first year at the school, as she realized that the situation at home was changing. She wrote to Theo: 'How strange it will be when now I come home, you are at Brussels and Vincent in London. I also would like to see a strange [foreign] country and hope I will once. But it will be very strange to miss my Theo out of circle of the family when I come back.'[21] Anna passed her English and handicrafts exams in the autumn, but at the end of the year, while she was in Helvoirt during the Christmas holidays, she wrote to Theo that she did not feel like returning to Miss Plaat's school, as she did not like her much ('Miss Plaat is so-so')[22] and she hated writing letters in English ('I should like to do it so much in Dutch').[23] During this holiday Anna was confirmed by her father in Helvoirt.[24] Confirmation is a rite in which a believer publicly declares his or her faith, usually by affirming several questions of faith during a church service. Anna was eighteen years old. At her

The 1874 class of the French School for Young Mistresses, Leeuwarden, with Miss Rebecca Plaat and Anna van Gogh (eighth from left). Photographer unknown.

parents' insistence, she returned to Leeuwarden for another semester to pass the French exam.

Unfortunately she would fail the exam, but early in the new year she appeared to have become more at ease at the school, and wrote that she needed to be more conscious of how fortunate she was with her family and education.[25] Despite this, Anna wrote on 20 January that she was not ready for her exams: 'I will not do my examination, I am not far enough to pass'. She returned to Lies and her behaviour: 'Either she regards you as a little boy and herself as a lady – not a young lady – or she does something which is not *comme il faut* [improper]. I know that she does not do the former for Lies had always wanted to look younger than she really is.'[26]

Lies had not been able to move to Helvoirt with the family, having contracted typhoid fever in 1871, when she was twelve. The situation was serious enough that she had to be nursed for some time in Breda. It is unclear whether she stayed with her grandfather and aunts on the Van Gogh side, or in a sanatorium. When her health improved, she wrote to Theo to thank him for his letter to her and apologize for her silence: 'I would have answered you earlier if I had not been ill. I am now in Breda restoring my health as it is called.'[27] While recovering in Breda she made new friends, and her family occasionally paid her a visit: 'When Pa and Anna were here, we drove to Zundert with Uncle Cent and were received cordially by everyone,' she wrote to Theo.[28] Lies apparently enjoyed being away from home and school. 'You can understand,' she confided in Theo, 'how kind everyone was to me; there was not a day that I did not go out, and to have those dear friends was enjoyable.'[29] After some time, her parents decided that Lies had enjoyed enough freedom, and arranged for her to return home to resume her lessons. They had appointed a governess, Miss Breunissen-Troost, who, according to Aunt Mietje, lived at the parsonage, later at Molenhage, and had in her charge the youngest Van Gogh girls Lies and Wil, as well as their cousins Fanny and Betje 's Graeuwen from the Molenstraat. Lies wrote to Theo: 'We have two new courses at school, namely natural history and literature...and now that you have changed from a schoolboy into a gentleman, you shall no longer care about these things.'[30]

In the autumn of 1874, when she was fifteen years old, Lies left Helvoirt to continue her schooling at the French Boarding School for Mistresses in Leeuwarden.[31] She, like Anna, found it tough, and recalled her youth in Brabant with melancholy and longing, especially the evenings that the entire Van Gogh family was there and sat around a beautifully decorated dining table. She wrote to Theo in October that she fully realized that there was no other option, but was sometimes sad that they had so little opportunity to 'talk confidentially with each other'.[32] The four eldest children had each followed their work or studies to a different city. For this reason, Lies emphasized the importance of regular correspondence, and sometimes found it difficult that Vincent did not answer her letters.

Although she often complained that she had limited contact with her brothers and sisters, Lies regularly corresponded with Anna and Theo, who in turn complained to each other that they seldom received letters from her. Anna had written to Theo from Leeuwarden in February 1873: 'How fond Lies is of you I nearly would be jealous, she wrote me such a mournful letter, and pitied so much you were gone.'[33] Unlike Anna, Miss Plaat forced Lies to write home in French. She wrote to Theo in April 1875 that she longed for home: 'Oh! Je languie tant de voir tout le monde et de parler, pas écrire, avec toi.' (Oh! I so long to see and speak to everyone again and to be able to talk to you and not have to write.)[34] She only had another twelve weeks, she told Theo and herself, until most of the siblings would return to Helvoirt for the summer vacation. Lies missed Brabant, and Helvoirt in particular: 'Long walks are taken with the young ladies from the boarding school, especially on Sundays from Leeuwarden to Marssum, Gorkum and Leersum, villages rather near the Frisian capital [Leeuwarden], but not one looks like our good Helvoirt, even though these villages sometimes have some beauty'.[35] In a letter from September 1875 she again wrote of her love for Helvoirt and the Brabant countryside when inquiring whether Theo still walked much: 'Do you remember those walks in Helvoirt and how we enjoyed them?'[36] Lies also faithfully maintained contact with her parents, and they always wrote back. This added much to her well-being. Maintaining family ties by writing letters and sending presents like a

Lies van Gogh, 1874–75. Photographed by H.A.K. Ringler.

picture of oneself facilitated looking forward to the future together, she thought, because 'we are all so of one mind, except perhaps for Vincent'.[37] It was Theo who would send her a small notebook with a number of transcribed poems and lyrics in it, which Vincent had started, just the way Lies used to do herself for their grandfather and for him. It was his way of helping Lies through nostalgic episodes at boarding school.[38] Like Anna, Lies had her picture taken in Leeuwarden by Hendrik Ringler and would have sent it to her loved ones.

Around this time Lies was developing a conciousness of rank and class, and of broad social developments taking place in the Netherlands. She commented in a letter to Theo from Leeuwarden that 'one has much to learn in this time, because everyone wants to end up in a higher class than one's own class'.[39] She liked learning, and emulated her two elder brothers and Anna when remarking she would like to one day be as independent as they were. 'Do not you think that things like this go much faster if you have a clear goal in life?' she asked Theo.[40] But, she continued, 'do you know what I find so vexing for us girls – that we can only be a deputy or governess.'[41] Her letters reveal a self-assured and ambitious young woman who wanted to earn money and work for herself, but felt despair at the limited options available to her. She would later be preoccupied even more by the subject of professions that were still barred to girls and young women.

While Dorus was able to pay for his eldest daughters to attend boarding school, there were times when one of the children was unable to come home for the vacation because of the cost of the railway ticket. When Pa and Moe received an invoice at the end of the school year for Lies's school fees in Leeuwarden, Moe bemoaned in a letter to Theo that they were struggling to raise the amount of almost 500 guilders[42] – over half of Dorus's annual salary. The three boys also put their parents to expense: Dorus paid 625 guilders[43] to keep them out of military service by paying for a so-called 'remplaçant' in February 1873. This payment meant that others would join the army instead of his sons.[44]

Dorus's father, Reverend Vincent van Gogh, died in Breda in 1874. His unmarried daughters – Antje, Doortje and Mietje – decided to move out of the house in which they had cared for him, which was emptied and sold. The chattels were divided among his children, and the proceeds from the sale of the house went to the three sisters who had worked so hard for their father in his last years, an arrangement agreed upon by all the Van Gogh siblings.[45] The sisters decided to use the money to build a house in Helvoirt. They bought the land from the De Jonge van Zwijnsbergen family, who lived across the road at Huize Mariënhof.[46] Their sister, Truitje, lived on the same side of the village at Villa Molenhuize. The parsonage where Dorus and his family lived was nearby, too. Pa would only live near his sisters for a short while, as he had already accepted a new post in Etten, but he would be closely involved in building their house. On 29 April 1875 he wrote to Theo: 'I was occupied planting and dressing the Aunts' garden from 5 to 12. It looks good now, but I am tired.'[47] Mietje, who appeared to want to avoid

Vincent van Gogh, *Vincent van Gogh, the Artist's Grandfather*, 1881.
Pencil, brush and ink and watercolour on paper, 34.5 × 26.1 cm (13⅝ x 10¼ in.).

the commotion of the move, stayed with her elder brother Johan in The Hague in the meantime. Antje and Doortje moved from Breda to Helvoirt on 16 April, accompanied by their maid, Kee. As the house was not yet finished, they stayed with Truitje. Mietje returned from The Hague on 21 May and stayed at the parsonage until the house was ready. As Moe had already started a class for young girls in their community some years before, teaching them how to knit and sew, her three sisters-in-law started a Sunday school for the children of the Protestant community of Helvoirt-Haaren. They sometimes awarded attentive children with prizes during this religious instruction, including drawings by their nephew Vincent.[48] The aunts were also very involved in their nieces' lives. Aunt Antje gave Anna, Lies and Willemien, and their cousins Fanny and Betje 's Graeuwen, some beautiful dresses.

The younger generation of Van Gogh siblings swiftly came to hold Helvoirt dear in their few years there. As well as their own house, the imposing Dutch Reformed church, the stately Jagtlust villa – whose residents regularly interacted with them – and the other beautiful houses on the Kerkstraat contributed to this. In their many letters from that time, and even years later, they wrote lovingly about Helvoirt and its inhabitants, and the nature surrounding the village, but above all about the parsonage garden, in which they invested much care. Lies wrote to Theo in May 1873: 'The bad weather is not good for the garden; last week's hard frost and snow have, we think, done much harm to the fruit that was otherwise most promising. The pots had also been taken out by the gardener, but Pa had to put them in the house because of the cold weather.'[49] In the same letter, she drew Theo's attention in a few sentences to an officer quartered at the parsonage: 'He was a kind person, who could talk and relate pleasantly.'[50] Since the end of the Belgian Revolution in May 1839, four quartered mounted field artillery batteries had conducted exercises in the Meierij van 's-Hertogenbosch, which included Helvoirt.

Wil also showed a love of gardening at an early age. In a letter to Theo, probably from April 1874, she wrote: 'Oh Theo my garden is so neat, I usually work in it every Saturday, if we do not go for a walk. I wanted you to see the chestnut trees. They are already completely green.'[51] Pa, too, mentioned the garden in his letters to Theo a few days later, writing that the chestnut trees had not yet blossomed very well as it was so cold. He thought it a shame, because 'the front garden is otherwise so beautiful, the grass has just been cut'.[52] He also reported that he had heard a nightingale early in the morning.

While their parents came from urban families in the predominantly Protestant northern region of Holland, it is remarkable to see how, within one generation, the Van Gogh children felt profoundly for North Brabant. Their love of the region, which had started in Zundert, was only deepened in Helvoirt. Vincent wrote to Theo on 26 August 1876, from England: 'Brabant is indeed Brabant, and the mother country is indeed the mother country, and the lands where one is a stranger are the lands where one is a stranger. And how friendly Helvoirt looked that evening, and the lights in the village and the tower between the snow-covered poplars, seen from a distance on the road to 's-Hertogen-bosch. But it's love that gives everything such great beauty and life.'[53] First from Leeuwarden and later from Tiel, Lies wrote extensively about her recollections of the walks they took in and around Helvoirt: 'How we enjoyed ourselves there'.[54]

Pa announced his move to Etten to the congregation in Helvoirt on Sunday 8 August 1875; the entire family was present, except for Vincent and Theo, who were in Paris. A meal at the parsonage after the service was attended by Uncle Cent, Aunt Cornelie and Aunt Truitje, as well as Uncle Bram 's Graeuwen. 'Anna had decorated the table so exquisitely and she and Willemien had made beautiful bouquets,' Dorus reported to Theo. 'You know how such things can be. We were well in the true sense of the word.'[55] But however much the Van Goghs loved Helvoirt, after four years another move beckoned.

CHAPTER 5

Cottages Covered in Ivy

London, Welwyn, 1873–1877

The artist, too, yonder on the slope of the shady hill,
Immersed in his work since the break of day,
[Heard] the Angelus sound, heralding the hour to retreat.
Slowly he wiped his brush and palette, packed them in his
    box with the canvas,
Folded his field stool and ambled dreamily down
    the meandering path
That led through the flower-filled valley to the village.
Jan van Beers, 'Eventide'[1]

Lies recited a poem on the occasion of Vincent's departure for England
on 12 May 1873. The excerpt quoted here comes from the first of the four-
part romantic poem *De Bestedeling* (The Boarder) by the Flemish poet Jan
van Beers. She copied the verse out, intending to give it to Vincent when
he was transferred from Goupil & Co.'s branch in The Hague to London.
Lies loved literature, and often referred to it at times of high emotion.
Two years earlier, on 23 March 1871, she had copied another poem as
a tribute to her grandfather, the Reverend Vincent van Gogh, who had
ministered to his congregation in Breda for sixty years. For him she
chose a verse by the little-known Reverend van Schaick at his jubilee.[2]

Theo had been living in Brussels since the beginning of January,
and was unable to attend the farewell gathering. Vincent had written
to him the previous Friday: 'My dear Theo, I'm leaving Helvoirt for
Paris on Monday morning and will pass through Brussels at 2:07. Do
come to the station if you can; I would like that very much.'[3] After he
had arrived in London, he told Theo about the poem he had received

58

from Lies. 'It's so perfectly Brabant, and I love it. Lies copied it out for me on my last evening at home.'[4]

On his way to London Vincent spent a week in Paris, visiting both of the Paris branches of Goupil and the Musée de Luxembourg. From Paris he went on to the Norman port city of Dieppe, where he boarded a ferry to Newhaven, and from there completed his journey from Brighton to London by train. He reported to Goupil at 17 Southampton Street.[5] Uncle Cent, who was living in Paris at the time, had accompanied the twenty-year-old Vincent on the journey, not only because of his nephew's youth, but also because he himself was of course a partner in Goupil. Cent had a major stake in the prosperous firm and, having no children of his own, considered his nephew and namesake a potential successor to his position.

During his time in London Vincent produced a drawing of the Dutch church Austin Friars, which King Edward VI had granted to the Protestant community in 1550. Vincent probably sent this small sketch, believed to be a copy after a photograph or print, to Anna with a letter, though he may also have given it to her in person when she visited him

Vincent van Gogh, *Austin Friars London*, 1873–74. Pen and brown ink on vellum paper, 10.4 × 17.2 cm (4 × 6¾ in.). Vincent made this drawing as a gift for his sister Anna.

59

in England a year later.[6] Anna had written to Theo in late February 1874, some time before completing her studies in Leeuwarden, to say that she was considering spending some time in England: 'Perhaps I already go in May to England.'[7] Vincent, who had by then been at Goupil in London for almost a year, was excited by the prospect. In March he wrote to his friends Caroline and Willem van Stockum-Haanebeek in The Hague: 'Now I have a piece of news for you; our Anna might be coming here. You can imagine how wonderful that would be for me, but it's almost too good to be true. Well, we'll just have to wait and see…I'd like so much to get to know her better than I do, for in the last few years we've actually seen very little of each other, and we only half know each other.'[8]

In the summer of 1874, when Vincent spent a couple of weeks' leave in Helvoirt, Pa and Moe put their heads together and decided to send Anna with her brother on his return to London. Anna was living in the family home, having left boarding school after failing her French exam, and her parents felt it was time for her to find employment. With her education, a position as governess seemed the obvious choice, and England offered more opportunities than the Netherlands for such work. She would move in with Vincent, who had taken rooms in the home of a Mrs Loyer and her daughter Eugenie at 87 Hackford Road.[9]

On 14 July Anna and Vincent travelled by wagon from Helvoirt to the railway station in the village of Oisterwijk, and set off for London. Almost every trip the Van Goghs made from Helvoirt was by carriage, wagon or tow barge; the latter was replaced by the train a

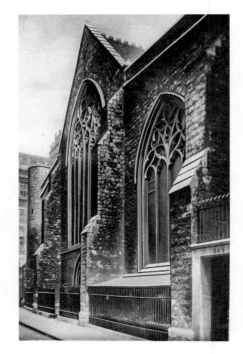

Austin Friars, London. Date and photographer unknown.

few years after the family's departure from the town. The train went via Breda to Moerdijk, a small village on the river Hollands Diep, where passengers transferred to a paddle steamer to cross from the city of Dordrecht to Rotterdam. In the 1870s, Rotterdam rapidly evolved into an important mercantile city, home to merchants and labourers. Port facilities were built on the south bank of the river Meuse, and shipping companies were soon running intercontinental services. Steamers gradually superseded sailing ships as the principal mode of water transport, and with the disappearance of vessels with tall masts it became possible to build road and railway bridges. The Moerdijk Bridge, the longest of its kind in Europe at the time, came into service in 1871, dramatically reducing the time it took to travel from North Brabant to the conurbations in the west of the Netherlands.[10] For Pa and Moe this meant quicker and easier access to their brothers and sisters in Holland, above the great

Moerdijk Railway Bridge, 1871. Artist unknown.

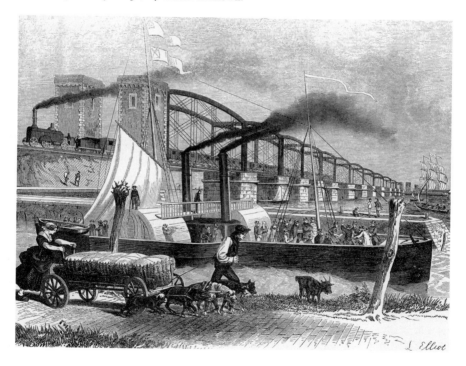

rivers. Rotterdam and Harwich had been linked by a ferry service for passengers, goods and livestock since 1863, but from 1872, after the opening of the New Waterway – a connection between Rotterdam and the North Sea created by digging a kilometres-long waterway through the dunes – this service was provided daily. A one-way first-class ticket cost 15 guilders; second-class fares started from 9 guilders.[11]

Anna and Vincent made the crossing – a turbulent one – from De Boompjes, the steamship terminal in Rotterdam. Before their departure Vincent made a drawing of the steamship on which they were about to leave, intended for Betsy Tersteeg, the daughter of his employer Hermanus Tersteeg at Goupil in The Hague. Vincent wrote, 'Next Monday I'm going back to London with my sister Anna and then I'll be travelling again on the little steamboat I've drawn here.'[12] The sketch has since been lost. Two years later, the ferry trip came to mind when Vincent was making his way via Rotterdam to Ramsgate in England to take up a position as an assistant teacher at a school for boys.[13] 'On the boat I kept thinking of Anna; everything there reminded me of our journey together...for now I found myself shuddering as I thought of the night in that stuffy saloon with passengers smoking and singing.'[14] He had set off on Good Friday, 1876. Perhaps he would have preferred to spend Easter with his family; whatever the case, at this stage of the journey Vincent's thoughts were of home and his eldest sister.

Anna was given the room next to Vincent's at Hackford Road, with a view of the back garden. She and Vincent spent much of their time together and enjoyed going for walks. Anna would sometimes accompany her brother to the Goupil gallery, and they visited the Dulwich Picture Gallery, where Vincent had once signed the visitors' book. He was impressed by the way his sister looked at art. He wrote to Theo that Anna was 'quite fond of paintings and has a rather good eye. She already likes Boughton, Maris and Jacquet, for example, so that's a start.'[15] Anna and Vincent also visited friends, among them the family of Charles Obach, the German director of Goupil in London. Anna wrote to her father about her life in London, and he relayed his eldest daughter's impressions to Theo: 'Anna writes about the Loyer ladies – they are good people who try to make things as agreeable as possible for us. Anna says,

Dulwich Picture Gallery, early 20th century. Photographer unknown.

I wish you could come to see my room. Last evening Vincent hung up a whole lot of prints. Altogether it's cheerful and pleasant. We go out walking every evening and always find nice new spots; the mist, which I used to picture as something beastly, also has a beauty of its own; in the evenings especially, when I accompany Vincent part of the way, the streets are really lovely. So you see, they're getting on well together and we must hope that all will end well.'[16]

Anna was happy in London, and enthused about the city to Theo: 'Oh, Theo! It's so delightful here. London cannot be compared to any other Dutch city. The cottages are all so quaint and snug, with little gardens in front. Nearly all of them are covered with ivy or creepers. I've already been to Vincent at the gallery three times and have seen some lovely paintings there, including the Marguerite by M. Maris, the one you've got a photograph of. We go on marvellous walks together;

now that evening is starting to fall earlier it's almost more beautiful than in summer.'[17] Though Anna and Vincent were perfectly content in Hackford Road, their parents were against them staying on, probably because Vincent had fallen in love with Mrs Loyer's daughter, Eugenie. The headmistress of a school in Brixton, Eugenie was already engaged to be married. As their parents were paying the rent, Vincent and Anna had no option but to comply with their wishes and look for new lodgings. They found two rooms in Lambeth, at an inn called Ivy Cottage at 395 Kennington Road, and moved there in August. Shortly after they moved out of Hackford Road, Moe wrote to Theo: 'I'm glad he's not there anymore, there were too many secrets and they weren't a family like ordinary people, but he must have been disappointed by them and unable to achieve what he was hoping for – real life is different from what one imagines it to be.'[18]

Anna was not to stay in Lambeth for long. She had come to London primarily for employment, but had struggled to find paid work. There was more demand for governesses in England than in the Netherlands, but the competition was stiffer. Vincent wrote to tell Theo that he and Anna would scour the newspapers for vacancies, and that he had even placed an advertisement himself – and moreover, Anna had signed up with an employment agency.[19] But none of these attempts had borne fruit, and Moe was fretting. At last, at the end of August, Anna was offered a position as assistant teacher and governess at a small school coincidentally named Ivy Cottage in Welwyn. The village was nearly 50 kilometres (30 miles) north of London, in the county of Hertfordshire. This necessitated leaving her brother, but she enjoyed the beauty of the countryside, especially in spring and autumn. She wrote to Theo: 'The terrain here is very hilly and to my mind that always makes a landscape nicer. The trees and shrubs are also more beautiful than in Holland, wilder and unpruned and hardier as a result. The sun setting behind the hills is always new and splendid.'[20] Though she was often kept too busy at Ivy Cottage to enjoy the surroundings, she found fulfilment in her work. Her main subject was French – the very subject she had failed in Leeuwarden. Anna had a room close to the schoolhouse, where she lived with the headteacher Miss Applegarth's sister Catherine Stothard and her four children at the left side of a large semi-detached red-brick building called Rose Cottage.[21] This would be her home for two years.

Despite her meagre income of £1 a month, Anna thoroughly enjoyed her stay in Welwyn.[22] This is clear from her letters home and to her brothers. She remarked to Theo, 'It must be marvellous to live in the art world; I wish I had more opportunity to learn more about it. But I have ample remuneration and this magnificent nature all around me.'[23] She was indeed in her element in Welwyn. She took well to the job; the headmistress, Miss Applegarth, left her in charge of the school when she went on an eight-day trip to London. She felt comfortable in the homely environment she was working in, but she also had a busy schedule. In the evenings she gave private tuition to Ernest Stothard, the eldest son of the family she was lodging with and Miss Applegarth's nephew, who needed French to go into business. Anna felt appreciated. 'Everyone here is so very kind to me,' she wrote to Theo.[24]

During the Christmas holidays of 1874 she went to see Vincent in London, but the visit was not a success. Ever since Anna had left for

Rose Cottage (left), Welwyn, *c.* 1910. Photographer unknown.

Welwyn, Vincent's behaviour seemed to have changed for the worse. His mother speculated in a letter to Theo that he must have been disappointed about having to leave the Loyer residence. On 28 April 1875 Anna also complained about her eldest brother to Theo: 'I believe that he has illusions about people and judges people before he knows them, and then when he finds out what they're really like and they don't live up to the opinion he formed of them prematurely, he's so disappointed that he throws them away like a bouquet of wilted flowers, without looking to see whether or not there are some among those wilted flowers which, when handled with care, are not quite rubbish yet.'[25] She looked back on that time with disappointment and sorrow in her long letter to Theo: 'I deeply regret having gone to him and been an encumbrance to him in the Christmas holidays. If I'd had any reason beforehand to think it would be like this, I would definitely have found one way or another to arrange things differently. I haven't told them at home; they're under the impression that he's very supportive of me and Pa and Moe seem to find that reassuring.'[26]

Anna encountered difficult times when Ernest, her pupil, suddenly fell ill. The boy had contracted diphtheria – which was still a common disease in the nineteenth century, with epidemics regularly sweeping Europe – and died on 9 April 1875. Anna described him as an amiable, good-natured child, who was missed by all. 'It's strange and incomprehensible, but we must trust that it's for the best.' She also wrote about a little girl, by her account a most adorable child, whose merry chatter helped her forget the adversities that are an inevitable part of school life. In spite of their unsuccessful Christmas in 1874, Vincent did visit his sister at Welwyn, and two years later recalled these events in a pensive letter: 'How kind she was to that family in Welwyn, in good times and bad, sparing nothing in her efforts to help and comfort them when that child was ill and passed away; I saw for myself how fond of her they all were....And Pa and Moe love her so much, and we all do too; yes, do let's stay close to one another.'[27]

In the summer of 1875 Anna went home to spend a holiday in Helvoirt. She would meet all her brothers and sisters there but Vincent, who was in Paris at the time.[28] Her parents had already announced that they would be moving to the village of Etten, where unfortunately there wasn't a suitable school for Willemien. During Anna's stay at the parsonage, her parents made an important decision: they felt that a few months in England would be the best thing for Wil. In a letter to Anna in late July, Miss Applegarth informed her assistant that, in appreciation of her services, she would amend the terms of her contract to allow her sister to stay with her at the school. On 11 August 1875, Pa observed in a letter to Theo 'how much Anna has changed for the better, compared to what she used to be like'.[29] She had become contented and gracious. 'It will surely do Willemien good to be with her and learn.'[30] Dorus was obviously pleased to see his eldest daughter more stable and mature. He also mentioned that 'Willemien loves her so dearly'.[31] He believed that Willemien's visit to Welwyn would be beneficial for both sisters.

Anna and Willemien left for England on Friday 13 August. They boarded the train at Oisterwijk station and arrived in Rotterdam at seven o'clock in the evening. At eight o'clock the following morning they sailed for Harwich. Willemien was acutely seasick on the voyage, but made a speedy recovery once they had reached dry land. Despite her best efforts, Wil's early attempts to speak English at Welwyn were disappointing. She did, however, find a small kitten, which kept her company and afforded some distraction. She had just turned thirteen and barely spoke the language, but that soon changed when she started attending school in Welwyn. The sisters managed to extend Wil's stay by almost six months; Wil returned to the Netherlands in May 1876, while Anna stayed at the school. Moe was pleased with the way that Anna had looked after her younger sister. She wrote to Theo in February: 'We sent Wil a little gold ring, partly from her own money, to give Anna as a memento of her stay with her.'[32]

Anna and Wil were still in Welwyn when Vincent moved to Ramsgate, but Anna was already preparing for a future in the Netherlands. Vincent and Theo placed an advertisement in a Dutch newspaper on her behalf, Vincent enclosing the text he had drafted in his first letter to Theo from Ramsgate. Theo had it published on 28 April in the newspaper of his choice, the *Opregte Haarlemsche Courant*: 'A young lady, minister's daughter, who has been in employment in England for a long period, seeks a job as a lady of company or to nurse a sickly lady. Address letters to: G.H.M. Post Office Welwyn (Herts) (England)'.[33] The *Opregte Haarlemsche Courant* was circulated throughout the country at the time. Lacking political or religious leanings, it was widely respected for its neutral character. Even though Vincent was not earning any money and Theo worked at Goupil in Paris, Vincent sent his brother a ten-shilling postal order to pay for the advertisement, a not inconsiderable sum.[34] In his next letter to Theo, sent a week later, Vincent reported that he had also put an advertisement in an English newspaper: 'Now we can only hope that something will come of it.'[35] Vincent did not seem very confident: 'I'll be glad when Anna has found something, but situations like the ones she is looking for are rather scarce. A sickly lady here who needed someone to look after her received 300 replies to her advertisement.'[36] Yet briefly it looked as if Anna would soon find a position; Vincent wrote to Theo early in May: 'Did you know that Anna has received an answer to her advertisements?'[37]

Anna in fact received three responses, two from Dutch families, and one English enquiry. She had by this time come to love England, and wrote to Theo in June 1876: 'Taking leave of everyone will take a great toll. Perhaps I'll stay on here until Christmas.'[38] Vincent also remarked that Anna was enjoying her time in England. After visiting her that June – having walked all the way from Ramsgate to Welwyn, via Canterbury, Chatham and London – he wrote to Theo: 'I was at our sister's at 5 o'clock in the afternoon and was glad to see her. She looks fine and you would be as pleased with her room as I was, with Good Friday, Christ in the Garden of Olives, Mater Dolorosa &c. with ivy around them instead of frames.'[39] Though Anna responded to the enquiries, she ultimately failed to secure a job. Still lacking work in October, she said in a letter to Theo: 'I still have not found a job. It is a matter of: "I recently saw it in our cat, / hours and hours she sat / waiting for a rat." Patience is the watchword.'[40] She remained in Welwyn until the spring of 1877.

CHAPTER 6

Quiet at Home

Etten, Tiel, Dordrecht, Soesterberg,
's-Hertogenbosch, 1875–1881

Dear Theo, I would like to add a few words for you to Pa and
Ma's letter, to once again say good day to you. It is quite a change
us going to Etten and me to England. How quiet it must be
for Pa and Moe. Now goodbye dear Theo, go well, love you fondly
as always. Wil.'[1]

Willemien wrote this note to Theo from Helvoirt on 11 August 1875.
In July that year Dorus had been offered the position of minister in
the village of Etten, which, like Zundert, is in the western part of the
province of North Brabant, not far from Breda. He had rejected an offer
from Nuenen four months previously, perhaps due to a serious conflict
between the church council and the Society of Well-Being over the
expulsion of one of the Society's lessees, who had been unable to pay
his rent due to health problems. The minister and the church council
took the tenant's side, while the Society wanted to maintain the rule
that rental arrears resulted in eviction. The situation would have been
an insoluble conflict of interest for Dorus, as both a minister and an
active member of the Society's board. Moe discussed Dorus's rejection
of the post extensively in a letter to Theo of 13 March 1875.[2] She formu-
lated the letter in her highly characteristic, somewhat incomplete and
associative manner: 'It is a nice working environment and Pa is very
coveted there, no wonder when you know how Pa is and works, the
salary was definitely higher but there was much to pay for rent and tax
and then a governess alone and nothing no contact for Wil, breaking
off music lessons etc. The combination very difficult due to distance

and road so that the latter objections weigh heavily for Pa's health and strength and the worries above all for Wil immediately had an effect.'5

Just four months later, a new opportunity arose. Three members of the Etten church council attended Dorus's service in Helvoirt on Sunday 11 July 1875. He must have made a good impression, because the council announced just a week later that it wanted him as Etten's minister. Dorus carefully considered the pros and cons, writing to Theo on 30 July 1875 that he had journeyed to Etten the previous day with Moe to inspect the village more closely: 'It was a long struggle for us, but the way of life is simpler and cheaper there, the salary is somewhat better and because we want to economize for the sake of educating the children, it appears to us to be our duty to take this post.'4 Dorus subsequently wrote a letter to the Etten church council, saying that he had 'decided to accept your call of duty after serious and prayerful deliberation.'5 Dorus had already had good experiences with the Dutch Reformed congregation in Etten. While a minister in Zundert, he had acted as locum tenens for some four months after the death of Etten's minister Rein Peaux, promoting the local congregation's interests and helping the church council find a new minister. In this capacity he had also led Pieter Peaux's inaugural service when he returned from Simonshaven to his birthplace of Etten to succeed his father.6

Although Dorus relinquished a successful position when he decided to go to Etten, and the Van Goghs were separated from a significant portion of their family and friends in Helvoirt, the new post had several beneficial aspects too. The salary was somewhat higher, and the costs for the parsonage, garden and staff were paid by the parish. Dorus also took care of the small Protestant community in the adjacent village, de Hoeven, a responsibility he shared with the Reverend Jan Gerrit Kam, for which he received an additional 75 guilders a year.7 The Van Gogh family would also live closer to Uncle Cent and Aunt Cornelie. They had built their home, Villa Mertesheim, in nearby Princenhage, which could be reached by foot from Etten. Leaving behind so many family members in Helvoirt was also ameliorated by the opportunity to renew ties with their extensive circle of friends and acquaintances in the Van Goghs' beloved Zundert. Pa and Moe saw another advantage

Vincent van Gogh and Cornelie van Gogh-Carbentus, *c.* 1860.
Photographed by Marie-Alexandre Adolphe (Adolphe Menut).

in Etten's railway connection, which would enable their eldest children to visit more easily and more often.[8]

One of the reasons that Reverend Pieter Peaux had left the village was the lack of a secondary school for his children. Adolescent children either had to rely on home schooling or go to school or boarding school in a nearby town, such as Breda or Dordrecht. But the four eldest Van Gogh children had left home by 1875, and Wil was going to England with Anna that year, so only Cor moved with his parents to Etten. According to Aunt Mietje's *Notes*, he attended the local primary school for the first year. The middle daughter, Lies, thought that Wil was too young when she was sent to England and that she should have stayed with Pa and Moe to facilitate their transition to Etten,[9] but for reasons unclear from the family's letters, boarding school or other educational opportunities outside the home were not available to Wil in this period. Perhaps it was a financial issue, or the family judged that she would not take to boarding school. It appeared to be a good solution for Wil to stay with Anna in Welwyn. Lies, too, had to admit that there was one major benefit for Willemien, writing to Theo: 'Wil shall have a good knowledge of English when she returns. It is wonderful for her that she is learning unawares, as actual learning is so difficult for her.'[10] On 26 September 1875, Lies wrote in a letter to Theo about the impending move: 'How busy it must be at home with packing. I think it will be good for Pa and Moe to really be in Etten. How difficult it shall be for them to leave Helvoirt. I am curious to know how Wil is faring. I do not think it agreeable that she and Anna write so little. It shall sometimes be strange for Wil too. How Ma must frequently miss her.'[11]

Dorus gave his final sermon in Helvoirt on Sunday 17 October. The family left for Etten the next morning, and on 22 October Dorus and Anna registered themselves, Wil (though she was in England at the time) and Cor at the municipality of Etten and Leur. The villages had around 5,700 inhabitants. Here, too, the vast majority was Catholic; only 158 Protestants were registered, and 8 in the small village of de Hoeven. Dorus van Gogh was confirmed as the nineteenth minister of the Dutch Reformed parish of Etten on Sunday 24 October 1875.[12] The parsonage the Van Gogh family moved to was built in 1652, next to the imposing St Mary's Church, a formerly Catholic institution that had been destroyed in 1584 and rebuilt for Protestant worship in 1614. The church became definitively Protestant after the Eighty Years War and had served the Dutch Reformed congregation ever since. Ma held sewing and knitting lessons in the building twice a week, and in the winter months Pa gave Bible lectures in the consistory, the room where the elders and the minister met.[13]

The parsonage the Van Goghs made their home was old and sometimes stank, but the building's façade was impressive. Thirteen windows, two chimneys and a large diamond-shaped skylight above the front door underlined the occupants' prominence. To the right of the house was an outbuilding with a large window that would become Vincent's first studio when he came to Etten from Brussels. The family lived close to the village centre and yet near the nature they so loved too, with only the cemetery and the church sexton's home between.[14] All of this can be seen on a map that Vincent and the then nine-year-old Cor drew together in 1876. It shows the area where the Van Gogh family lived in Etten, as well as the winding road to Leur, lined with the pollard willows that Vincent often drew. Vincent annotated the map with a series of family names: members of the Dutch Reformed community.[15] The Kaufman family lived on the Leurse Laantje; their son Piet was the parsonage gardener and later one of Vincent's favourite models.

Most of the inhabitants of Etten and Leur worked in agriculture and lived in moderate or extreme poverty. Only a small fraction paid taxes and, consequently, had the right to vote. The minimum amount that had to be paid for the right to vote was 20 guilders[16] a year – only 4 per cent of the population met this requirement. Reverend Van Gogh paid 9 guilders in 1881,[17] making him one of the better-heeled people in the vicinity, but he was still not entitled to vote. It was necessary for him – and many others – to maintain his own kitchen garden and potato plot to feed his family. Moe wrote to Theo in the spring of 1876: 'Our back garden is sown with spinach, carrots, lettuce and shallots, parsley and other bits and pieces. It is very easy. And some berries and raspberries; it is ample for us.'[18] Dorus's post meant he was also the secretary of the Etten church council, and therefore was responsible for resolving disputes about the allocation of plots of land. He of course represented the interests of the Etten Protestants, but, as always, attached great importance to maintaining a good relationship with the Catholic majority. Dorus himself used the same tool as his eldest and youngest son in 1876: copying a map from the village archive on which he indicated exactly which land belonged to the Dutch Reformed parish.[19]

Fourteen-year-old Wil's nine-month stay with Anna in England must have been a long separation from home for her. In Welwyn, the sisters wrote letters to their parents and siblings, about the weather, school and walks they took in the area. The only surviving letter from Willemien to both Vincent and Theo dates from this period, and a few letters written jointly by both sisters have survived. Wil and Anna wrote to Theo, who had broken his leg shortly before: 'Is your leg completely better now? We are currently reading *Het huisgezin van Dr May*, I think it is very good. Do you have rather a lot of time to read. It is very cold here, it snows at any time, yet snowdrops are already open. I hope you shall write to us again soon. We have already worked a bit in our little garden.'[20] Anna added beneath Wil's text: 'We were fine here, but very quiet. It's always beautiful here, we have just recently devised a new walk, to a moor, it was magnificent there. There are gravel-pits and chalk-pits here and that has something very beautiful about it. We are busy working again, from morning until late at night. How wonderful it is that it is so much lighter in the morning. Are you getting up early? We see the sun rise over the cemetery from the living room window. How wonderful it shall be to see each other again. And now it is Pa's birthday on Tuesday.'[21] Wil wrote to Theo three months later: 'I am very happy that I am going home so soon. Around two weeks now and maybe I shall already be at home. I shall certainly have forgotten how to speak Dutch....The trees are already starting to become very green. It's very rainy today. We frequently take lovely walks in the woods, which are full of flowers. I thank you for your most recent letter. Anna has had two letters from Vincent, it seems that he is enjoying himself [in Ramsgate].'[22]

After returning from England, Wil attended lessons with her youngest brother, Cor, at Reverend Jan Gerrit Kam's house in Leur, even though she was already too old to do so. Kam had engaged a 'governor' for his children, which the Van Goghs felt offered a better education than Cor was receiving from the village school he had been attending in Etten.[23] Lies also changed school around this time. The French School for Young Mistresses was to become a girls' secondary school at the beginning of the next academic year, which would mean it could no longer accept pupils from outside the Leeuwarden area.[24] Thus after a year in Leeuwarden she moved to an expensive boarding school for girls from the upper classes in Tiel, an old town in the neighbouring province of Gelderland. A report by the Tiel school committee praised the school as being 'in flourishing state': the number of students had increased; the teachers were talented; and the financial contributions that the headmistress, Marianne Antoinette Brugsma, demanded from pupils' parents maintained her school's high standards.[25] One of the 'junior mistresses' who had worked in Miss Brugsma's employ was Anka Maria (Annemie) Schuil, former governess of the Van Gogh family while they were living in Zundert.[26] But Annemie had already left Tiel before Lies arrived, as she married in 1872, which meant the end of her working life.[27] In principle, this was the case for all upper-middle-class women. Only women from the lowest classes continued to work after marrying, as they relied on this income to support their families. They worked in factories, or as washerwomen, housekeepers or seamstresses in cottage industries.

While Lies sometimes appeared to do better at this school than in Leeuwarden, she was regularly sick and complained about the 'funereal faces around her';[28] yet she also eulogized her time in Tiel, and evidently had some happy times there. She wrote to Theo after the feast of St Nicholas in 1877 to thank him for the beautiful little wallet he had sent her, and mentioned how she had thoroughly enjoyed the festivities in Tiel.[29] Named after the third-century bishop of Myra, this popular annual feast day has been celebrated on 5 December in the Low Countries since the fourteenth century. Lies had celebrated the evening with five other girls and two teachers. She was showered, she informed Theo, with a total of sixteen presents; she also described the jokes in the verses they had written for each other. Like Anna and Theo, Lies had sent some St Nicholas gifts to Etten, among others a photograph of herself and another woman,[30] 'and they appear to have been rather delighted with them at home'.[31]

As in Leeuwarden, Lies was often homesick in Tiel. Nevertheless, she had to prepare for the exam for the assistant teacher certificate of aptitude. In September she wrote to Theo about the pending exams, and reproached herself for a lapse in her correspondence: 'I must also say that it is more than shameful not to write you for so long, but you surely know that confessing one's guilt is halfway to forgiveness?'[32] Anna accompanied Lies to Arnhem on the day of her exam, 11 October 1877.[33] Lies passed, and was thus entitled to call herself an assistant teacher or deputy (a teacher who assists the head of a boarding school). Despite such successes, Lies's doubts about herself and her academic achievements got on top of her. When she failed her English and French exams in May 1878 Miss Brugsma was confounded, as Lies was one of her best pupils, especially in French. Moe, worried about her daughter, travelled to Tiel to collect her.[34]

Lies found it unexpectedly hard to say goodbye to Tiel after such a long time there: 'I cannot comprehend that my final school years are now almost over. They have given me wonderful memories, and it is hard for me to leave Tiel, where I have always received such love and kindness, but what I recently read in a German book is true: *You see yourself, you get to know each other, you love each other, and you must part.* Pa and Ma know this too, watching everybody leave them, and watching them proceed around the wide world.'[35] Although Lies had failed her exams, Miss Brugsma still had faith in her abilities, and recommended her as an assistant or junior teacher to Miss Troost, head teacher of a girls' advanced elementary education school in Dordrecht. Advanced elementary education was a new kind of school that had come into being after the Education Act of 1857 was passed. The schools focused on the practical skills that people needed in a time of rapid modernization, teaching Dutch, French, English, German, algebra, geometry, geography, history, biology, physics, business calculation, accounting and gymnastics. Lies was able to assist there and study for an MMS diploma, especially for English and French. The MMS, Middelbare Meisjes School (Girls' Secondary School), was a five-year secondary education for girls. The first MMS school opened in Haarlem in 1867. It was the equivalent of the HBS, Hogere Burger School (Higher Civic School), which was mainly for boys. While working as an assistant teacher in Dordrecht, Lies continued to study, finally gaining her MMS diploma in July 1878.

Lies was content with her new job and wrote to Theo: 'Does it not sound dignified: my sister who works as a deputy at the advanced elementary education school in Dordrecht.' Theo was in Paris at the time, and Lies thought that it was affecting him considerably; while still in Tiel she had written him: 'Boy, boy, how you must be spoilt, and not seen much anymore. When you once again set eyes upon your humdrum sisters, you should not compare them to the droll Françaises whom you have certainly come to know.'[36] Lies was not only happy that she had found a job with favourable circumstances, but also that, like Theo, she could alleviate the financial pressure on their parents: 'Like you, I can now also work, and somewhat reduce the worries at home'.[37] Lies lived at the home of the Latin school rector, Baron Van Hövell, sharing her room with a former classmate from Tiel who also worked at Miss Troost's school. The lessons were given on the ground floor of the distinguished patrician's house. Yet it soon became clear that Lies was unable to settle here either: 'If my everyday philosophy is not faulty, it is such a pleasure to be satisfied with the present. I am too, but only goodness knows what I shall develop into, for I shall never become a true thoroughbred pedagogue.'[38] By this she meant a somewhat strict and pedantic schoolmaster. In spite of her own misgivings about her skill as a teacher, she was given a permanent appointment, and though she only moderately enjoyed the job, this did give her satisfaction: 'I am starting to make pleasant acquaintances here. Including a widow with two daughters, the eldest of whom is consumptive [has tuberculosis], and who live above us, so I can walk there if I want. It means a great deal to me, even though I need a pleasant environment much less than I did in Tiel.'[39] Lies also returned to a plan she and Theo had once hatched to visit their sister Anna in Leiden, which had fallen to pieces: 'Pa was so opposed to it, because I had been here for such a short while.'[40] There is no indication of whether the siblings ever made this trip.

Lies spent the Christmas holidays with her parents in Etten. Shortly after her return to Dordrecht in January, she had her picture taken by the famous photographer Johann Georg Hameter in the daylight studio on the roof of his building, on the corner of the Voorstraat and the Visbrug (bridge). Hameter also photographed Willemien. Lies appears rather old-fashioned and distinguished for a nineteen-year-old, leaning on a dining room chair. The seventeen-year-old Wil, grimacing, looks a little sick and worried. Photography, invented at the beginning of the century, had become increasingly popular among the middle and

Lies van Gogh, 1879. Photographed by J.G. Hameter.

upper classes; people sent portraits taken by professionals to friends and family as gifts or mementos. In this period, in which the Van Goghs no longer saw each other as a matter of course, these photographs taken in photographers' studios supplemented the family correspondence. As boarders in Leeuwarden, Anna and, a year later, Lies had had photographs taken by the local photographer Ringler as mementos for their parents. Multiple copies were probably made. 'For Theo', underlined with an elegant curl, is written in ink on the back of one picture of Anna. When, in 1875, Anna was unable to attend the family Christmas, she asked Vincent to put the most recent portrait photograph of their youngest sister, Wil, together with letters from the sisters in England, on their parents' plates on New Year's Eve, so that they would discover them at the meal when they returned home after the New Year's Eve service at the church in Etten.[41]

Willemien van Gogh, 1879.
Photographed by J.G. Hameter.

Lies found teaching hard going, in part due to her poor health. 'I have of late been downhearted and annoying and coughing badly,' she wrote in a long letter to Theo on 21 February 1879. 'I called the doctor one evening who examined me and declared that my lungs were well, but my windpipe had been affected.' The doctor forbade her 'to speak for the first while, so that I must now go to Etten for four weeks, and cannot study for a year, because everything has to do with overstrained nerves....You can understand how hard this order is for me,' she continued. 'First of all, terminating the study, stopping my work, and then this intolerable time in Etten, where everyone pities you, tells you about God's providence, sets you to work at the wringer or mending stockings.'[42] Lies had tasted an independent life in a town, with a job and a varied social life, as well as an advanced education. She clearly regarded her return to the village of Etten – where she was condemned to household drudgery, which she had never liked anyway – as a step backwards. Finally, she wished Theo a pleasant Sunday and week, but not before announcing a portrait photograph of herself. This was the portrait made by the photographer Hameter. Lies said about it: 'It is not cheerful and contains a trace of misanthropy and repentance, but it does correspond to my present mood.'[43]

Early in the summer of 1879, when Lies was feeling better again, Moe and Pa decided to employ her as Willemien's governess. Wil had left the Etten village school in April: 'It was not good anymore in the long run...commotions, no order or authority, and she had outgrown it.'[44] Moe hoped that her daughters would teach each other a little at home, before Wil was possibly to continue her education in Breda after the summer. But Lies struggled as a governess, her role complicated by the familial relationship with her pupil, and so the arrangement only lasted a short time. This was to spell the end of her career in education. She found an advertisement for a job in Soesterberg, a small village located between the towns of Utrecht and Amersfoort. While the position may not have been her first choice, she seized the opportunity to leave Etten with both hands: she was to become the companion of Catherina van Willis, wife of Jean Philippe du Quesne van Bruchem, the deputy cantonal judge in Amersfoort. Lies van Gogh registered in Soesterberg on 21 February 1880 and went to live with the family at their estate, the Villa Eikenhorst.[45] This would turn out to be a decisive step, considerably changing the course of her life.

PENSION

Huize EIKENHORST, Soesterberg.

Villa Eikenhorst, Soesterberg. Date and photographer unknown.

CHAPTER 7

Memories of the Garden

Etten, Hengelo (Gelderland), Leiderdorp, 1876–1881

'Dear Vincent and Theo, My heartfelt thanks to you both for your last letters, which we were very glad to receive. How wonderful it will be at home at Christmas. It's been very cold here, but now it's very mild. Theo, how awful about your leg, is it now completely better? We'll probably have a Christmas tree. Our holiday begins on Thursday. And now, goodbye dear Vincent and Theo, I wish you both a very merry Christmas.'[1]

Thirteen-year-old Wil wrote this letter from Ivy Cottage, Welwyn, where she and Anna were spending the first Christmas of their lives without their family. The upcoming holiday reinforced their longing for home and hearth, especially since Pa, Moe, Theo and Lies were all suffering various physical ailments at the time. Fortunately, the Van Goghs still had several wonderful moments ahead of them in the Etten years. The whole family would gather for Christmas the next year; Pa and Moe celebrated their twenty-fifth wedding anniversary; Anna would marry and give birth to the first grandchild, Sara, who was baptized in the village; and Willemien returned from England and was confirmed by her father.

Vincent left London in December 1875, while Anna and Wil were still living in Welwyn, and went to work – without much pleasure – at the Goupil branch in Paris. His employment there lasted only a few months; he increasingly disliked the art trade, particularly dealing with customers, and returned to his parents' home in Etten on 1 April 1876 after falling out with his boss.[2] That he was unemployed aged twenty-three greatly worried Pa and Moe, who wondered what would become of him. In the course of long discussions with his parents back in Brabant,

Vincent decided to return to England and seek employment as a teacher. After several unsuccessful applications, he was offered an unpaid job as a teaching assistant at a boys' school in the seaside resort of Ramsgate.[3] He accepted for lack of an alternative. He did not earn any money, but at least was provided with food and board, and was training to become a teacher. Vincent took a steamship from the Netherlands on 14 April. He remained on deck for a long while as the ship departed, apparently in a reflective mood: 'How much I thought of Anna on the boat; everything there reminded me of our journey together. The weather was clear, and on the Maas especially it was beautiful, also the view from the sea of the dunes, gleaming white in the sun. The last thing one saw of Holland was a small grey tower'.[4] He eventually went below deck, as he was getting cold.

Soon after arriving at the school, Vincent described his new surroundings in a letter to Theo. The room in which he was to teach looked out onto the sea, and the whole class – around twenty-four boys between the ages of ten and fourteen years old – took a walk along the beach

Vincent van Gogh, *View of Royal Road, Ramsgate*, 1876.
Pencil, pen and ink on paper, 6.9 × 10.9 cm (2¾ × 4¼ in.).

every day after dinner. Vincent wrote that it was beautiful there. The daily walk was in keeping with his own preference for travelling by foot. He was only too glad to no longer have to work in the art trade.[5]

During his stay at Ramsgate, Vincent became increasingly engrossed in the Bible. He was struck by a passage from the Gospel of Matthew displayed on the wall of a church he visited: 'And surely I am with you always, to the very end of the world' (Matthew 28:20).[6] It was at this time that Vincent decided to follow in his father's and grandfather's footsteps and become a minister. He seized his chance when given the opportunity to move to Isleworth, near London, to become an assistant minister to a certain Reverend Thomas Slade-Jones. Slade-Jones let him teach Sunday school, and eventually also allowed Vincent to preach in his church at Turnham Green, as well as other churches in the area. During this time Vincent gladly took the opportunity to draw the churches at Turnham Green and Petersham.[7] He seemed happy, writing to Theo, who was ill and staying at Etten: 'I'm really very glad that Mr Jones has promised to let me work in his parish, and that I'll eventually find the right thing.'[8] Although Pa and Moe had their reservations about this unpaid job, Vincent regarded it as an opportunity to see whether he had the potential to become a minister instead of a teacher.

Pa and Moe celebrated their twenty-fifth wedding anniversary on 21 May 1876.[9] Lies and Cor were living at home with their parents, and Wil had arrived that week on the steamship *Batavier* from London.

Letter from Vincent to Theo van Gogh with a sketch of Westminster Bridge above the Goupil & Co. letterhead, sent from Paris on 24 July 1875.

Letter from Vincent to Theo van Gogh with a sketch of small churches at Isleworth, sent from Isleworth on 25 November 1876.

Dorus was unable to pick her up due to an appointment in the nearby village of de Hoeven that afternoon, so had asked Theo, also visiting for the occasion, to collect her from the port of Rotterdam, where her boat disembarked at around six o'clock in the morning.[10] Vincent and Anna both stayed in England.

The eldest sons gave Pa and Moe a print for their anniversary. This was Theo's idea; Vincent wrote to him: 'I think your plan to give Pa and Moe "Après le départ" [After the Departure] by Sadée is very good; that's agreed, then.'[11] The original canvas was painted by Philip Sadée in 1873 and displayed in the 1875 Salon des Artistes, an annual exhibition inaugurated at the Louvre in Paris in 1667 on the instruction of King Louis XIV. This exhibition would later be held at the Grand Palais, built in 1900. It brought together the best work of the French painters, sculptors, engravers, photographers and architects of the day. *Après le départ* is a brightly coloured photogravure of fishermen's wives and children on the beach at Scheveningen, The Hague. The assembly are watching the departure of their menfolk's boats. The print was published by Goupil in 1875. Pa and Moe were very pleased with this gift, and hung it in the drawing room of the parsonage in Etten.

Dorus and Anna enjoyed life in Etten. In the autumn of 1876, the minister was asked to return to his first post, his beloved Zundert, but he announced during a service that he would reject the offer.[12] The couple had only moved to Etten a year previously, and moreover it was unusual for a minister to return to an earlier post. Dorus occasionally stood in for his colleague in Zundert, but that was as much as he would do. He and his wife were also caring for Theo, who had returned home that autumn with some illness; the nature of his condition is not known. Its symptoms were sustained fatigue and attacks of fever. He was nursed conscientiously by Moe and Wil. Vincent, then in Isleworth, felt for his brother: 'I heard from home that you were ill. How much I'd like to be with you, my boy.'[13] His cousins Vincent Willem and Johannes van Gogh, Uncle Jan van Gogh's sons, regularly visited Theo.

It was during Theo's convalescence that Dorus walked to Hoeven in extreme winter weather in November. The ground had frozen and was so slippery that the carriage Moe had ordered could not come, and so Pa was unable to attend to the members of his congregation any other way. Though his brother Jan, who was visiting Etten at the time, tried to persuade Dorus not to go, he was adamant, and so Jan decided to accompany him. 'It was a hard journey,' Pa wrote later to Vincent, 'but Uncle Jan rightly said: the devil is never so black that you can't look him in the face.'[14] Once home, Dorus wrote, 'I cannot describe how wonderful it was to sit so cosily in a nice warm room in the evening, resting after work – that dear Theo was still with us then'.[15] When Vincent heard about it, he was so impressed by his father's accomplishment that he was overcome by nostalgia, recounting the episode to Theo and concluding: 'Shall we, too, go once again to some church *in this way*? As sorrowful yet always rejoicing, with everlasting joy in our hearts because we are the poor in the kingdom of God, because we have found in Christ a friend in our lives that sticketh closer than a brother, who brought us to the end of the journey as to the door of the Father's house'.[16]

The winter might have been very cold, but it was cosy in the parsonage. In December Wil wrote to Theo, who had recovered sufficiently to leave Etten on 14 November and gone to The Hague: 'I received a great deal for St Nicholas. 0.75 [guilders] from Pa and Moe, a pretty bag from Fen and Bet, from Lies too, many exquisite photographs from Uncle and

Aunt, and for Cor and me together much cake and candy.' Willemien was spoiled at school too; the teacher gave her a book. But she missed her middle brother; she thanked him for the soap he had sent her, and was already looking forward to Christmas: 'Lies and Vincent will be coming in eight days on Saturday.'[17] When Vincent returned home to Etten at Christmas 1876, the whole family was present: Pa, Moe and 'the little ones' were there, and Anna had travelled from Welwyn, Lies from Tiel and Theo from The Hague.[18]

It had become increasingly difficult to gather all the family members at once as the eldest children had left home one by one. They tried to maintain contact by writing to each other between family gatherings, and had been looking forward to the upcoming holidays since November. In their letters the siblings repeatedly mentioned how fond they were of Christmas and how they longed to be at home with the family. Anna wrote to Theo in October: 'How wonderful it would be for us all to be at home again for Christmas, which is such a convivial time to have vacations.'[19] Christmas had been a sober festival for Dutch Protestants in the early nineteenth century: the nativity scene was taboo because of the figures in it, especially that of the newborn Christ, and Christmas trees and decorations were a rarity in Protestant homes. Yet times were changing, and many Protestants – including the Van Goghs – began to decorate their homes for the festivities. Yet the siblings were not drawn home by Christmas trees or nativity scenes. For both Protestants and Catholics, Christmas was a celebration of family; families came together, and, as well as attending the service at church, ate together at a festively bedecked table. The siblings wrote to each other again after the holiday that they had enjoyed it so much. Vincent wrote to Theo on New Year's Eve: 'Now, old boy, dear brother, what good days those were when we were all together, have a good New Year's Eve and believe me, Your loving brother Vincent'.[20]

It was decided over this Christmas that Vincent would not return to England, as his work in Isleworth as an assistant minister was voluntary and therefore unpaid. Pa and Moe were also shocked by his physical and mental condition. Lies expressed it more bluntly, noting that Vincent's letters were pervaded with biblical quotations and had taken a rather sermonical tone: 'He has grown dull from piety, I do believe.'[21] Once more, Vincent had to look for a job, and once more Uncle Cent came to his aid, finding him work as an errand boy at the Blussé & Van Braam bookshop on the Voorstraat in Dordrecht. His father came to see him as soon as he had started there in the new year. They visited the Dordrechts Museum together – founded in 1842, it is one of the oldest museums in the Netherlands – and had an enjoyable day. In a letter Dorus suggested to Theo that he visit his brother in Dordrecht, and not the other way around. Vincent's return to the Netherlands had been costly, and since he wouldn't accept any money from his father, he was broke.[22]

Anna finally returned from England a few months later, in the spring of 1877, having found work in the Netherlands. She left Etten on 6 April to move to the village of Hengelo in the province of Gelderland, where she would work for a Mr and Mrs Van Houten and their nine children, who lived in Huize Meenink, on the road between Hengelo and Vorden.[23] She was to become Mrs Sara van Houten-van Heukelom's companion on the estate. While in Hengelo, Anna met the twenty-seven-year-old Joan van Houten, who was the director of a lime kiln in Leiderdorp, just outside the town of Leiden. On 9 July 1877, just three months after she arrived at Huize Meenink, Anna and Joan were engaged. Pa, Moe and Theo appeared very satisfied with Anna's choice; Pa wrote to Theo full of praise about his future son-in-law: 'We are extremely pleased.... We were delighted to meet him when he visited us with his father last Wednesday....We are so happy and grateful for our dear child's engagement.'[24] Only Vincent seemed cautious, writing to Theo: 'She'll perhaps be very happy one of these days, may she have made a good choice and one not to be repented of. The best we can do for the time being is, I think, simply be very happy about it.'[25] Pa had a different idea of Vincent's impression. He wrote to Theo: 'Vincent is so looking forward to this too.'[26] Like Vincent, Moe was surprised by the rapidity of Anna's decision. Anna and Joan had only been courting since Whitsuntide, on 20 May. Even though Joan regularly accompanied Anna on family visits to Etten – the Van Goghs had come to know him well in this short time – their engagement was apparently unexpected.

The wedding took place on 22 August 1878. Anna had struggled with her health in the weeks prior to the celebration and, according to Moe, looked rather 'delicate and thin'.[27] Vincent noticed this too, writing to Theo one month before the wedding: 'Anna is but poorly, she's so quiet and sometimes looks so very weak – poor sister – it seems to me that it's better to be well and truly married than to be engaged, and I should sincerely wish for her sake that she were already safely three years or so further along in life – may God spare her and protect her from all evil'.[28] Anna was suffering from lethargy and abdominal pain. Joan consulted a doctor, who told him that Anna must not exert herself in the weeks before her marriage. As a result, she temporarily moved from Huize Meenink back to her parents' home in Etten.[29]

On 7 August, Anna and Joan took out the banns in both Etten and Leiderdorp, as it was customary for betrothed couples to do so both in their place of residence and where they were getting married. Moe and Theo exchanged much correspondence on the upcoming marriage. Moe said she had heard that 'one will shoot'[30] for Anna, by which she probably meant shooting carbide, a ritual in the south and east of the Netherlands in which gunpowder was detonated in a milk can encased in gut, traditional on New Year's Eve and other celebrations.

Vincent observed in a letter to Theo a week before the wedding that Anna looked much better since she and Joan had registered their banns in Etten. The rest of the family was busy making preparations. To Pa, Moe and Anna's great sadness, Theo was unable to attend the wedding due to obligations in Paris, but he sent Anna and Joan a letter with good wishes. Pa and Moe gave Anna and Joan the Sadée print that their eldest sons had gifted them for their silver wedding anniversary, which had hung in the drawing room in Etten for two years: a memento for Anna of her parental home. Because of his absence, Theo also intended to send a gift of several prints. Pa informed him in a letter on 5 August that they had not yet arrived, and Moe added that 'Such a bloom is needed'[31] as a little reminder of him on the festive day. Besides Vincent, Willemien was the closest of the siblings to the bride-to-be: 'Wil is faithfully at Anna's side, everything for her is now ready, her widow's weeds too, and nothing is missing.'[32]

Pa and Moe described the preparations and wedding day to Theo in great detail. Leafy branches were placed above the parsonage's front door and on the chimney to evoke a guard of honour or laurel wreath, as at Pa and Moe's wedding in 1851. Pa and Wil arranged flower pots, while Joan brought the bouquets. Vincent tried to help, too; he planned to suspend hanging nets for the flowers and make the letters of Anna and Joan's first names from branches. He started working on this well before the wedding day: Dorus wrote to Theo on 5 August that Vincent was already working away in the study room. The gardener Willem brought flowers to decorate the large front room.[33] The daybed was moved, and a gift table installed.[34] According to Moe, it had 'masses of cards' and felicitations on it,[35] as well as a mantel clock and a tray with a decanter and glasses: all gifts for Anna and Joan's home in Leiderdorp. The newlyweds were to move into the director's residence of the lime kiln.

Joan indicated more than a week before the wedding took place that their honeymoon was to be shortened because of Anna's health; they even had to cancel their plans to visit Theo in Paris owing to Anna's frailty. Both Anna and Theo appreciated the wisdom of this decision, but it was a pity, given that Theo had been unable to attend the wedding and was very close to his eldest sister. Joan wrote to his future brother-in-law: 'We should so much have liked to have been able to see you discharging your duties there and you would have been such a good cicerone [guide], but it is too exhausting, which is why we shall not go further than Brussels. Incidentally, all of these places should be packed too as they shall be celebrating in honour of the royal couple at the same time we are coming. They have set a good example for us, having chosen the 22nd as our wedding day.'[36] Joan was referring to the twenty-fifth wedding anniversary of the Belgian King Leopold II and Marie Henriette of Austria, which was being celebrated lavishly in Belgium that August.

Theo's wedding gifts had finally arrived in Etten by then, and Joan thanked him for the beautiful prints in black and brown frames. The couple was very pleased with them, Joan writing that they would 'make a beautiful addition' to their living room in Leiderdorp.[37] Some of the more fragile items were sent directly to their new home rather than to

Etten. Joan wrote gratefully and with satisfaction that they had already received tables full of goods to be able to run 'their little household' together. Anna had remained calm and was already 'a real heroine'. Joan signed his letter to Theo, adding: 'Receive greetings and a handshake, I shall write, your brother Joan.'[38]

Joan expected some twenty family members at the wedding, including three brothers, his sister Saar van Houten and a sister-in-law. His mother, Mrs Van Houten-van Heukelom, was absent from the ceremony, possibly still in mourning, as her husband had died on 30 June of the same year, aged seventy-two.[39] Uncles and aunts from both sides were expected at the wedding, as were old acquaintances and neighbours. Although Joan's mother's absence would have set some tongues wagging, more attention seems to have been paid to an absence on the bride's side: Aunt Cornelie. She had a stomach ailment that precluded her from travelling by coach or train, and so she was unable to come to Etten for the big day.[40] Aunt Willemina Stricker-Carbentus, Moe's sister in Amsterdam, was not present either. Part of the company had arrived on Wednesday 21 August; at half past eight in that evening a brass band played an hour-long serenade to the bride and groom in the parsonage garden.[41]

The couple needed the consent of both the bride and groom's parents to get married. Dorus and Anna van Gogh's presence at the wedding testified to their consent. Joan seemed to be a desirable match, 'a kind and decent person' according to Pa,[42] with a good job and a nice house. A young woman could not do much better in this day and age. Joan's mother expressed her consent in a letter. A certificate was also submitted attesting that Joan had fulfilled his compulsory military service. The civil servant then ascertained that Anna and Joan's upcoming marriage had been proclaimed correctly, two weeks before the date of the wedding, on 8 August, in both Etten and Leiderdorp. Anna's witnesses were her eldest brother and her uncle, the two Vincents. After the civil wedding the whole company went to the Dutch Reformed church, where Dorus solemnized his eldest daughter's marriage. Straight after the wedding ceremony, at twelve o'clock, everyone enjoyed the wedding breakfast, with 'fine dishes'[43] arranged by Uncle Cent. The young couple departed for Brussels at half past three. Dorus was satisfied with the way the day had gone; he wrote to Theo that everyone had participated in the ceremony with interest and 'contentment', and that his daughter had looked 'refined and dear'.[44]

By this time Vincent had resolved upon his ambition to become a minister. He left the bookshop in Dordrecht and moved, in May 1877, to Amsterdam to learn Greek and Latin. As he had failed to complete secondary school, this would enable him to prepare for the gymnasium state exam and a university degree in theology.[45] He stayed in Amsterdam with Uncle Jan van Gogh, a vice-admiral and officer in the Military Order of William, at the naval yard at Kattenburg.[46] Another uncle in Amsterdam, Reverend Jan Paul Stricker, arranged for him to have lessons with a classical languages teacher, Maurits Benjamin Mendes da Costa,[47] who would become a famous Dutch writer. He was to prepare Vincent for the state exam. Moe worried that Vincent lacked the necessary qualities to become a minister. She was proved right – it soon became clear that Vincent was not well-suited to this kind of schooling. On 27 July 1877 he wrote to Theo that it was not easy doing Greek lessons in the heart of the Jewish quarter on a sultry summer afternoon, and he longed for the beach and the cornfields of Brabant.[48] In the end he didn't show the endurance needed to master his studies, and dropped out, definitively precluding any possibility of becoming a minister. He attempted to solve this problem by taking a short evangelist training course in Belgium, travelling in December 1878 to Wasmes in the Borinage, a mining region near the French border in the southern Belgian province of Hainaut. But he was unable to secure a permanent position after his training, and increasingly focused on art – a career move possibly initiated by Theo.[49] Not long before, Vincent had thought he would choose a life resembling his father's, but now the twenty-five-year-old Vincent turned his back on Dorus, and even appeared to dislike him at times. This discord was fed by the limited sympathy his parents were able to muster for his next career choice: becoming a professional painter.

Pa and Moe's concerns about Vincent's career were punctuated by a joyful event: the birth of their first grandchild. Sara Maria van Houten, named after her paternal grandmother, was born in Leiderdorp on

22 July 1880.[50] Grandfather Dorus led the baptismal service in Etten on 29 August.[51] On 28 December of the same year, Wil did her confirmation with her father, also in Etten.[52] By this time Vincent had moved from the Borinage to Brussels, where he lived at the expense of Theo and his parents while he pursued his new artistic ambitions. He returned to Etten at the end of April 1881 to live at the parsonage, using the ivy-covered outbuilding looking out onto the garden as a studio. The building can be seen in three surviving

J. Goedeljee, *Sara Maria van Houten*, 1888.

drawings. Two of them were by Vincent – he drew one, depicting the entire parsonage, in 1876 (pl. IV), and the other, entitled *Tuinhoek* (Corner of a Garden), in 1881.[53] The third was by Willemien, who copied Vincent's first drawing and gave it her own interpretation by colouring it in more, adding buds to the trees and leaving out certain details (pl. V). Wil made several drawings over the course of her life; her own creativity in this respect was discussed in detail many years later in a letter from Lies to her Van Houten nieces.[54]

In 1879 Wil attended the Mann sisters' school in 's-Hertogenbosch to train in handicrafts, among other things. She received her diploma in April 1880.[55] Upon her return home she soon became Vincent's favourite model. After several months in Etten, during which she posed for Vincent frequently, she moved to Weesp on 2 July 1881 to work as a governess for the widow Mrs Scheffer-Michielsen and her five daughters.[56] Her new employer's family had returned from the Dutch East Indies upon the death of her husband, who had been the director of the botanical gardens in Surabaya, a city on the island of Java. Vincent regretted Wil's departure and wrote to Theo: 'Willemien has left and I'm sorry, she poses very well, I have a drawing of her and one of another girl who

Vincent van Gogh, *Anna van Gogh-Carbentus*, 1888. Oil on canvas, 40.5 × 32.5 cm (16 × 12¾ in.).

Anna van Gogh-Carbentus ('Moe'). Date and photographer unknown.

stayed here.'[57] After a short period in Weesp, Wil moved with the Scheffer family to Haarlem, but she worked for them for only a year and a half.[58]

Vincent stayed with his parents until the end of 1881. Life was cheap in Etten, and he was able to fully focus on his sketches and drawings. Several of the villagers were prepared to model for him. He also drew the parsonage's lush garden many times, and would draw it from memory during his stay in Arles in 1888, painting his mother and Wil in *Memory of the Garden at Etten* (pls VI, VII). Years later he wrote in letters that working on this painting had reminded him of the plots of land connected to the parsonages in Etten and Nuenen where the Van Gogh family had lived between 1875 and 1885. Homesickness prompted him to make the painting, which he hung in his bedroom as a reminder of home.[59]

Memory of the Garden at Etten recalled his family life in Brabant, but could not be taken too literally, Vincent explained to Wil, saying that it was more a poetic, dream-like visual representation based on lines, shape and colour: 'The figure in the Scottish plaid with the orange and green checks standing out against the dark green of the cypress, this contrast even more exaggerated by the red parasol, gives me an idea of you, vaguely a figure like those in Dickens's novels.'[60] He also wrote that he had not 'intended to render the garden in its vulgar resemblance but draw it for us as if seen in a dream, in character and yet at the same time stranger than the reality.'[61] The elderly woman in the painting was very similar to the photograph of Moe he had received a month previously from Willemien. Painting this portrait in October 1888 made a deep impression on Vincent, as he and his mother had not seen each other for almost three years by then. Vincent wrote to Theo while working on it from Arles: 'I'm writing to you in haste; I'm working on a portrait. That's to say I am doing a portrait of our mother, for myself. I can't look at the colourless photograph and I am trying to do one with harmonious colour. As I see her in my memory'.[62]

CHAPTER 8

Great and Holy in his Final Rest

Nuenen, Leiderdorp, Soesterberg, 1882–1886

Pa received a second request to relocate to Nuenen on 2 April 1882. This time he agreed with little hesitation. The salary of 1,100 guilders[1] was the highest he would ever earn, and having only thirty-five members in the congregation, the Nuenen posting presented another challenge for the minister to build and strengthen the Protestant community of North Brabant. Additionally, the eye-catching parsonage was to be renovated according to the Van Goghs' wishes before they arrived. The monumental eighteenth-century building was in the centre of the village, and the surrounding countryside was beautiful and varied. There were meadows, forests and moors, arable land, uncultivated land and a watermill that Vincent drew in 1884 (pl. ix). Vincent, Pa, Moe, Cor and two servants registered at the municipality on 7 August.[2]

Only the twenty-year-old Willemien found Nuenen less favourable than Etten. She would not easily find work there, and would have to rely on her parents. She readily pitched in when the family needed her; such a supportive role was often left to the youngest daughter in the nineteenth century, especially regarding the care of elderly parents. But Wil would also look after other family members, including Theo, Lies and later Vincent.[3] Cor was enrolled at the HBS in Helmond, which was easy to reach from Nuenen by railway.[4] There he became friends with Naud Carp, the son of a big cigar manufacturer; the Carps were among the most important families in the nearby textile town of Helmond and, like the Van Goghs, were Protestant. Cor regularly visited Naud's family home.

Cor graduated in August 1884, after which he started looking for employment. He applied for a post at the machine factory Stork Brothers

& Co. in Hengelo (in the province of Overijssel, in the east of the country) because it did not charge an apprenticeship fee, but he was rejected,[5] and considered continuing his studies at the technical college in Delft, but the tuition was too expensive.[6] However, Nuenen had a major advantage lacking in Dorus's previous posts: a railway station connecting it to larger towns in the vicinity (though Etten had a railway station, it was not near a large town). In particular, the towns of Helmond and Eindhoven had plenty of opportunities for Cor. Dorus devised a compromise and enlisted Cor as a student at the Begemann machine factory in Helmond, where he could complete his technical training somewhat more cheaply than at the technical college, though still for a not inconsiderable sum: '300 guilders apprenticeship fee, 150 guilders tuition fees and 360 guilders board and lodging.'[7] There were additional costs for clothing and school supplies, but Dorus was prepared to invest a great deal in his youngest son's career; he and Moe were optimistic about Cor's future: '[he] resolutely appears to want and knows from close hand, [from] the young people he associated with in Helmond, that one must work with energy there. If only he succeeds! And this first step leads to a happy and honourable future....We must not hesitate and pray for blessing.'[8] On Monday 21 July Pa paid Mr Begemann – who had already announced that he would accept Cor – a visit to discuss the fees.

Nuenen's advantages were also attended by several drawbacks, including the size of the municipality, which Reverend Dorus would often have to traverse on unpaved roads to visit members of his congregation. Disagreement also arose in Nuenen in 1880 over the inspection of the Society of Well-Being's goods. Dorus was officially called to his new congregation on 8 June 1882. It is likely that he was thought well placed to solve these problems, partly due to his years of experience with the Society. He was officially inducted on 11 August 1882 in Nuenen's small octagonal Protestant church, as the congregation's eleventh minister. A verse from the Epistle of St Paul the Apostle to the Corinthians was the starting point of his first sermon: 'For Christ sent me not to baptize, but to preach the gospel' (1 Corinthians 1:17).[9] As on previous occasions, many of Dorus's relatives attended the service. Aunt Antje van Gogh, Aunt Truitje 's Graeuwen and her husband Abraham, along with their children

Antje van Gogh, before 1883.
Photographed by Ferdinand Reissig.

Fanny, little Betje and Bram, travelled from Helvoirt in a wooden cart. 'They greatly enjoyed' the trip of some 40 kilometres (25 miles); 'It was so exciting and pleasant,' Aunt Mietje wrote in her *Notes*.[10]

The Van Goghs' move to Nuenen took place during a turbulent period in Dutch history. A major agricultural crisis caused by the import of enormous quantities of cheap grain and other agricultural products from the United States lasted throughout the 1880s. In addition, the mechanization of agriculture resulted in many field labourers losing their jobs and livelihoods. These people migrated in large numbers to urban centres, where they sought work in factories or service in the army. Some of them ended up in the small-scale textile industry that was developing in that period, particularly in North Brabant and Twente, a region in the east of the country. In Nuenen, weavers working from home produced cloth for manufacturers in towns. There were plans to open a modern textile factory in the village, but it failed to materialize. Nuenen's failure to modernize meant that weavers' orders declined, and eventually almost completely disappeared.[11] It is not by coincidence that Vincent made many drawings and paintings in this period of men and women at the loom, as well as of spinners: the women who spun the threads for the weaving process. Most of them were agricultural labourers trying to generate some additional income by producing semi-finished products for the textile industry, especially during the winter, when the cattle were in cowsheds and the ground could not be worked. Changes in the agricultural industry also had other consequences: the cultivation of grain, particularly rye and buckwheat, was declining and there was an increase in potato cultivation, as it was an easy crop to grow. The high price of bread caused dietary changes: rye bread and buckwheat pancakes and porridge were replaced with potatoes. At meals everyone took a potato from the pan with a tin fork and dipped it in bacon fat. People sometimes ate potatoes twice a day on working days, freshly cooked at the main meal at noon and reheated at the end of the day.[12] In 1885 Vincent combined the atmosphere of the communal meal with an emphasis on its main element by painting *The Potato Eaters* in Nuenen (pl. x).[13]

In these years, at around the age of seventeen, Willemien started having regular contact with people outside her immediate family circle. Through the Van Goghs' social network she befriended Margaretha Meijboom, the daughter of a minister from Amsterdam, who taught at a Sunday school. Margaretha was at first friendlier with Lies, and had already visited the family in Etten. She would often accompany Aunt Wilhelmine Stricker-Carbentus when she was visiting her sister, Wil's mother, in Brabant.[14] Wil and Margaretha became close friends, initiating at this time an intimate correspondence that would continue for years; at least forty-six letters from Margaretha to Wil are known, though unfortunately none of Wil's responses has survived. Margaretha lived in The Hague and for a time was engaged to Paul Stricker, a cousin of the Van Gogh family, although the betrothal would be broken off. Margaretha wrote later, in 1887, to Willemien: 'He rejects my sympathy for strong, unruly female behaviour, and actually rejects my hatred of small-mindedness. He loves those "thousand trifles that are so sweet about a woman" and I believe I miss 999 of them. Not that I like it; I would love to be gracious, lively, convivial, sharp, etc., but I am not and now prefer to become untrue and unnatural by studying or rather imitating the qualities of other women that I lack myself. And now I can hardly believe in a love that does not understand and hurts.'[15] Margaretha and Wil corresponded on subjects that occupied many women's discussions in the nineteenth century: family, health, literature, music and their own physical and mental condition. It would later become apparent that the latter subject in particular brought them together: 'I love having been, and being able to continue being, something for you, but do not call me pure, because it stifles me. I have to fight so much against my irregularity

Willemien van Gogh, 1878.
Photographed by J.F. Rienks.

of temperament, against gloominess, against my own vehemence which is sometimes so great that it shocks me, against a hundred egoistic and petty thoughts which I find ugly and suppress but are there anyway. My ideal is [to be] a calm and powerful and gentle woman, which I do not yet fully resemble! But it is nice that we have virtually the same difficulties to fight against and want to go in the same direction. Let us therefore firmly hold and support each other and keep each other informed of our progress.'[16]

Why Wil stopped working for the Scheffer family a year after their move from Weesp to Haarlem cannot be deduced from Wil's or others' letters from the time. Without new employment, she was dependent on her parents once more and returned to Nuenen on 22 November 1882. Only occasionally in these years do we gain insight into Wil's well-being or activities, from her letters or others'. Aunt Mietje mentioned her in a letter to Theo in February 1883. Mietje was staying with the family in Nuenen, while Willemien was at her sister Anna's home in Leiderdorp, helping with the birth of her second niece, Anna Theodora, born on 12 February. Mietje was very pleased that Wil had gone to Leiderdorp: 'Wil is now doing good work at Anna's; it is strange that she is not here.'[17] She addressed Lies's condition in the same letter: 'I also saw your Lies for a while, she looks a little better than in the autumn, I received a delicate, sensitive verse from her.'[18] Lies had sent her this verse to console her when her sister, Aunt Antje, died.

After her return from Leiderdorp, much of Wil's time was spent caring for her parents, who were in their mid-sixties by then. Lies also returned from Soesterberg to be nursed by Wil later in the year.[19] The root of Lies' poor health and fatigue is unclear. It may be that she was overstrained; she found the endless cleaning of the seventeen rooms in the Du Quesne family home in Soesterberg and caring for the sick Mrs Du Quesne taxing. Yet Wil was not always a pillar of strength in the house; she was also incapacitated at times, forcing a reversal of roles. For example, Lies thanked Theo on behalf of Wil in a letter dated 9 December 1883 for the 'most beautiful prints' she had received from him for the feast of St Nicholas. Wil was bedridden with severe stomach pain, Lies wrote, 'which is why she does not thank you for herself'.[20]

Anna Theodora van Houten, 1895. Photographed by J. Goedeljee.

Moe Van Gogh broke her femur when disembarking from the train in Helmond in January 1884. Aunt Mietje came to stay in Nuenen to keep her company and assist around the house, and later described in her *Notes* how Cor, who worked in Helmond, enlisted Helmond minister Lakeveld's help after Moe's fall. Cor and the minister brought a doctor with them, who applied a temporary splint to Moe's leg, after which the doctor, clergyman and patient went to Nuenen in a carriage. Their doctor in Nuenen was informed in the meantime, so that he could 'prepare' the family members at home and set up Pa's study as a sick room.[21] Vincent was full of praise about the way Wil nursed their mother through her recovery. He wrote to Theo at the beginning of March: 'At the outset the doctor said it would be six months before the leg had healed – now he's talking about a good 3 months – and he said to Moe – "but that's your daughter's fault, for I seldom, very seldom, see such good care as she gives". What Wil does is exemplary, exemplary, I shan't easily forget that.'[22] Wil was responsible for almost all the care and Vincent assured Theo she had 'spared Moe a great deal of misery....And I assure you that the chores she has to do aren't always pleasant.'[23] Aunt Mietje cast more light on Lies and Wil's health problems in her *Notes*: 'The girls' discomfort was, as it were, corrected by this shock [Moe's accident]. Wil and Vincent were of great assistance.'[24] Lies soon recovered and returned to Soesterberg.[25] As Moe was being well cared for and Lies and Wil felt better again, Aunt Mietje was able to report in April: 'Everything is going very well in Nuenen, ten weeks after the fall the patient is starting to learn to walk with much assistance, she also has a cart with which she can be taken around the garden and can sit there.'[26]

Moe's rehabilitation took a long time, but was so successful that, even aged sixty-five, she learned to walk with a stick and 'could move quickly for years to come'.[27] Pa said that it was nice to see Moe progressing so well and persevering. In a letter dated 30 December to Theo, he remarked that the accident was the most important event of the year for him. He added that it was 'a great blessing that she should be able, at least as far as we are now, to recover. Lying tires her more than being occupied; it is a strange thing.'[28] He wrote that they took walks together, sometimes for longer than an hour, and she managed well. It was a good thing that Moe had regained most of her mobility, as Wil was suffering severe toothache at the time, and had to rest. This was a pity, as she appeared to have found purpose in giving Dutch and French lessons. She gave these two-hour lessons three times a week, but to whom and where is unclear. Ma wrote to Theo on 21 January 1885: 'She has much satisfaction, she is doing well.'[29]

In the summer vacation of 1884 Wil stayed with Anna and Joan and their daughters Sara and Anna Theodora in a guesthouse in Noordwijk aan Zee, a seaside resort on the coast of the province of South Holland, not far from Leiden.[30] Theo paid for his youngest sister's vacation – as he paid for many other things for his siblings. Noordwijk was primarily a fishing village until about 1866, when visitors started flocking there to take advantage of the beneficial effects of sea air on the body and mind. Bathing in the sea – a new practice – was also believed to contribute to good health. It was even the fashion at the time to drink sea water. Bathers initially boarded at people's homes, and later in guesthouses. The first foundations of the Huis ter Duin hotel were laid in 1883; it opened in 1885. In 1884, Willemien, Anna, Joan and the children stayed with Mr Maarten Verloop at 52 Noordwijk aan Zee. Verloop was a carpenter who also hosted bathers, making him one of the first guesthouse owners. The weather was magnificent, and they had a wonderful time, walking a great deal during this two-and-a-half-week vacation. The holiday at the sea apparently had a great impact on Wil's health, though she began to deteriorate again just as she was due to return home. Pa wrote to Theo on 19 July: 'Wil is likely to come back home this coming Thursday. They have had much enjoyment, but Anna has complained of late that Wil was again tired and now seemed less well. Yet she was able to go to The Hague, where she was invited to witness the Prince's funeral.'[31] He was referring to the recently deceased crown prince Alexander, who was transferred from the palace in The Hague to the Nieuwe Kerk (New Church) in Delft on 17 July 1884, to be buried in the House of Orange-Nassau family vault. Alexander had died of typhus at the age of thirty-two, leaving his almost four-year-old half-sister Wilhelmina the heir to the throne.

Vincent went to Nuenen in early December 1883. He had been painting in the northern province of Drenthe for three months, but the loneliness of the remote countryside and financial hardships brought this to an end. He stayed at the parsonage in Nuenen until May 1885, first using the laundry room as a studio and later renting two rooms from the verger Schafrat of the Catholic Church of St Clement, where he could withdraw from the family and so fully dedicate himself to his work. He slept more and more often in the drying loft above his studio in Schafrat's house.

Vincent made several paintings of the parsonage, the garden, the neighbourhood and the locals during his time in Nuenen. Long before he went to live there himself, Vincent had heard from Pa, Theo and Wil's letters how wonderful the nature around Nuenen was. In a reply to Theo, Vincent expressed how he was looking forward to painting the old tower and surrounding cemetery with its wooden crosses. Vincent also painted the octagonal Dutch Reformed church, dating from 1842, where the family attended the weekly service and where his father preached. He sketched the composition in a letter to Theo,[32] and gave the painting to his mother. Moe was very attached to this painting, and kept it for the rest of her life.

Vincent painted the parsonage where the family lived more than once. He made at least ten drawings of the garden behind the studio, including two pen drawings of the garden in snow in 1884. The Nuenen winters were cold and white, and Vincent painted them beautifully. During the Christmas holidays Cor came home with a few other students to go ice skating. Dorus enjoyed having them in the parsonage; he liked seeing how well they got along. He was fond of having a large and harmonious company around the table, and wrote to Theo that they had hosted 'the young people' for a meal on Boxing Day – Cor, his Begemann colleagues and Wil, who was 'so revived, after her toothache had gone again'.[33] The boys were rehearsing a comedy that they would perform at the Begemann's warehouse on New Year's Eve.

The year 1884 had been difficult for Anna and Joan, coping with two small children and the death of Joan's mother on 27 November in the city of Arnhem. Yet Pa and Moe did not appear very affected by the Van Houten family's circumstances. On the subject of the death of Mrs Van Houten Dorus wrote to Theo simply 'I think I have heard that this does not change the financial situation', before entreating Theo in the following sentence to come to Nuenen again in the new year.[34]

In that same year, Vincent drew the back of the parsonage for the first time. This drawing would later belong to Lies, who wrote extensively about it in her memoirs in 1910. She said she could see in the drawing, which she calls both 'masterly' and 'anxious and mysterious', that Vincent was unhappy and uneasy at the time: 'From the old-fashioned, gently subsiding building, from the well-cared-for, friendly garden, he created a haunted house enclosed with wild grasses.'[35] The wind is swaying all the trees to one side, and it is not possible to tell from the figures whom Vincent was depicting.

All of the family but the two elder brothers gathered in the parsonage on Shrove Tuesday in February 1885. The Van Goghs did of course not celebrate the Catholic festival, but most factories, shops and government buildings were closed for the religious holiday, so Cor did not have to go to Helmond and Pa had little to do. Lies had come from Soesterberg, and Wil was at home to help Moe. Dorus reflected sadly on Vincent's absence to Theo, who by that time was back in Paris: 'It seems as though he is becoming increasingly alienated from us...his irascibility hinders any conversation, and this in itself indicates that is not normal.'[36] He concluded with the lamentation that they hoped 'and prayed for light and wisdom and for him, oh could it be so! to live a bit contentedly again.'

Vincent was fully engrossed in his painting in Nuenen. Having his own studio at some distance from the parsonage made an important difference, and he made some of his most famous works during this period, such as *The Weaver* and *The Potato Eaters*.[37] The inhabitants of Nuenen were often his models, as in these works. His family and other influential townsfolk were embarrassed that he used the local population as models. It was not considered proper for a minister's son to be so involved with the peasantry. Moe also objected to Vincent paying for his models, because he usually did so with Theo's money – the paintings were still not selling, after all.

There was a great deal of conflict between Vincent and his family in this period, which culminated in September 1885. The Catholic Father Andreas Pauwels had intervened, trying to convince Vincent not to fraternize with people from a much lower class than his own, but Vincent rejected his advice. Pauwels eventually ordered the Catholics in Nuenen not to pose for Vincent anymore. He was even willing to pay them money to forego modelling for Vincent. Moe and Theo worried about the situation, wondering why the priest was interfering. 'May Vincent soon find something else suitable,' Moe said.[38] Everyone to whom Theo showed his work said that it certainly had potential – he must just keep going! It seems that their mother did not wish for him to stop painting altogether – although the family found his behaviour socially unacceptable, and she found his art hard to understand, she kept a collection of his work for herself until her death. Of course, it was not Vincent's art alone that caused these tensions to rise to the surface in the autumn of 1885.

Theo received a letter from Nuenen on 25 March 1885. Moe reported that Pa was 'extremely busy', including preparations for Cor's confirmation and that of some of his friends.[39] Wil had just returned from a two-week stay with Anna and added a cheerful section to Moe's letter: 'Dear Theo, I would like to thank you with a few words for the beautiful set of photographs that you sent me on my birthday, I am very happy with it and I think it is so beautiful, and there are so many of them. And I thank you very much for your friendly letter. We long to hear about your summer plans; as we have already said, it would be nice if Lies and you could be here at the same time. Anna shall probably also come for a while in the summer. I was in Leiden with great pleasure. The children are so cute. Little Anna is now walking a great deal; it is so pleasant that they are so seldom sick nowadays, it was such a concern for them. We are rehearsing for a Comedy piece. It would be very nice if it were to go rather well, it gives a bit of variety. And now, dear brother, I shall leave it here, a warm kiss from your so loving Wil.'[40]

Quite unexpectedly, a sad and dramatic event would cause all the children to go to Nuenen the next day. Pa's sudden death on 26 March 1885 would have far-reaching ramifications for the Van Gogh family. Vincent would have the quarrel with Anna that resulted in him leaving the Netherlands for good; and Moe and Willemien would be compelled to move to Breda, and eventually to leave their beloved North Brabant.

Lies wrote of Pa's death in her memoirs: 'The unexpected death of Vincent's father – a heart condition of which he was unaware, which killed him in an instant – hastened Vincent's departure. Vincent did not leave the bed where the dead, great and holy man lay in his final rest in the days preceding the funeral. "It is better to die than to live," Vincent said, when a faithful soul walked in on tiptoes to see the deceased once more.'[41] A little further on she wrote of her brother's 'eccentricity' and 'withdrawal from communal life', which could mainly be seen at the table, where Vincent sat separately during dinner. She was incensed by fellow villagers, particularly in Etten: 'The supposedly interested friends and family members bothered Vincent's parents with indelicate questions. – It was not about a young man of his age not yet earning his living; they had to deal with him differently; he should not isolate himself; he should dress better; he should be like everyone else; – as though it is not sometimes a privilege not to be like many others! – His father should have put him in an asylum. – That is what the thousand-witted Cruelty, called the World.'[42] Not only Lies, but Wil and Anna were also very affected by the quarrel. After she and Moe had moved to Breda Wil wrote to her friend Line Kruysse about its aftermath: 'He took it so badly that we have not heard from him since. I hope he will forget his grievances gradually, because it is such a sad relationship, and something like that so easily leads to disunity.'[43]

The family had to attend to several practical matters after Dorus's death. One was making an inventory of the parsonage, which was the responsibility of the local notary Abraham Schutjes.[44] In 1851, the year of his marriage, Dorus had written a will stating that half of his belongings should go to his widow and the other half be split among his (future) children. But the will had not been registered, despite having been drawn up in the presence of a notary.[45] Nevertheless, the execution of his estate was done in the spirit of his decision. Only Vincent, Wil, Ma and Uncle Paul Stricker were present when Schutjes described the estate.[46] The contents were valued in their entirety rather than per object. The inventory gives the impression of a somewhat bourgeois middle-class home. Apart from the many prints, which were not included in the inventory owing to their modest value, there was a mirror or painting in every main room in the parsonage and there was a clock on every mantelpiece. It is also striking that the items in all the main rooms for both day (the living and dining rooms and studies) and night (the bedrooms) were valued more or less equally; one would expect the more expensive objects to appear in the living room or the study. The inventory also revealed that some of the best furniture was in the guest room, which was unusual for the time. As well as household effects, the catalogue included the deceased minister's portfolio holdings. Pa had a large number of Austro-Hungarian gold and silver bonds, and bonds for the construction of railways in Russia and the United States.[47] It was a varied collection of investments, which left the heirs a reasonable balance after deducting liabilities and debts.

The Dutch Protestant Church at Nuenen, between 1880 and 1910.
Photographer unknown.

Vincent was not faring well physically in the months after his father's death. He suffered from stomach complaints and had at least ten bad teeth requiring urgent treatment. His dental problems were the result of a medical treatment he had undergone in Antwerp: mercury baths. He used his financial position as an argument for not going to Nuenen to help settle his father's estate: 'Let's consider whether or not any help they might get from me would be worth the journey there and back'.[48] Apart from practical considerations, it had become clear to Vincent that his presence in the parsonage in Nuenen was not desired by all at the time and was even considered burdensome by some: 'If I encountered opposition and scenes like I got before I left, I would be wasting my time there'.[49] Vincent eventually travelled instead to Paris to join his brother, who had been working there as an art dealer since 1878.

CHAPTER 9

My Greatest Ambition is
to Write Something Original

*Soesterberg, Middelharnis,
Amsterdam, Paris, 1885–1888*

In August 1885, six months after Dorus's death, someone new came into the lives of the Van Goghs. Johanna Gesina Bonger, called Jo, had grown up in a liberal family in Amsterdam, with nine brothers and sisters. Her parents lived at 137 Weteringschans, diagonally opposite the new Rijksmuseum, which had opened in the summer of 1885. The younger sister of Andries Bonger, a friend of Theo's in Paris, Jo was destined to play an important role in the family as Theo's wife, as a friend of the sisters and as a fourth daughter to Moe. It was Jo who would ultimately keep the Van Gogh family name alive and preserve Vincent's legacy.

Jo met Theo on 7 August 1885, while she was visiting her brother Andries in Paris. In October, on Theo's suggestion, she and Lies struck up what was to become a lasting correspondence; Theo suspected that the two women's shared interests would result in a close relationship, and indeed they quickly brought each other into their confidence. 'My conscience never troubles me more than when I recall, in my childhood, the countless books that were hidden away from me in every nook and cranny of the house, and which I just as often managed to lay my hands on; of those times in bed when I devoured them, shivering with fear, and of the remorse I felt when I was caught.'[1] Lies wrote these words to Jo on 17 November 1885 from the Villa Eikenhorst in Soesterberg, where she had spent the past six years as a nurse-companion to Mrs Du Quesne-van Willis.[2]

Lies loved literature. As a child she would not allow a day to go by without spending at least an hour on poetry. At fourteen she was writing verses about nature and, like her two sisters, she kept a poetry album, which contained contributions from her family, her classmates and friends, a few of the Du Quesnes and one or two acquaintances. These were the people with whom she surrounded herself at the age of twenty-six.

Jo shared Lies's love of literature. She had trained as an English teacher and was working as a translator when she met Theo and began to correspond with Lies. This encounter between the future sisters-in-law, conducted on graph paper, developed into an enthusiastic exchange that lasted throughout the winter. They did not set eyes on each other until a few months later, in Amsterdam. The letters that they shared before this meeting conjure up an image of two young women eager to offer a glimpse into their hearts and minds, Jo explaining: 'That is why I shall enjoy professing my beliefs on the subjects of literature, painting, music, all those things I sadly know so little about, but that I passionately enjoy, that make my life so rich and pleasurable.'[3]

Their letters were more than academic exchanges about the arts. They also discussed their appearance and vanity, their experiences of love, having a job and earning money, and their aversion to housekeeping and especially spring-cleaning – a duty that women were expected to perform. Lies wrote to Jo, 'To begin with, your wanting a decent job, your desire to do something other than repetitive household chores in the same monotonous sequence – I felt the same before I came here! And yet, like you, I love my home. I wonder whether you find cleaning as tiresome as I do. But nor would I pretend to be a bluestocking; I have the temerity to admit I'm not; I sometimes even sew my own dresses, though only when I can't afford to have them made. I should far prefer not to.'[4] In the same letter Lies talked about her feelings for her brother Theo, which ran far deeper than her affection for Anna, Wil, Vincent or Cor. She likened this devotion to Jo's love for her brother Andries. 'Do you also have such a yearning to love? We often deceive ourselves because of it, and yet we so easily make the same mistake again. The one person I have loved always and constantly is, like you, my brother Theo.

Neither of my sisters nor any of my other brothers could ever compare with him.'⁵ And, a short time later, 'You mentioned Eliot in your letter. Have you read *The Mill on the Floss* by her? I do hope so. Don't you think it describes the love between brother and sister beautifully?'⁶

At Jo's insistence, Lies gave a description of herself: 'What I look like? In one respect you were right, i.e. that I am petite, nowhere near as tall as Theo and more slightly built! But I am not blonde. When my housemistress during my years at boarding school felt called upon to say something hateful to me, she would say I had red hair. I, however, would say it is a good brown, perhaps what people might call chestnut. She knew perfectly well that she was touching a sore spot, that beastly woman; I, who actually fancied it was my one asset because I didn't have to put it in curlers.'⁷ Jo replied in kind. 'Now I owe you a description; build – quite tall, taller than your brother – eyes – dark brown – hair even darker, black in fact, and I was foolish enough last week to have it cut short, so at the moment you must picture me looking like a boy. Oh, here comes another confession – I should like so much to be beautiful, truly beautiful, not for silly coquettish reasons, but from a purely aesthetic point of view. But it is definitely good that I am not, for I would surely have been vain; some busybodies say I already am, I am teased for looking in the mirror so much. As you see, I tell you everything, and to be honest I must say that I like looking as attractive as I can, and if I could afford it, I would always be beautifully turned out. I like seeing someone who is well turned-out, for which colour harmony is all-important; I get so cross with people who spend lots of money and the result is tasteless nonetheless! Sometimes I have moods of puritanical simplicity and fancy that I would have made a good nun who has forsworn the world and its vanities.'⁸ Lies's reply was just as frank. 'The first thing I do when I am alone is look in the mirror to see what I looked like or to fathom how people would have seen me.'⁹

Lies's reflections on her years at boarding school had a slightly bitter undertone. She compared her teachers to Hans Christian Andersen's Snow Queen: 'You go there with an unblemished heart nurtured by the fires of home, sensitive to any unkind word, totally unacquainted with the meanness of the woman who presents herself in the prospectus as one who loves the girls entrusted to her care like a mother. Let me hold my tongue as to how that young heart, so eager to grow attached and accustomed to warmth, is turned away by coldness. I hope you know Andersen's fairy tales? As a child I learnt them off by heart and I still think they are unforgettably poetic and beautiful. Do you know the one about the Snow Queen, how she pressed the little girl to her icy heart until love and everything good in the child's heart was frozen. Every schoolteacher is a Snow Queen like that, you see, at least everyone I've come across in that category.'[10] She returned to the subject of boarding school in a later letter, writing about an unwelcome, but ardent admirer. 'I was only thirteen when I went to boarding school in Leeuwarden, though we were living in the south of Brabant. I was so homesick that Pappa kept me there for one year only and then sent me to Tiel, where I stayed up to the time of my exam. I went out all the time there, as a lady who had taken me "en amitié" used to take me everywhere. I loved her as I would a mother and she adored me. Unfortunately, there was a youngster lodging in her house, well he wasn't even all that young but he had moved in when he was still a boy. He was extremely formal and aloof, seemed never to take any notice of me, but felt called upon to advise me on lots of things, which I had absolutely no desire for him to do, and why I found him frightfully annoying, as I made abundantly clear. In spite of that he made a passionate declaration, which astonished and unsettled me and which I immediately discussed with my friend.'[11]

Later, Lies confessed to another romantic escapade – this time the feelings were mutual – which had made it difficult for her to leave the city of Dordrecht in 1879. The name of the young man is never revealed. 'Our relationship was secret,' she confided in Jo, until a friend found out and wrote to Pa about it. Pa came from Etten in all haste. 'I was eighteen at the time, found myself in a most agreeable milieu where I felt happy and felt completely at home, those wretched school years were behind me...I met a young person, he was the same age as me and about to become a student; he wasn't exceptionally clever, but exceptionally handsome, and what really attracted me was his directness and decency. He had already seen much of the world and circumstances had made him older than he was. Oh, Jo! How I loved him, how I loved him. No one knew about our liaison until a friend of mine, so-called of course, found out and wrote home about it. Pa came down at once, spoke to me, spoke to him. Though he was wealthy and believed in what he wanted, he was too young for a girl to make a commitment, all contact was to be broken, correspondence strictly forbidden. Pa found it difficult, as he liked him too and thought him a decent chap who had taken it well. Oh well, the age-old story. I have never heard from him since. Once, when I could no longer bear it, I wrote to him. He replied in a few words, saying he had given his word to Pa as a man and didn't want to break it. At the time he loved me with all his heart, but now? How could a young man who has the whole world in his hand, who is admired and sought after, remain true to a love so far in the past? After that, I retreated here, where I have never since met a single member of the opposite sex.'[12] This was a remarkable thing for her to say, considering what was happening at the Villa Eikenhorst in Soesterberg at the time. But that only came to light later – and for some family members even decades later.

Besides their appearance and matters of the heart, the future sisters-in-law wrote mainly about their love of books. Jo wrote: 'My greatest ambition is to write something original, but it is such a high ambition that I might never attain it. For consolation I remind myself that George Eliot only started writing later in life but – I'm already twenty-three and if I am ever to accomplish anything, then now is the time. Your brother has told me a little about your literary work (you see, you weren't a complete stranger to me) but I should like to hear more about it.'[13] She later added that literature, more than anything else, provides an outlet for our need to 'confide in someone all our uncertainties and worries and troubles....My books satisfy that need best of all. From Eliot in particular I always find encouragement and comfort, but there are so many! Do you love Longfellow the most! I am not sure; I think Shelley is my favourite poet, but I love them all from Beets and De Génestet to Goethe and Shakespeare. Goethe! Do you know of anything more moving than Gretchen!'[14] Jo loved several Dutch preacher-poets, such as Nicolaas Beets, also known by the pseudonym Hildebrand, and Petrus Augustus de Génestet, as well as foreign literary giants, but had little affinity with French writers: 'Now I have to confess to another aversion,

François d'Albert-Durade, *George Eliot*, 1850–66, based on a work
of 1850. Oil on canvas, 34.3 × 26.7 cm (13½ × 10½ in.)

one that might strike you as odd. I do not like French literature at all. How
often I have been the butt of ridicule for this from André [her brother
Andries], who thinks I am being narrow-minded, but what can I do. I
am not talking about poetry, for that is indeed pleasing to the ear and
charming, enchanting even, but prose! I keep dipping into it, but it makes
me so despondent, disappointed with humankind and everything that
it is beyond words. On the face of it French society is elegant, graceful
and civil and on the inside so superficial, decadent and hollow, ugh.'[15]
Lies admitted that she was not fond of French novels, either.[16]

Besides reports on family, the city and their lives, every letter touched
on their passion for literature and their favourite writers. Lies wrote,

'I love Dickens, don't you? Would you please answer this? I so enjoy hearing you talk about writers, for though I agree entirely with your opinion, I could never express it as comprehensively and clearly as you do.'[17] To which Jo replied, 'I believe we see eye to eye on that point, because I love him, too. Copperfield, Dombey and Nickleby are my favourites par excellence. I well remember reading Copperfield for the first time. I thought my heart would break from pity.'[18] Lies responded enthusiastically to Jo's love of books, clearly feeling that she had found a kindred spirit: 'Just imagine, impossible though it may be, that we were to write a book together...I am sure our words and ideas would be so absolutely identical that the public would assume that one and the same author had produced the work! Oh! My dear Jo, what I would not give to see you! Never have I dared talk to my sisters or to anyone else as I do to you; they would surely laugh at me.'[19]

Lies van Gogh, *c.* 1880. Photographed by J.W. Wentzel. From the family album kept by Theo van Gogh, and inscribed: 'with my best wishes for my brother Theo'.

Lies's motivation to write was not, by her own admission, purely literary: 'I must be honest and confess to something I am ashamed of, because in truth it is at odds with my indifference to money, but my main reason for writing is?...to earn! No doubt you will turn your nose up at the mere thought of a woman who writes for a living. I would, too. Are passion, talent and art not given to us for a purpose other than to be sold? I cannot but agree with you entirely. Even so, for me life would be so much more worthwhile if I knew there would never come a day that I might be dependent, when my wish to be able to do more for others was fulfilled. So you see, dear Jo, why I should like to earn, and without a reputation, without acquaintances or sponsors in the literary world it is not possible in this country for one whose main genre is poetry. I infinitely prefer writing verses to novels, although I have discovered that the latter are at least paid for when they are published in instalments. Still, I have no complaints and am truly satisfied with the reviews; but if I could, I would turn my hand to translating.'[20] Lies enclosed a poem with this letter to Jo, 'a few lines I wrote on the beach':

THE SONG OF THE SEA
A song of joy, a song of woe,
sings the beautiful sea,
sings the azure sea.
It is the song of life
It is the song of love;
In strange tones
Infinitely beautiful and melodious
It is the song of hearts
of strange smarts none understand,
The song of flowers withered too soon
A song of the grasses
It is the song of the waves,
Of brave men sent
To early graves.
The stream of life carries away all!
So sings the sea.[21]

This is presumably the poem Lies had sent to Theo a few weeks earlier. However, Theo read 'graves' instead, probably, of 'grasses'. He wrote back to Lies. 'But if I may say so, your little poem is merely a succession of thoughts which, for others to understand them properly, needed some explanation. "The song of flowers, the song of graves" is not very clear. But again, if the sea inspires such thoughts in you, it shows you are more sensitive than most people. You say you would like to be a boy so as to be exposed to different points of view, but you are very much mistaken if you think it is so easy for us to find people with whom we can exchange ideas.'[22]

Jo's response to the poem was more complimentary: 'How I envy your gift to write poetry. My heart can be so full when something beautiful affects me, but even then I can't express it. How often have I stood on the beach listening to the song of the waves, trying to understand what whispered and rustled inside them, but never have I been able to put it in words, never give it shape as you do. Oh, what a wonderful gift it must be, lucky, three times lucky, those who possess it. But that song of the sea was a peach that makes one want more!'[23]

The two young women finally met in Amsterdam in January 1886. Lies was excited about it, though she admits to having felt like a provincial. After returning to the Villa Eikenhorst, she wrote: 'It was delightful walking out together. I had pictured that in my mind so often. But it was far too short, don't you think? Those moments simply flew by! But what shall not be lost is the memory, the lasting impression it made on me....You have no idea how childishly gauche I felt when I came to meet you in Amsterdam and how afraid I was of not finding the way. But whether or not one feels comfortable on one's own depends on one's routines and habits, and I, who have lived only in villages and in Tiel for a couple of years, found the bustle of the city rather overwhelming.'[24] Amsterdam's population nearly tripled between 1810 and 1900, from 180,000 inhabitants to 520,000. This was caused by the decades-long natural increase in the population and the growth in trade and new industries, which attracted impoverished rural workers to the city.

Jo replied nine days later, saying that she actually found the city soothing. 'I can imagine that the turmoil of A. unsettled you for a while; I felt exactly the same and it took me time to calm down (how our brothers would laugh at us if they heard this). You know, a city makes one feel impossibly small, foolish and insignificant; never have I been more aware of my own insignificance than I am now!...No, sweetie, I didn't take the tram; I strolled home drowsily; the daylight began to fade, and the street lanterns were lit – I love the city at that hour – and so many thoughts went through my mind. How many footprints have I left on the Keizersgracht, where our secondary school used to be and the business college that André attended. We always used to walk there – a wonderful time.'25

Two days later Lies wrote from Soesterberg, 'My mother and sister are staying in Amsterdam. I did not know until this morning and still thought they were snowbound in Leiden. They shall not be here very long as Mama is missing home. They shall only have a brief spell of peace there because there shall soon be all the commotion of the move [to Breda].'26 It took Jo a month to write back. On 21 February 1886 she sent an apologetic reply. 'I go out far too much and then toil during the day to make up for it. I went to the students' ball and the Winter Fair, last evening I was dancing again until three o'clock; in March there is still the *bal masqué* and, in between, the opera, theatre and concerts. It is dreadful of me, but such fun going out!...Shortly after receiving your last letter my mother and I, as you may have heard, paid a visit to your mama, whom we fortunately found at home. I need not tell you what a pleasure it was to meet her. You look very much like your mother, dearest, and her voice reminded me very much of yours. Would you believe I sometimes imagine that I hear you talking!'27

Like Lies and Jo, Wil had an avid interest in literature, and even tried her hand at writing. In a letter from Paris in late October 1887, Vincent recommended a number of authors she might enjoy, such as Émile Zola, Guy de Maupassant, Honoré Balzac, Voltaire, Shakespeare, Harriet Beecher Stowe and Leo Tolstoy. In the same letter he commented on a short story she had written about 'the plants and the rain', in which she likened people to grains of wheat, and on her plans to study Dutch and write books: 'Now, to get back to your little piece, I am reluctant to accept for my own purposes or to recommend to others for theirs the belief that powers above us intervene personally to help or comfort us. Providence is a strange thing, and I must tell you I really don't know what to think of it. There is also a certain sentimentality in your piece and its form, in particular, recalls the stories about providence mentioned above, many of which are implausible and can easily be refuted....Most of all, I find it worrying that you feel you need to study in order to write. No, my dearest sister, learn to dance or fall in love with one or more notary's clerks, officers or whoever is within your reach. Rather, far rather, commit a few follies than study Dutch. It serves no purpose whatsoever other than to make a person dull, so I wish to hear nothing more about it....People who are in love and do nothing besides are perhaps more earnest and holier than those who sacrifice their love and their hearts to an idea. Be that as it may, to write a book, to do something meaningful, to produce a painting with life in it, you have to be someone who lives life yourself. So for you, studying is of secondary importance, unless you don't want to get ahead....If I were living near you, I would try to convince you that it might be more practical for you to paint with me than to write; that might sooner be the way for you to express your feelings. I, in any event, can do something about painting, but as for writing, it's not my metier. Anyhow, it's not a bad idea for you to aspire to become an artist, because someone who has fire inside, and soul, can't survive in a cinder-box – one would rather burn than suffocate. Whatever is inside has to come out. Take me, for example. Making a painting enables me to breathe, and without that I'd be unhappier than I am.'[28]

Avid readers and keen correspondents, the Van Goghs sometimes sent each other several letters a day. Vincent and Theo took pains over their writing; their sisters, too, though to a lesser extent. They discussed family and all other kinds of matters, often the books they were reading and literature in general, and recommended publications that impressed them. They were also in the habit of lending or giving each other books. None of this is surprising; the Van Gogh children had grown up with books in a home with a well-stocked library, and had uncles who were bookbinders or booksellers. Moreover, the times were conducive to reading. Besides the edifying literature they were accustomed to, new genres were starting to appear, such as detective stories and popular fiction with a historical, psychological or social slant. Women were gaining prominence in literature, both as writers and protagonists of novels: *Madame Bovary*, *Anna Karenina*, *Eline Vere*, *Wuthering Heights*, *Jane Eyre* and *Sense and Sensibility*. During their stay in England, Vincent, Anna and Wil discovered the works of English writers such as Jane Austen, the Brontë sisters and Mary Ann Evans (who wrote under the pseudonym George Eliot, as Jo and Lies seem to have been aware, unlike Vincent, who had taken George Eliot for a man).[29]

Vincent was always eager to share his enthusiasm for art and literature that appealed to him. He would urge his siblings, Willemien and Theo in particular, to read books he had enjoyed. In a letter to Theo of 5 August 1881, he says, 'I don't know whether you read English books. If you do, I can highly recommend Shirley by Currer Bell [the pen name of Charlotte Brontë], the author of another book, Jane Eyre. It's as beautiful as the paintings of Millais or Boughton or Von Herkomer. I found it at Princenhage and finished it in three days, though it's quite a big book. Reading books is like looking at paintings: what one considers good with conviction, without doubt, without hesitation, is good.'[30]

Vincent sometimes drew parallels between his own experiences and those of characters in books like *Nicholas Nickleby* or *Madame Bovary*. Though he rarely mentioned Dutch authors by name, we can presume from his references to specific episodes and characters that he had read Multatuli (Eduard Douwes Dekker), Hendrik Potgieter and Frederik van Eeden. He wrote about Potgieter's protagonist Jan Salie, for example, and quoted Multatuli's paradox, 'Oh God, there is no God.'[31] Both during and after his visits to England, the writers he most frequently recommended to his family were Charles Dickens, Shakespeare and the Brontë sisters. Like Jo and Lies, he enjoyed George Eliot: 'I'm reading *Middlemarch* by Eliot. Eliot analyses like Balzac or Zola, but English backdrop and with an English feel.'[32] His other favourite was Charles Dickens, and he was greatly saddened by the author's sudden death in 1870.[33]

Harriet Beecher Stowe's ground-breaking and shocking *Uncle Tom's Cabin* was published in the United States in 1852. The book made a huge impression on Vincent, who read it for the second time during his stay

Harriet Beecher Stowe, 1862. Photographed by William Notman.

in Arles. Stowe describes the plight of the men and women taken into slavery and the young girls who were forced to produce future generations of slaves. The main female protagonist, Eliza, strives to improve her lot and does everything within her power to deliver her child from bondage. In May 1889, Vincent wrote to Willemien saying he had reread Stowe's book with close attention precisely 'because it's a woman's book, written, she says, while making soup for her children.'[34] In the hope of arousing Wil's interest, Vincent copied a poem for her from Stowe's book *We and Our Neighbours*,[35] published in 1875.

Vincent also read and frequently re-read work by the American poet Walt Whitman. Writing to Wil in August 1888, he remarked that 'everyone's talking about it'.[36] He loved Whitman's 'Prayer of Columbus', which

Line Kruysse, between 1889 and 1894.
Photographer unknown.

appeared in the acclaimed anthology *Leaves of Grass* in 1881. Whitman, he wrote, 'is totally honest and makes you think about God and eternity.'[37] A couple of months after receiving this letter, Wil wrote to Theo from the village of Middelharnis that she had found Whitman's poetry 'so sublime that it spoilt, or rather dispelled my enjoyment of lighter poetry for the time being....These poems are so solid and wide-ranging, nothing can compare with them; they are suffused with a wholesome, powerful effective joie de vivre, refreshing. I enjoyed them and Lien [Line], who was with me, liked them too.'[38]

While living in France, Vincent immersed himself in French literature. Towards the end of October 1887 he wrote to Willemien from Paris: 'Like me, for instance, who can count so many years in my life when I lost all inclination to laugh, leaving aside whether or not this was my own fault. I for one need above all just to have a good laugh. I found that in Guy de Maupassant and there are others here, Rabelais among the old writers, Henri Rochefort among today's, where one can find that – Voltaire in Candide....On the other hand, if one wants truth, life as it is, the works of Edmond de Goncourt and his brother Jules, for example, in Germinie Lacerteux, or Edmond's La fille Elisa, Émile Zola's La joie de vivre and L'assommoir and so many other masterpieces paint life as we experience it ourselves, satisfying the need we have for people to tell us the truth....The work of the French naturalists Zola, Flaubert, Guy de Maupassant, De Goncourt, Richepin, Daudet, Huysmans is magnificent and one can scarcely be said to belong to one's time if one isn't familiar with them. Maupassant's masterpiece is Bel-Ami; I hope to be able to get it to you.'[39] Vincent depicted books by Zola, De Maupassant and several other writers in some of his later works.

In November 1888, Vincent painted *Liseuse de romans* (The Novel Reader; pl. XII). It was done *de tête*, from memory, like his *Memory of the Garden at Etten*, and as a result it is difficult to determine who the woman, so intently reading her novel, was supposed to represent. Could it be Willemien, who often wrote to Vincent about literature and aspired to become a writer herself? She was his favourite sister, and had posed often for him in Etten. Vincent also discussed the painting with her at great length in one of his letters, including a sketch of the work (pl. XI). He explained that the yellow book the woman is reading was a yellow-cover Naturalist novel published by Charpentier, whose stable of authors included Zola, De Maupassant and Flaubert. 'I've painted a "woman reading a novel" as well. A mass of very black hair, a green bodice, sleeves the colour of wine sediment, the skirt black, the background all yellow, library shelves with books.'[40] It was inspired, he said, by Rembrandt's *Holy Family*, also called *The Bible Reading*, of 1640. A reproduction of the Rembrandt hung in his bedroom in Paris; he later gave it to Theo and Jo because he felt it symbolized harmonious family life, though it lacked 'the personal and intimate qualities' of modern art. He also presented a copy to his sister Anna. And his middle sister Lies seemed to know it too, as she writes about it in a letter to Theo.[41] His own picture of a woman reading a novel, rather than the Bible, perhaps hints at the domestic contentment that eluded him at this stage of his life.

CHAPTER 10

Every Family Has Its Secrets

Breda, Saint-Sauveur-le-Vicomte, Soesterberg, 1886–1889

Dorus's death gave rise to several major changes in the family, both financial and personal. The Van Goghs were no longer entitled to live in the vicarage. They were compelled to look for more modest accommodation, with Dorus's successor, Reverend Casper Everhard Crull, due to move into the house in the summer of 1886.[1] They considered Leiden, so as to be closer to Anna, Joan and the children. From there it was only a short train journey to The Hague, where Moe had spent the first thirty years of her life and where the family still had many relatives and friends. But things turned out differently. While visiting her sister Wilhelmine Stricker-Carbentus at her home on the Gelderse Kade in Amsterdam, Moe heard that a suitable apartment had become available in Breda. She was obliged to leave without delay, as there were other interested parties, cutting short her stay with her sister and brother-in-law Paul, who had been extremely helpful in winding up Pa's affairs after his death. Moe set off for Breda, returning to familiar territory for the Van Goghs.[2]

With the repeal in 1874 of national legislation governing urban fortifications, Breda had cast off its medieval straitjacket and expanded beyond the confines of the historic city walls. The Concordia Theatre and a series of town houses were built behind the inundation sluice that had formed part of Breda's defence line. One of these properties, located on the corner of Wapenplein and Nieuwe Ginnekenstraat, had just been completed the previous year. Apartment number 2A, on the top floor of the building with a view over both the square and the adjacent street, was the dwelling Moe went to view. Although it didn't have a garden, it met with her approval, and she and Wil moved in on 30 March 1886.[3]

Less than two days later, Wil's brother Cor joined them. He had been employed at the Egbertus Begemann factory in Helmond for over a year and was now to work as an unpaid apprentice at the Backer & Rueb factory in Breda. But by June 1887 he had moved to Amsterdam, 24 Wagenaarstraat, to take up a job in another factory.[4]

Moe's move to Breda was not celebrated widely in the family. Theo had reservations about his mother's decision right from the start: 'Is it now definite that Moe is moving to Breda?' he asked Lies on 28 December 1885. Breda, in his opinion, was dreary. 'As long as she

Cor van Gogh, 1887.
Photographed by Ferdinand Reissig.

has managed to find a pleasant home, because the streets of Breda do not appeal to me very much and I am worried that she shall be even more unhappy if she is cooped up there.'[5] And yet there was much to attract Moe. Uncle Cent van Gogh and his wife, Aunt Cornelie, lived within walking distance of the centre of Breda, where Moe could easily reach them. The elderly, childless couple were extremely wealthy and wielded great influence in the international art world. Cent's stately manor house had an outdoor sculpture garden and a gallery for his collection of Barbizon and The Hague School paintings. The Barbizon School of artists worked in the period from approximately 1830 to 1870 in the environs of the French village of Barbizon, near the town of Fontainebleau. They painted realistic and unadorned landscapes as a reaction to Romanticism, using colours to convey mood. The Hague School was a movement of like-minded Dutch painters who worked between 1860 and 1900 in The Hague. Its members also rejected the Romantic tradition and its idealization of reality, which reached its acme in Dutch painting around the middle of the nineteenth century. They worked outdoors, as did the

Barbizon painters, and the works also communicated the artists' mood. Physically ailing and increasingly housebound in his retirement, Uncle Cent was at least able to enjoy his art.[6]

Cent and Cornelie's home became a place of refuge for Moe during her years in Breda. She whiled away the hours reminiscing with her sister and basking in the luxury of their surroundings. On occasion she stayed in the house when the couple went away. As the years passed, Cent's health continued to decline. He suffered from a pulmonary disease and various other afflictions.

Lies had more urgent matters on her mind at the time that her mother and younger siblings moved to Breda. She had been working at the Villa Eikenhorst in Soesterberg for six years, tending the seriously ill Mrs Du Quesne. Contrary to what she had told Jo in her letters, there was indeed a man in her life – one too close for comfort. Lies had been having an affair with her employer's husband, Jean Philippe du Quesne, and was now carrying his child. Mrs Du Quesne was apparently oblivious

to the whole situation. After much consideration – initially only Moe was aware of Lies's predicament – it was decided that the pregnancy and the birth of the child would be kept secret. On the pretext of going to England, as Anna and Wil had done, Lies left the Villa Eikenhorst in early July 1886.[7]

Lies described her journey to England, via the Channel Islands and northern France, in letters to friends and relatives. She informed them that she was travelling in the company of a Miss Van Epen and

Vincent (Uncle Cent) van Gogh. Photographed by Stanislas Julien Ignace Ostrorog ('Walery'). Date unknown.

Jean Philippe du Quesne van Bruchem and Lies van Gogh,
c. 1895. Photographed by J.W. Wentzel.

her canary, called Pietje, transported in a cage that fit neatly into a
woven basket. Lies's first letter to her family dates from 8 July 1886.
She and her companion had by then landed on the Isle of Wight, but
as Lies thought it too expensive they had gone on to Jersey. Lies had
thoroughly enjoyed the voyage. The pair continued to Coutances on the
Normandy coast. From there Lies sent a breezy letter to Moe and Wil:
'This is a strange country, very primitive, with the most extraordinary
old buildings one could imagine; ancient towers of dilapidated castles
converted into dwellings...and all the countryside hilly and wooded,
with lovely cows in the meadows.'[8]

Villa Mertesheim, Princenhage, near Breda, from the side (ABOVE) and from the back (BELOW), showing the garden, greenhouse and picture gallery. Date and photographer of both images unknown.

In response to Wil, who had asked after the canary, Lies wrote from Carteret, near Cherbourg, 'Your interest in my Pietje left me far from unmoved, Wil...I take my Pietje wherever I go and even though his basket is closed, completely closed, every now and then he surprises our fellow travellers by singing a resounding song at the top of his voice. Once, however, he managed not to hang himself, when he poked his little head through the rods at the top, intoxicated by the fresh sea air. I had to push his head down, but fortunately it didn't harm his common sense.'[9]

Of course, the journey was no ordinary holiday jaunt, nor was Pietje a bird. By then the baby was almost due, and Wil had been let in on the secret. Lies was in two minds about having a child, as we see from her ambiguous, coded references to the imminent birth. Nor was she travelling with a Miss Van Epen. Her companion on the journey was none other than Mr Du Quesne, as the Van Gogh expert Benno Stokvis deduced in 1969.[10] Lies first publicly touched on the subject in her book *Proza* (Prose) in 1929. Under the heading 'Every family has its secrets' she listed a number of key words that, cryptic though they may be, related to her own life and experience: 'It is the family secret – inheritance, resemblance to distant generations, impoverishment, profligacy, envy, murky misdeeds, intemperateness, slander – and sweet secret liaisons, marital fidelity and parental love, modesty, piety as winged seeds stirred by autumn breezes, thoughts, perceptions evoked by the Family Secret.'[11]

The baby arrived before the couple were able to embark for the crossing to England. Hubertina Marie Normance was born in the Hôtel de la Victoire in Saint-Sauveur-le-Vicomte at eleven o'clock in the morning on 3 August 1886. The birth was registered by the proprietor of the hotel, Mrs Jean, accompanied by Dr Pierre Bellet, the local physician who delivered the baby. On Bellet's recommendation Hubertina was placed in the care of the twenty-two-year-old widow Balley, who ran a grocery store in the village and already had two children of her own. Mr Du Quesne offered to contribute financially towards her upbringing and education, and is believed to have done so until she reached adulthood.[12] Hubertina came to be known as Hubertine, the French variant of her name.

On 7 August 1886, four days after Hubertine was born, Lies wrote to Moe from La Hay-du-Puits saying she would only return to the

Hubertine van Gogh with her stepmother Mme Balley, 1890s.
Photographer unknown.

Netherlands, via England, in mid-September. She apparently wanted
to take advantage of the opportunity to visit the village of Avranches
and the medieval abbey of Mont-Saint-Michel, which crowns a rocky
tidal island.[13] As things turned out, Lies and Du Quesne never made it to
England. After spending another five weeks in France, they returned to
Soesterberg, without the child. The fact that Moe contributed from her
modest means to the costs of the journey and the birth bears witness
to the importance she attached to bringing the episode to a discreet
end and avoiding, at any price, a scandal that would have embarrassed
everyone involved. She was never to meet her third grandchild.

The three members of the Van Gogh family living in Breda each went their own way. Moe spent much of her time at Uncle Cent and Aunt Cornelie's home, and Wil sought ways to occupy her time. Her correspondence with her good friend Margaretha Meijboom, then living in The Hague, was helpful in this quest. Margaretha suggested that her friend might consider applying for a position as a florist in the Tesselschade-Arbeid Adelt (TAA), (Labour is Ennobling), an association established to promote women crafters of modest means. Years later, in 1898, the TAA was one of the organizers of the Nationale Tentoonstelling voor Vrouwenarbeid (National Exhibition of Women's Labour), in which Wil was actively involved. Margaretha's suggestion suited Wil perfectly. She loved arranging flowers; her parents had praised her talent in letters to other members of the family when she had decorated Vincent's and later Dorus's farewell dinners in Helvoirt and Anna and Joan's wedding in Etten.[14] Wil was evidently excited by the idea, as Margaretha wrote, 'I am so glad the florist plan appeals to you. This morning I spoke to Miss Tak, who told me the following: an examination is not required. The previous lady florist número 1 was trained there. Her mother was in Amsterdam. She received an allowance and had lodgings in Baarn (or Bussum, I do not remember) at the home of a florist. She did practical work there, regular gardening and received some tuition in French from one of the ladies from Tesselschade. Two years later she knew everything about plants and went to Van Rijsewijk here in the city [The Hague] to learn how to make bouquets. She was there for less than a year and now has a position with De Sitter in Amsterdam, at the shop that makes bouquets, and earns 800 guilders a year.'[15] Margaretha thought a similar arrangement might be suitable for Wil and asked what Moe thought of the idea. Margaretha felt it would be good for Wil to get out of the house and have something to occupy her. And though there was no 'mathematical certainty of a position,' florists were in demand and the TAA's influential members would surely find employment for Wil.

Wil sent her application letter to Margaretha, who replied: 'I sent your letter to Miss Tak. Did she not answer you? How extraordinary!'[16] Nothing more is known about the application or its outcome. But Wil's passion for flower arranging did not suffer. In September 1887, she wrote

De Hollandsche Lelie, first edition.
Amsterdam, 6 July 1887.

an article for *De Hollandsche Lelie* (The Dutch Lily), a weekly journal for young ladies. Published under the title 'Making bouquets', it was an unconventional guide to flower arranging: 'This is not to say I don't like bouquets made by florists, who understand and love their profession. I just prefer more loosely arranged flowers so that, when grouped together, the individual qualities of each stem nevertheless stand out....Moreover, bouquets needn't necessarily consist of cultivated flowers.'[17] And Willemien did not forget Margaretha, repeatedly thanking her friend with bouquets of dried flowers. They always had the effect of lifting her spirits, she said.

Wil was lonely and unhappy in Breda: by then most of the family had left home. She discussed this at length with Margaretha. Wil was articulate and Margaretha, who suffered from bouts of depression herself, responded with tact and insight. On 22 April 1887, she wrote, 'Your letter has done me good, Wil. I sat down quietly in my study and read it undisturbed. And when I had finished, I sat nodding off for a while, something that seldom happens to me in our merry-go-round lives, though there are times I need it so badly. This morning I had a gratifying feeling that I had been of help to you and I understand now how that came about. I had kept writing to you because I love you dearly, with no ulterior motive. I had absolutely no intention to influence you and was unaware that I was doing so. And I thought how good it was that I had not vanished from this world in those years after 1879, as I had so often wanted to do. I had to smile when I read that you thought my life so much more agreeable.'[18]

Wil travelled as often as she could to escape the stifling atmosphere of Breda. She went to The Hague, Paris, Brussels (with Cor), the village of Middelharnis in the province of South Holland to visit the Korteweg family and to her sister Anna and her young family in Leiden.[19] She also arranged to stay with Anna in Leiden in August 1887, when Moe was visiting Aunt Cornelie and Uncle Cent in the countryside again. During their absence, Moe and Wil were informed that their landlord was intending to sell all his property, including the house at Wapenplein, which they would accordingly have to vacate in April of the following year. Luckily, they soon found an apartment on Nieuwe Haagdijk, in a new suburb on the western outskirts of Breda. The house was within walking distance of the Villa Mertesheim, where Aunt Cornelie and Uncle Cent lived. Though considerably smaller, it was nicely situated on the ground floor and had a garden,[20] which pleased Vincent: 'It's excellent that you and Ma dispose over a garden, with cats, tomcats, sparrows and flies, rather than an extra flight of stairs to contend with.'[21] Wil wrote to Jo Bonger, her future sister-in-law and by now her friend and confidante, that the back of the house overlooked the Capuchin monastery.

Margaretha Meijboom expressed an even stronger opinion. Just after Moe and Willemien moved to their new residence, she wrote: 'Say Wil, where exactly is Haagdijk? Haven't we walked past it together and doesn't it debouch into Princehage? You need to tell me that at once, will you? How pleasant that you finally, well and good, are over now'.[22]

Moe engaged a local man, Janus Schrauwen, to transport their possessions to the new apartment, not

Margaretha Meijboom, *c.* 1900.
Photographer unknown.

suspecting that the family would have far more to do with him in the future. Several crates containing Vincent's early works went into storage at Schrauwen's. These boxes had been kept in the chicken coop at the Nuenen parsonage after Vincent's studio in Schafrat's house was cleared out. Along with Vincent's own works, the crates contained prints, sketches, photographs, books and magazines that he had acquired for study purposes. He had collected some while living in England, such as prints from the illustrated magazine *The Graphic*, which he followed obsessively.[25] The decision to leave the crates with Schrauwen may have been purely pragmatic; their new apartment, like the last, had no storage space and, besides, Willemien had discovered that the crates were infested with woodworm. But a more important factor may have come into play: the fact that Moe still had reservations about Vincent's work. It was not that she did not like it; she simply did not know what to make of it. When Vincent was still living at home, she had thrown away some of his sketches and drawings. That she had also kept some of his work only transpired later.

While in Arles, Vincent occasionally wondered what had become of the work he had left behind in Nuenen. From time to time he would ask Theo and Wil about his early works, or the books and prints from which he drew inspiration. He could not yet afford to engage models, and wanted to draw on material from his old collection instead. He appears not to have known that the crates were in storage at Schrauwen's, writing to Wil more than two years after the move: 'Tell me, talking about clutter. Perhaps it would be a good idea to salvage anything that's worthwhile among that rubbish of mine that Theo says is still somewhere in an attic in Breda. But I don't feel I can ask you and perhaps it's been lost, so don't worry about it…but this is the question. You know, Theo brought a whole batch of woodcuts with him last year. But a couple of the best portfolios are missing and the rest isn't so good because it's not complete any more. Of course, woodcuts from illustrated magazines become increasingly rare as the issues get older. Enough, that rubbish isn't entirely unimportant to me; for example, there's a copy of Gavarni's Mascarade humaine, a book Anatomy for artists, anyway, a few things that are actually far too good to lose. But I'll start by assuming they are lost; anything that might turn up will be a windfall. When I left I didn't know it would be for good. Because work wasn't going badly in Nuenen, I just needed to persevere. I still miss my models and still love them, if only I had them here now – I'm sure my 50 paintings would be spot on. Please understand, I'm not angry with the human race because they think I'm this or that – I'll say right now that I agree with them, but it saddens me that I don't have sufficient means to get the models I want, where I want and for as long or as short as I want.'[24]

Besides Moe, Wil, Theo and Vincent no one knew that the crates existed. When visiting his mother, Theo dropped by at Schrauwen's to cast an eye over them, but he too left them where they were. Three years later, when Moe and Wil moved again, they collected the furniture stored at Schrauwen's, but the crates were left behind. They were never returned to the family. Decades later, as Vincent's reputation grew, the family tried to retrieve them, but by then it was too late. Jo Bonger, Theo's widow, took legal action but even that was unsuccessful. Schrauwen had presumably sold Vincent's works, sending the reams of prints, newspaper cuttings and drawings among them to be pulped. The mystery of the Breda crates is being resolved, gradually and piecemeal, but no one knows exactly what they contained or what became of their contents.

After a prolonged illness, Uncle Cent died on 28 July 1888. Moe took care of Aunt Cornelie. The will was read a couple of weeks later. Generous to the end, Cent had provided even for distant relatives and domestic staff, but he had explicitly disinherited Vincent, his nephew and godson. His will states: 'I intentionally direct that it is my will that Vincent Willem van Gogh, the eldest son of my brother Theodorus van Gogh, shall not be a beneficiary of my estate.'[25] Another clause again excludes Vincent and his progeny. When drawing up his will Cent may have been under the impression that Vincent had had a child by a woman called Sien Hoornik, a friend of his from The Hague. But he was probably even more disappointed by Vincent's failure to accept the many career opportunities he had offered him.[26]

There was a separate legacy for Moe and Theo. Under the terms of the will, a quarter of Cent's substantial estate was to be shared by Vincent's five siblings. Theo was dismayed that his brother had been cut off. For more than a year, the Van Goghs bickered over the inheritance. Willemien was anxious to avoid repeating the mistake she believed she had made in 1885 when, after the violent quarrel between Vincent and Anna, she had sided with the family rather than with Vincent, despite her own misgivings. She wrote to Margaretha about Cent's will and received the reply: 'Actually, Wil, I wholly agree with you on the matter of the inheritance....I saw it as a vote of no confidence, perhaps justified, but it's exceedingly hurtful.'[27] Wil was apparently so upset by the friction that Margaretha invited her to The Hague. 'Are you "in tune" again? I suspect not. I'm afraid the whole business about the inheritance had a sting in the tail. Yes, come here quickly if you feel troubled. We'll go walking in the woods and Mother Nature will heal us both.'[28]

Willemien took every opportunity to get away from the house at Nieuwe Haagdijk, which she described as dreary and cold, and redoubled her efforts to arrange outings and trips for herself. Around 15 August she set off to visit Theo on her first visit to Paris, and in October, she went to stay with the Korteweg family in Middelharnis, where she had spent a happy fortnight in 1884. From there she wrote to Theo: 'As you see, I've flown the coop again. Ma is staying in Princenhage until aunt leaves, and I do not feel like being there all the time, I would turn into a kind of dullard, and it is dismal staying at home on my own. I like it here and enjoy being in a congenial homely environment, because things have not been so good with us lately, even though it was fine. Ma has actually been away all the time, ever since I got back from Paris. The Kortewegs are all delightful people...I feel fine here, really like one of the family and not like a house guest. Today I am even in charge until tomorrow. Cor and Korteweg have gone to a party in Heenvliet. And I am at home with the three children, all boys, sturdy, healthy, good-natured little chaps, rascals at first but, even so, loveable children.'[29] The Cor Willemien was referring to was Cor van der Slist, an orphan who had been at boarding school with her in Den Bosch in 1879 and 1880. After leaving school the two friends continued to spend holidays together.[30] In Middelharnis they attended a meeting of Dorcas, a Protestant women's association founded to help the poor, especially the elderly, and combat poverty. In December, Wil went to stay with her sister Anna in Leiden, as she had done the previous year.

Like Wil, Moe soon grew tired of Breda. After Uncle Cent's death, Aunt Cornelie had moved to Menton on the French Rivièra, so there was little reason for her to remain in the city.[31] Anna's husband Joan van Houten rallied his contacts to find a suitable home for Moe and Wil in Leiden. Something turned up in early 1889, but the landlord was playing two interested parties off against each other, and the deal ultimately fell through. Moe was disappointed, and Wil even more so. Jo, who was now seeing more of Theo and corresponding regularly with Wil, was apparently well aware of this. No further opportunity presented itself before the end of the year, though Wil was urgently in need of a change. She was lonely in Breda, and felt unable to stay there any longer. In a letter to Jo she said that being preoccupied with too many things could make one's head spin, and that she felt dreadful when it happened to her. Knowing that Jo led a busy life, Wil assumed she would understand what she meant by saying she needed to clear her mind, as she had done when feeling lonely the previous week. She brightened when Jo announced that she would visit them in Breda. Wil replied, 'Everything's all right again…and I hope it stays like that for a long time to come. Still, I was very pleased yesterday to have Moe back safe and sound, and now it is most agreeable.'[32] Jo was reassured after seeing things for herself. Her fortnight's stay made a world of difference to Wil. Jo, too, enjoyed her visit and the chance to strengthen her friendship with her future sister-in-law.

Theo and Jo admired Moe's ability to take things in her stride. She never complained about her reduced circumstances and social standing, so different from what she had been accustomed to during her youth and the years of her marriage.[33] Yet Breda did not offer what she had hoped for, and Joan's efforts to help her find a new apartment encouraged her to make a fresh start, close to friends and family. Leiden beckoned.

CHAPTER 11

I Just Can't Imagine You in Paris

Soesterberg, Leiden, Paris, 1889–1890

In the spring of 1889, Wil often joined Lies in Soesterberg to help look after Mrs Du Quesne. 'My dear Sisters,' Theo wrote from Paris on 24 January 1889, 'I shall just write this to both of you, now that you are in it together, sharing the good times and bad. From what I hear, this must be a sad time for you, and Mrs Du Quesne's condition sounds extremely worrying. So it is good, I am sure, that you have got each other...I hear from Ma that she has decided that she is going to live in Leiden. That is splendid because Breda has nothing more to offer and never had much going for it anyway. What is more, the house looks nice. Do you like it, Wil? From Vincent, fortunately, the news is good, and his letters are more lucid than they ever were before.'[1] Mrs Du Quesne died on 17 May of that year at the age of fifty-one. In June, Joan van Houten found a suitable home for Moe and Wil in Leiden.

The ground-floor apartment of the house at 100 Herengracht had a view of the water with ships sailing past, and a small garden at the back. Adjacent to them at number 102 was their landlord Barend den Houter's warehouse; Houter himself lived at number 78. In Wil's opinion, as she mentioned to Jo, the rent of 250 guilders a year was not excessive. Given the many advantages of their new Leiden home, she and Moe regretted having to wait until the beginning of November to move in.[2] Unhappy as Wil was in Breda, she kept her spirits up by thinking of better times to come. On the evening of her birthday, 16 March, she wrote a letter to Theo, thanking him for the gifts she had received from him and asking about his impending marriage to Jo.[3]

Theo had been introduced to Jo by her brother, his friend Andries Bonger, in Paris in 1885. Though he was interested in her, she was seeing another man, and so they had no further contact for some time, although at his recommendation she and Lies had struck up their lively correspondence. Jo was urged to do the same by her brother Andries. Lies confided in her new pen friend her greatest wish for her brother Theo: 'I should so much like to find a nice woman for him, but that means he must have a secure future and that has to come first. Otherwise misery, all misery.'[4] Another meeting between Theo and Jo in 1886 prompted Theo to present himself, unannounced, at her parents' home on the Weteringschans in Amsterdam on 25 July 1887.[5] Expecting to spend an hour or two discussing art and literature with him, Jo could not believe her ears when Theo proposed to her. She was in love with another man and declined, with apologies for hurting him. That day, she wrote about the incident in her diary: 'I received him pleasantly and then he suddenly began to make me a declaration. It would sound improbable in a novel, and yet it is the case that having known me for no more than 3 days [Theo had also seen her in 1885 and 1886] he wants to spend his whole life

with me, he wants...to put all his happiness in my hands. And I'm so terribly sorry that I've had to cause him pain. He's been looking forward to coming here all year and pictured so much to himself, and now it ends like this. How downhearted he shall be when he returns to Paris.'[6] Yet her relationship with the other man did not work out, and after another meeting on 21 December 1888, Theo wrote to his mother to tell her that they would be getting married.[7] On 2 January 1889, Vincent sent Theo a letter from

Andries Bonger, 1885.
Photographed by Ernest Ladrey.

the hospital in Arles. He wrote it from the office of Dr Félix Rey, the resident physician who was treating him. Still recovering, Vincent penned only a few short lines expressing his approval. He had ended up in hospital after severing his ear on 23 December.[8] From the short note Dr Félix Rey had added to the letter, it would appear that Vincent was on the road to recovery. He had read Theo's account of his meeting with the Bongers several times and stated it to be perfect. He underlined his approval with a written handshake and continued that: 'As for me, I'm content to remain as I am.'[9] The engagement party was to be held in Amsterdam a week later, on 9 January, and the wedding would take place on Thursday 18 April, also in Jo's hometown.[10]

The letter Wil wrote to Theo on her birthday contained a warning about the arrangements for his approaching wedding. 'Moe, I can tell you, frets day and night about you not getting married in church.'[11] Theo and Jo were intending to have a civil ceremony, and the devout Moe was understandably distraught. Though Wil tried to persuade her brother to concede for the sake of the older generation, her arguments were not very convincing: 'You cannot have it at the Bongers' home. Just go ahead with it [in church], otherwise it will be a terrible blow.... If you do not want to kneel, you do not have to; just tell the minister. Then it is nothing more than a gesture. After all, you are not on earth just to please yourself. Just do this.'[12] As for herself: 'No, I shall carry on for a while without anyone who wants to share my life. And for the first time that is what I choose to do, so that is fine. Though it is right that you are setting a good example.'[13] And 'Theo van Parijs', as Aunt Mietje wrote in her *Notes*, did indeed set that example, marrying Jo in Amsterdam on 18 April 1889.[14] The couple did, however, persist in their decision to have a civil wedding.

After the wedding, Jo moved to Paris, where she and Theo moved into a new apartment at 8 Cité Pigalle. From her new home she wrote a long letter to her sisters-in-law Lies and Wil: 'My very dearest sisters, I wish you could just see right now how nice and snug Theo and I are, sitting in our living room drinking tea and writing letters at the same time. The lamp stands on the table between us; the shimmer on the new teapot is a joy to behold. We are so wonderfully at peace and contented, so perfectly

Theo van Gogh. Date and photographer unknown.

happy after the twilight hour...you shall have to come soon and see for
yourselves. The guest room is so much nicer than I had expected that
I do not mind inviting anyone at all, and believe me, it is truly not a
"cubby-hole".'[15]

Theo and Jo made their home comfortable and attractive. Vincent's
'beautiful peach trees in blossom' decorated a wall in the bedroom; 'a
Mauve still has to be hung beside it', Jo wrote. The living room, which
was more colourful, had 'warm yellow curtains, a red shawl on the
mantelshelf – paintings in gilt frames (some), above the fireplace, instead
of a mirror a tapestry with all sorts of beautiful things on it including
a lovely yellow rose by Vincent.'[16] Jo's closing words show yet again
how close the sisters-in-law were: 'My dear sisters, thank you again for
all the affection you have lavished on me. Lies and Wil a loving kiss.'[17]

Before moving into his new home with Jo, Theo had lived at various addresses in Paris. Two of these were 25 rue Laval and 54 rue Lepic, where Andries Bonger had been one of his housemates. Paris was the preeminent artistic hotbed in the nineteenth century; representatives of various schools of art gave expression to what could be called the start of modern painting. Romantics, Realists, Impressionists and later Post-Impressionists exhibited their work at the various Salons which were at their apogee in nineteenth-century Paris. These artists initially worked predominantly in their own studios, but public spaces would become a key part of artists' work environment. Among the famous artists working in Paris while Theo lived in the city were Delacroix, Renoir, Monet, Manet, Degas, Courbet, Toulouse-Lautrec, Gauguin, Redon, Fantin-Latour and Pissarro, but the city also attracted artists from abroad, who came to study or exhibit their works. Lucien Pissarro drew Vincent and Theo in 1887 and Henri de Toulouse-Lautrec painted Vincent in that same year. Over the centuries hundreds of Dutch artists were drawn to the French capital, including Gérard van Spaendonck, Ary Scheffer, Jacob Maris, George Hendrik Breitner, Johan Barthold Jongkind and of course, Vincent van Gogh. They would play an important role in inspiring the art scene and artists at home, as well as offering to their French counterparts new subject matter, colours and approaches that reflected Dutch sensibility.

Andries Bonger had moved to Paris at the age of twenty-seven to take up a position as an insurance broker. He was passionate about art, and became friends with Theo in 1882. When he and Theo visited Pa and Moe van Gogh in Nuenen and stayed at the parsonage in 1885 Andries met Vincent, with whom he later had frequent contact. He and Vincent even stayed together for a time at 54 rue Lepic (pl. XIII). By the time he left Paris in 1892 he possessed at least seven works by Vincent, making him one of the first collectors of Vincent's art.[18]

On 15 August 1888, the year before Jo and Theo's wedding, Wil paid her first visit to Theo in Paris. It left her with extremely happy memories.[19] Vincent wrote to her during her stay. He was overjoyed that she had arrived at Theo's in Paris, and hoped she would see a lot. He instructed her to go often to the Musée du Luxembourg, and to see the modern paintings in the Louvre so that she might better understand Millet,

Lucien Pissarro, *Vincent van Gogh in Conversation with his Brother Theo* (to the right, with top hat), 1887. Black chalk on paper, 18 × 23 cm (7 × 9 in.).

Breton, Daubigny and Corot.[20] In addition he warned her that the sun shone far more strongly in the summer in Paris than it did at home in North Brabant. What precisely Willemien did during her first stay in Paris remains largely unknown, but Vincent concluded the visit had been a great success. In a letter to Theo he reflects on the possibility of Wil marrying an artist: 'that wouldn't be bad. Well, we'll have to go on urging her to untangle her personality, rather than her artistic abilities'.[21] He forestalled a meeting with Willemien by suggesting they meet in Arles a year later. He appeared to have been distancing himself from his family, according to his letter to Theo of 3 April 1888, in which he refers to his family and friends in Holland: 'and it calms me down to say to myself that we'll do some paintings for there. And after that I'll forget them and I'll probably think only about the Petit Boulevard.'[22] Be that as it may, Willemien never went to the south of France and never saw Vincent again.

Earlier that year, on 30 March, his thirty-fifth birthday, Vincent had offered to give Willemien a painting of his for her birthday and had asked her to choose one. He reminded her of this on 14 September, saying he would keep a small study aside, which Theo would pass on to her. The work he went on to describe was probably the *Blossoming Almond Branch in a Glass with a Book*, which he had painted earlier that year (pl. xiv).[23] Besides this work, Willemien possessed another three paintings, which she may have chosen during this visit to Paris. They included the *Orchard Bordered by Cypresses* (pl. xv), the *Edge of a Wheatfield with Poppies* and *A Public Garden with People Strolling*.[24] For her part, Willemien gave Theo a photo of her mother to be passed on to Vincent, who was delighted with it, as he wrote to Theo on 21 September of that year. He said he could see Moe was keeping well and still looked full of life, but added that it was difficult to get the colours right in a painting after a black-and-white photo.[25]

Wil must have told Margaretha Meijboom that she was enjoying her stay in Paris, as Margaretha replied, 'I must tell you that I think of you every day and enjoy the idea of you roaming around Paris. Isn't it wonderful! At least, if Theo and you are getting on together. Of course, I have no reason to, but I suppose you are...I simply cannot imagine the two of you in Paris. Wil and Theo strolling through streets and museums, but not as if you lived there. Don't you think you would never feel at home there? You shall get homesick for all the beauty....Just be happy that we are both enjoying ourselves and thinking of each other faithfully. And trust me, always.'[26] But it was perhaps not the case that Wil could not feel at home in Paris. In a letter to Theo from Middelharnis, Wil reflected on the emotions that Paris aroused in her: 'that is the wonderful thing about Paris, I think. It is so full of life. I like that, even though it treats you harshly now and again. I prefer that to a life that is too quiet.'[27]

During her three-week stay in Paris Willemien had got to know Theo better. Vincent, however, had fled the city a few months before she arrived. Paris was too hectic for him, and he had quarrelled with everyone he knew. For those reasons and perhaps lured by sunnier climes, he had left for Arles in February 1888. In late December, three months after returning to the Netherlands, Wil received the news – probably from Theo – that Vincent had severed his own ear and had been admitted to an asylum. She was devastated and wrote about it to Margaretha, whose brother Meinard also had a history of mental health problems. Margaretha was shocked. 'That poor fellow, how dreadful. So ill – I mean, in that way – and on top of it so far away. Oh yes, my sweet, I understand your feelings perfectly. I always think you and Vincent are like Meindert and me....Going to a sanatorium sounds harsh, but did you know that any expert would recommend not postponing it for too long? Patients suffer less because they get the right treatment. We know the supervisors at the sanatorium in Zutphen very well. And they have often told us that nearly all patients calm down immediately and that merely the knowledge and tact of the nurses does them a power of good. Apparently it is so hard to know what to do that, even with the best intentions, things go wrong in nearly all families. Did you know that? What a blessing that he was not alone but had help. Who shall let you know what is happening now? [Paul] Gaugain [sic] or the doctor at the asylum?...Meinard has just asked so sympathetically, "Could it be a brain disease that will pass?" Might that not be the case?'[28] Wil struggled with the feeling of being far away from her brother and being unable to reach out in a situation like this.

The following September, shortly before Moe and Wil were due to leave Breda, Wil decided to spend some time with the Kortewegs in Middelharnis again. The sea and fresh air lifted her spirits: 'Now, on holiday, I am clearing up all those things in my mind and every now and then a small ray of light breaks through. I did not have time throughout the summer to collect my thoughts, and it was all such a dreadful muddle that I did not know my own mind. Now I shall be completely rested when I go home on Thursday; it feels wonderful.'[29]

Wil had no reservations about the move to Leiden. It was not as if she were leaving any friends behind in Breda, as she wrote to Jo Bonger exactly one month before the event. She was the only child still living at home, with no friends of her own age. She would miss the glorious Mastbos and moors, the beautiful Oude Kerk (Old Church) where her paternal grandfather had preached, and the good-natured people of North Brabant, but there was much to make up for these losses: the excitement of big city life, and the proximity of family and friends – Line Kruysse and Margaretha Meijboom in particular – most of all an end to the loneliness she would not have been able to endure for much longer.[30] The convoy of removal vehicles set off on 2 November 1889; Wil and Moe were the last Van Goghs to leave the province of North Brabant.[31]

Wil had high expectations of the opportunities that would open up for her in Leiden. She would be able to study, and it would be easier for her to find employment. The apartment on the Herengracht was spacious, with two adjoining rooms on the ground floor. The room at the back looked out on the garden, where Moe was able to indulge her passion for flowers and the outdoors. She filled the space with plants and shrubs, along with a medicinal lemongrass plant Theo had given her. Wil considered taking a cutting for him back to Paris.

Joan and Anna welcomed Moe and Wil to Leiden with open arms. The apartment was soon furnished and decorated, and Moe was delighted. 'We are living in a lovely suite and we planted our garden ourselves.'[32] Joan's business was flourishing. In January 1880, he and his business partner Peter Zillesen had established Van Houten & Zillesen, which produced shell-lime by a process of calcination. Rapid industrialization and urbanization had boosted the construction sector, increasing the demand for bricks and mortar, and lime mortar was favoured for its good cohesive and adhesive properties. The social housing sector was growing as well, driven by private-sector investors who formed corporations and associations to build low-rental housing for working-class families.[33] One of the suppliers to profit from projects of this kind was Joan's shell-lime plant. Joan, well-to-do from birth, could now conduct his own household and the upbringing of his children in the same comfortable manner in which he had been raised.

A few weeks after Moe and Wil's move to Leiden, Theo invited Wil to Paris for a second visit. Jo was expecting their first child, and Theo hoped that Wil might help out during the pregnancy and the weeks after the birth. Willemien welcomed the prospect of some distraction. She packed a little cardigan for the baby and took the train to Paris on

2 January 1890.[34] In the summer of 1889, Jo had asked Vincent to be the child's godfather. She was convinced that the baby would be a boy, and wanted to name it after her brother-in-law. Yet she had reservations about the pregnancy. Her anxiety was not about starting a family, but rather her and Theo's poor health, which she feared would affect the child's well-being.[35] Wil's competent ministrations would be a godsend in the late stages of her pregnancy and during her confinement after the birth.

The Paris that Wil returned to was at the height of what the French had been calling the *fin de siècle*. The art of this period was characterized by an explosion of styles and forms. This included the growth of Impressionism and Art Nouveau in painting and building, advancements in cinematography and the invention of the cancan in the performance arts and dance. There were also various developments in science and sociological theory, which regularly conflicted with conservative traditions: Darwin's theory of evolution contradicted the Bible; the rise of Socialism threatened the power of the bourgeoisie; and Freudian psychology posited that humans harboured impulses that they would rather deny. These tensions gave the middle classes an ambivalent attitude. The dawn of a new century was hailed with both hope and trepidation. In art this ambivalence led to an escape from reality to luxury. This excessive prettiness gave the period, which would continue until the outbreak of the First World War, its name, La Belle Epoque. When the war came to an end it had brought so much suffering that the beauty of the preceding period was only more striking by contrast.

Paris was proudly known as the Cité de la Lumière, the City of Light, not in reference to luminaries like Voltaire or Montesquieu, but because of the foresight of an absolute monarch of a century earlier. To improve public safety and surveillance King Louis XIV had introduced street lighting in every boulevard and alleyway in the city. Renovated by Baron Georges-Eugène Haussmann between 1853 and 1870, the city was growing rapidly, due in part to an influx of migrants from rural France. Property prices in the centre soared, displacing large numbers of people who were now forced to seek more affordable housing on the outskirts of the city. By 1890 Paris had expanded to encompass the village of Montmartre.

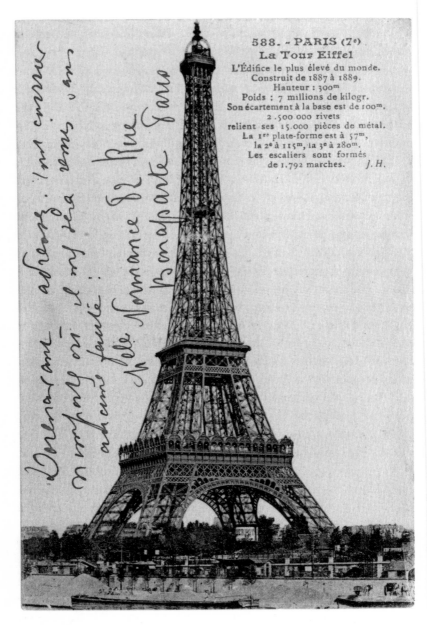

588. – PARIS (7e)
La Tour Eiffel
L'Édifice le plus élevé du monde.
Construit de 1887 à 1889.
Hauteur : 300m
Poids : 7 millions de kilogr.
Son écartement à la base est de 100m.
2.500 000 rivets
relient ses 15.000 pièces de métal.
La 1re plate-forme est à 57m,
la 2e à 115m, la 3e à 280m.
Les escaliers sont formés
de 1.792 marches.   J. H.

Postcard showing the Eiffel Tower, sent by Hubertine van Gogh. Date and photographer unknown.

The city's emergence as a modern metropolis was showcased at the Exposition Universelle (World's Fair) of 1889. Vincent wrote to Willemien twice about the Fair in 1888, while he was living in Arles and she was visiting Theo in Paris, first on his birthday, 30 March, and then again on 20 June.[36] He said he was working very hard so as to be able to present sufficient works. The World's Fair would take place the next summer; the Eiffel Tower was built for the occasion.[37] Wil must have seen it under construction. 'My dear sister, I'm writing in haste to let you know without further delay how delighted I am that you're in Paris, and I imagine you'll see a great deal of it in the coming days. Next year, when I'm living with my friend Gauguin, it's not exactly impossible that you might also come down to the Mediterranean. I'm sure you would like it here.' He concluded by saying, 'I'm busy with my sunflowers and can't actually think of anything to say, so I'll end by wishing Theo and you a splendid time and fine weather.'[38] The wrought-iron Eiffel Tower, which was completed in early 1889, loomed over an exhibition site that covered almost a full square kilometre. Visitors were transported around the pavilions by steam train. The future had arrived and there was no turning back. Paris at the turn of the century was still grappling with the aftermath of the Franco–Prussian War of two decades earlier, while the destruction, deprivation and catastrophic carnage of the First World War were yet to come. But this interbellum was characterized by optimism, prosperity and *joie de vivre*. This was the Paris that Willemien visited.

Throughout Wil's stay in Paris, Vincent wrote to her from the asylum in Saint-Rémy-de-Provence. On 4 January 1890 he wrote to say how happy he was that she had arrived in Paris for the second time.[39] On 20 January he asked: 'Are you enjoying yourself in Paris? I could very well imagine that it would strike you as being an over-large city, too muddled. That's what always vexes us, we who are rather accustomed to simpler surroundings. Write to me one of these days if you'd like to, for I very much want to hear you say that you're better. I fear a little the effect that Paris will have on me should I return there, as will probably be the case in the spring. For all through the year I've forced myself to forget Paris as much as I could from the point of view of the disturbance and excitement a prolonged stay causes.'[40] In the same letter he asked her if she had already met the painter Émile Bernard, a dear friend of his who he remarked was as memorable a character as one would find in one of Alphonse Daudet's adventure novels.[41]

Vincent often thought of the three of them – Theo, Jo and Wil – while recovering from his attack of delirium in Saint-Rémy, and hoped the 'big event' would go well for Jo.[42] He was happy to be working again, and intended to paint flowers – daisies, violets and dandelions – and trees. He had sent a painting of women picking olives to Paris for his mother and Wil (pl. xvi). Vincent remarked that he had chosen it for them 'so that they might have something a little studied.'[43] He sent the painting to Theo to prepare it for them, and advised him how to frame the work. 'If you use a white frame, I think you'll see that the contrast with the pink and green gives it a soft glow.'[44] He said he would be sending 'more mountains' and 'a garden with tall pine trees'.[45]

Theo often went out with his youngest sister during her stay in Paris. On 17 January 1890, he took Wil to Edgar Degas's studio, near the artist's home at 19 rue Fontaine.[46] Degas's reputation for being difficult and reserved had not prevented Theo from asking him for work to sell at Boussod, Valadon & Co., the gallery that had bought Goupil & Co. Degas was popular, and his paintings were fetching high prices. Around 1890 he painted the first of a highly successful series of dancers in blue costumes (pl. xvii). His dancers – executed in oils, gouache, chalk and, since the early 1880s, as three-dimensional sculptures – were doing particularly well.[47] The sculptures, in bronze or wax, must have made an impression on Theo and Wil. There would have been several of them in Degas's studio, each roughly the size of an adolescent girl. Degas was experimenting with unconventional combinations of different materials and achieved an astonishingly life-like effect. His bronze dancers from that period wear textile pointe shoes and real tutus. Their close-fitting bodices and short skirts reflect the prevailing fashion in ballet costumes. In line with the more permissive attitudes of the time, the traditional calf-length white skirt had been shortened to the knee to reveal the dancer's legs and sometimes even her bottom.

On 19 February 1890, Vincent replied to a letter Wil had sent him while still in Paris: 'I think you were lucky to see Degas at his home.'[48]

Theo had written to him about their visit on 9 February 1890, the day of Wil's departure for the Netherlands.[49] Wil's features had evidently reminded Degas of women in paintings by the Old Dutch masters, which made the great artist long to visit the museums in the Netherlands. He went to a great deal of trouble for her – a young woman he had only just met – bringing out one work after another to show her. Wil liked them, Theo said, adding proudly that she had a good eye for the female nudes – not least for a minister's daughter from Nuenen![50] For Wil, the whole visit must have been an extraordinary experience.

Theo had known Degas for some time. In July 1886, he had bought his *Woman Seated beside a Vase of Flowers* for Boussod, Valadon & Co., and in January 1888 had held an exhibition of Degas's work at the gallery. In the following years, he kept in touch with Degas and bought many more of his works. The two men met from time to time and must have corresponded about business matters like supply dates and payments, though the only surviving tangible evidence of their acquaintance is a telegram from Degas requesting payment and one of his business cards inscribed with a note to the same effect (pl. XVIII).[51]

The newest member of the Van Gogh lineage arrived on Friday 31 January 1890.[52] It was close to midnight when Theo and Jo's son was born. He was called Vincent Willem, after his godfather, who had been named after both of his grandfathers. The pregnancy and birth had exhausted Jo. She needed time to recover her strength and was having difficulty nursing the child. In April, Theo wrote to tell his mother and Wil that his son was doing well. 'He is growing out of all his little bonnets....We are giving him cow's milk twice a night now, as Jo could not cope. I was in favour of bottle-feeding him occasionally during the day as well, but so far she prefers to give him the breast.'[53] Anna assured Jo that she had known a child who had been raised on bottled milk and was doing perfectly well.[54] So there was no need to worry about little Vincent. Powdered baby formula would have been another option: it was as readily available in Paris as in the Netherlands.

In the five weeks that Wil spent with Jo, supporting her during her confinement, the two women got to know each other well. Jo wrote that her youngest sister-in-law's help had been invaluable and, above all, that

Jo van Gogh-Bonger and Vincent Willem van Gogh, 1890.
Photographed by Raoul Saisset.

they had got on so well together. The family doctor also commented on
the benefits of Wil's presence. He called in regularly to visit the young
mother, and remarked that Wil was 'much too good to get married'. It
was probably meant in jest, but Theo took it to heart, and in a letter to
Vincent written on the day that she departed for home he made a point
of saying how happy he would be if she did.[55]

Dear Sister, Dear Vincent

Paris, Leiden, 1888–1890

'My dear sister, Thank you very much for your letter, which I had been looking forward to. I'm reluctant to give in to my inclination to write to you often or inveigle you to do so. All this correspondence doesn't always help to buttress those of us of a nervous disposition when we are immersed in the kind of melancholy you were referring to in your letter and which I too experience now and again.' Vincent composed this letter to Willemien over the course of four days in Arles in June 1888.

Although it is known that Vincent kept up a keen, if sporadic, correspondence with his sisters, especially Anna and Lies, few of the letters they exchanged have survived. Some years earlier, in 1881, a flurry of letters had passed between him and his youngest sister. In October of that year, Vincent told Theo he was 'in constant correspondence with our sister Willemien.' They had another spell of intense contact in the autumn of 1887, but only a few of these letters, from Vincent to Wil, have been preserved, along with twenty-two letters he wrote to her between 1887 and 1890, one of which

Willemien van Gogh (right) and an unknown friend. Date and photographer unknown.

was never sent. Three further letters addressed to Wil and his mother jointly were written at this time. The only surviving letter from Wil to Vincent (and Theo) is one she had sent while visiting Anna in England in 1875 at the age of thirteen. There is a note Anna sent from Welwyn, and two drawings that Vincent may have sent her at that time.[2] No letters from Vincent to Lies exist. We know only that he enclosed a note for Anna and Lies in a letter to Theo on 4 September 1877. He asked his brother to 'add a few words and send it in time for Moe's birthday.'[3] Though he never wrote directly to his mother after the death of his father and his own departure from Nuenen, he assumed she would read some of his letters to Wil and communicated with her in this manner. Presumably in response to Vincent's note, Lies wrote to Theo, 'But I sometimes feel decidedly alienated from Vincent. I have so little inclination to write to him and so little affinity with the spirit in which he typically writes letters.'[4]

Wil and Vincent were close in spite of the distance between them as Vincent travelled from Holland to England, Belgium and eventually France, and Wil stayed largely with her mother or relatives in the Netherlands. They were frank with one another and wrote not only about art and literature, but also about love and finding a partner. Vincent often reminisced about his lost youth. When he wrote about it, his tone was melancholy. 'My fates have ordained that I shall make rapid progress in growing into a little old man, you know, with wrinkles, bristly beard, a few false teeth &c. but being as I am I often work with pleasure, and I see the possibility glimmering through of making paintings in which there's some youth and freshness, although my own youth is one of those things I've lost. If I didn't have Theo it wouldn't be possible for me to do justice to my work, but because I have him as a friend I believe that I'll make more progress and that things will run their course.'[5] Other passages on the same subject touch on the forces that drive his work. 'As for me,' he wrote, 'I keep having the most impossible and unsuitable love affairs which, as a rule, leave me battered and bruised...[but] through my love of art true love disappears.'[6]

Vincent and Willemien formed a strong bond when they lived together at the parsonage in Nuenen. But for a time after their father's death in

1885 and his quarrel with Anna, Vincent wanted nothing to do with Willemien. He wrote to Theo around that time: 'I find them at home (I know – contrary to your opinion and contrary to their opinion) very far, very far from sincere, and since there are also other things I object to for what I believe are sound reasons, I think Pa's death and the settlement of the estate is a point at which I will withdraw very discreetly.... Do you remember how sympathetic I was to Wil when I wrote to you when Moe was ill. Well, it was over in a trice – and it's frozen again.... I can see that you're doing your best to reconcile us. Even so, my dear fellow, I really wish her no harm and I really won't do them any harm. Only I have no desire to try and persuade them, firstly because they don't understand, but secondly don't want to understand.'[7]

However, after moving to Paris in late February 1886, Vincent found himself missing his mother and Wil, and resumed his correspondence with his youngest sister. He was proud that she and Lies were looking after the ailing Mrs Du Quesne in Soesterberg.[8] From the long letters he sent Wil from France we can deduce what she must have written about it to him, illuminating their shared interests.[9] He wrote to her as an elder brother, protective and ready to advise, but his letters were also humorous and cheerful. He and Wil often exchanged ideas on literature, love, colour, the sun, southern Europe and, needless to say, art. Their correspondence in this period was warm and communicative. Wil was interested in her older brother's ideas about his work not only from a personal point of view but also because she apparently drew inspiration from his style and choice of subject matter for her own experiments with drawing. After receiving two drawings from Wil, Margaretha Meijboom wrote to her: 'I am returning the Sunflower to you. I do not think it as good as the previous ones. The draughtsmanship of the Mother and Child lacks confidence. These are not ordinary people, but nor are they fantastical beings. The mother with her yellow paper flower is simply dreadful. Her saying, "The sun has set in my son's garden," is incongruous there. The style, too, is inconsistent. One moment you are up in the air, fearless and proud, and then suddenly you go and sit on the ground. All in all, it makes me dizzy because of the many bad transitions. And, to my mind, you could certainly present the idea in nicer, more suitable packaging. I would advise you not to send it. Am I getting "the children" on loan? I'd say I deserve it for my blunt grumble about "the Sunflower".'[10] Margaretha's frank evaluation of these drawings indicates that Wil shared her artworks with her friends, and was open to criticism. Indeed, she apparently made a point of explaining how she chose her subject matter and working methods: 'Now I understand that the inconsistencies in your drawing of that mother were deliberate, and the Sunflower too, but your intentions were not clear and that is why it looked wrong. At least to me, but then I do not consider myself an authority.'[11]

Margaretha was apparently fond of Vincent and saw something of herself in him. In 1888 she wrote, 'Glad that Vincent's doing so well. I should be delighted if he were to come again. I have always felt an affinity with him and his struggle with the world.'[12] Wil forwarded some of Vincent's letters to Margaretha, who commented on one: 'Vincent's letter is quite extraordinary. I had not realized he was so cultured, Wil! Or so deep and well-read! And how highly he thinks of Theo! I can imagine that it must have been extremely gratifying to have that glimpse into his soul. I completely disagree with his views on love. Life has forced me to accept what he calls love. Well, I can live with that, but there is also another kind, purer, loftier and nobler than he has in mind, which makes one's whole life sunny and bright whenever it shines through the mist, as powerful and invincible as a storm, yet still not egoistic, which takes you much further as an artist, whereas his concept [of love] does not offer much, I believe. Besides that, I agree with him that an artist learns more from life than from study....Nice what Vincent says about serenity and about burning rather than suffocating. The same idea in a different form came to mind when we were sitting at the seaside. Tired as I was from all the struggle and turmoil, I nonetheless thought "sooner be crushed by waves than wither away on a rock."'[13]

Margaretha was commenting on a letter that Vincent had sent to Breda in October 1887 and Wil had forwarded to her. In it, Vincent had advocated that young women should lead relatively conventional lives. He rejected the idea of studying in order to become a writer or painter, and offered his sister advice on how to find happiness, suggesting that she should enjoy herself, live life to the full and avoid anything that might give rise to pessimism. But he appears to have been ambivalent. On the one hand, he was trying to curb Wil's ambition, whereas Margaretha was encouraging her. At the same time, he wrote, as Margaretha acknowledged, 'Whatever is inside must come out.'[14]

Vincent and Wil were each aware of the other's struggles with their mental health and their discussions of the topic were frank and compassionate. On 31 July 1888, Vincent wrote, 'Are you in good health? I hope so. The main thing is for you to spend a lot of time outdoors. I'm often troubled by not being able to eat, more or less like you that time. But I manage to steer clear of the rocks. If you're not strong, you have to be smart; you and I, with our constitutions, should take that to heart.'[15] Vincent was referring to the months in 1884 when Wil was confined to bed with severe abdominal pains.[16] He wrote to her again in late April or early May 1889 – in French, which he preferred to Dutch by then – and told her that he would be admitted to the hospital in Saint-Rémy 'for three months or less', after having suffered three 'attacks'. He had lost consciousness on those occasions 'for no plausible reason' and had no recollection of what had happened or what he had said or done.[17] Later, Vincent wrote that he felt unable to explain exactly what he was suffering from: the symptoms included anxiety attacks, a feeling of emptiness, fatigue and depression with no apparent cause.[18] He adopted the formula prescribed by his literary hero Charles Dickens to banish thoughts of suicide: a daily glass of wine with some bread and cheese, and a pipe of tobacco.[19] In October 1889, he told Wil that, according to the doctor Theo had sent to examine him, he was not insane, nor was his moodiness precipitated by alcohol. His seizures were epileptic.[20] His mother's sister, Clara Carbentus, had been diagnosed with the same disorder a few decades before.[21]

In a letter to Wil of 20 January 1890, while she was staying with Theo and Jo in Paris for the second time to help with the birth of Vincent Willem, Vincent expressed concern about his sister's health. He himself had found Paris 'too big and disorientating', and feared it might have the same effect on her.[22] Reading Vincent and Willemien's correspondence, as well as what others wrote about them, it is tempting to diagnose their afflictions. Yet psychiatry was still a new field in the late nineteenth century. The German doctor Johann Christian Reil had invented the term to describe a new branch of medicine focused on researching, treating and curing mental illnesses in 1808, but understandings of the causes and treatments of psychological problems were in their infancy. Mental illnesses were no longer all diagnosed as 'lunacy', but a very different language was used to describe mental health disorders, or 'brain sufferers', as people with a mental condition were called. Work by Wilhelm Griesinger and Emil Kraepelin led to the classification of psychiatric syndromes; dementia praecox (schizophrenia) and manic-depressive psychosis in particular were recognized as specific syndromes. Other common diagnoses in this period were hysteria and neurasthenia.

Vincent and Wil discussed far more than the state of their health. They wrote about art and literature, the paintings Vincent was working on, and people they both knew. Vincent's letters were generally quite serious in tone, especially when he wrote about his work. This was the period, first in Paris and later in Arles, in which painting became his mission in life, and he wrote several letters that discuss nothing else. Wil and Theo were the first to know what was on his mind or what he was busy painting – sunflowers, the postman, the terrace of a café. In a long letter to Wil composed over 16 and 18 June 1888, Vincent described the environs of Arles, extolling the landscape and the light: 'The colours here are actually very fine. When the vegetation is fresh it's a rich green the like of which we seldom see in the north, calm. When it gets scorched and dusty it doesn't become ugly, but then a landscape takes on tones of gold of every hue – green-gold, yellow-gold, red-gold, ditto bronze, copper, in short, from lemon gold to the dull yellow of, say, a heap of threshed corn. That with the blue – from the deepest royal blue in the water to that of forget-me-nots. Cobalt above all, bright clear blue – green-blue and violet-blue.'[23] And in the same letter: 'I spent a week on the Mediterranean; you'd like it. What strikes me here and what appeals to me about painting here is the clarity of the air; you can't imagine what it's like because it's exactly what we don't have at home – but an hour away from here you can distinguish the colours of things, the grey-green of the olive trees and the grass green of the meadows e.g. and the pink-lilac of a ploughed field. At home we see a vague grey line on the horizon; here, the line is sharp and the shapes are recognizable even from far, far away. This gives a sense of space and air.'[24]

Vincent admitted to Wil that his exuberant style and palette were not to everyone's taste. 'Uncle Cor has seen work of mine more than once and he thinks it atrocious.'[25] But Vincent was undeterred in his delight in his chosen subjects: 'I'm working on a portrait of a postman in his dark blue uniform with yellow. A face rather like Socrates', hardly any nose, a high forehead, bald scalp, small grey eyes, strong-coloured full cheeks, a big beard, pepper and salt, big ears. The man is a fervent republican and socialist, reasons well and knows a great deal. His wife gave birth today, so he's as pleased as punch and beaming with satisfaction.'[26]

Vincent started to make paintings, especially for Willemien. On several occasions, he asked her to choose a painting for herself from among his recent work when she visited Theo in Paris, which she would then take back to the Netherlands. More often, however, he sent his work to the Netherlands via Theo, though Willemien may already have known from Vincent's letters what they would represent. In March 1888, two weeks after her twenty-sixth birthday and on his thirty-fifth birthday, he wrote to her from Arles: 'As for me, I too must wish you a happy birthday – as I want to give you a work of mine that you'd like, I'll set aside a small study of a book and a flower – the same subject as my painting Parisian Novels [which is] in a larger format, with a whole mass of books with pink, yellow, green covers and fiery red. Theo will bring it for you.'[27] The works Vincent was describing are his *Blossoming Almond Branch in a Glass* and its pendant the *Still Life with French Novels and a Rose*, also known as *Romans Parisiens*. Another letter followed in June informing Wil that he had sent her a drawing, 'the first rough sketch for a fairly large painting.'[28] This was a study for the painted *Harvest Landscape*. On one occasion that we know of, Vincent painted Willemien a copy of another artist's work. In a letter from Saint-Rémy-de-Provence, Vincent wrote: 'I thought of sending you yourself a sketch of it to give you an idea of what Delacroix is. This little copy of course has no value from any point of view.'[29] As we now know, a copy of Delacroix's Pietà indeed did end up in Willemien's collection.[30]

In September 1888, Vincent suggested that Wil should take one of the paintings he had made in Saintes-Maries-de-la-Mer to the Netherlands. Just over a year later, in October 1889, after his mother and Wil had announced their intention to move to Leiden, Vincent wrote to Wil from Saint-Rémy-de-Provence saying he would send her seven paintings via Theo in Paris: 'Very soon I'll send Theo the painted studies I had promised, and he'll get them to you in Leiden. This is what I have: An olive grove, Wheatfield with reaper, Wheatfield and cypresses, Interior, Ploughed fields, morning effect, Orchard in blossom, and a portait of me. Let's say that during the course of the next year I send you as many, that would make a little collection with the two that you have, and if you had enough room I would urge you to keep them together, since you'll probably see artists from time to time in Leiden, and other studies would, I dare believe, soon join mine.'[31] As far as Vincent was concerned, she could hang them in the corridor or in the kitchen or beside the staircase. But they should be displayed in simple surroundings, he explained. He had tried to make them in such way that they would look right in a kitchen or a living room. It did not matter to him either way.[32] He also wanted Wil to have *The Red Vineyard*, which was still at Theo's in Paris.

Sometimes when Vincent painted especially for Willemien, he intentionally adapted his style to cater to his sister's preferences. In December 1889, he wrote: 'I have 12 large canvases on the go, above all olive groves, one with an entirely pink sky, another with a green and orange sky, a third with a big yellow sun.'[33] This olive grove with a completely pink sky was the first of three versions of *Women Picking Olives*. Vincent told Theo that he painted the third version for Willemien and his mother. This last iteration was more abstract and simplified than its predecessors, a trait which it shared with other repetitions made for Willemien and his mother, that he intended to send to Theo in late September.[34] In the accompanying letter he wrote: 'the sixteen paintings in the shipment, should give them a good start, and I think this will give both you and me some pleasure to ensure that our sister or

Vincent van Gogh, *The Red Vineyard*, 1888. Oil on canvas, 75 × 93 cm (29½ × 36⅝ in.).

sisters have a small collection of paintings.'[35] Shortly thereafter, Vincent wrote to Willemien about this painting: 'I hope that you'll quite like the canvas I'm doing for Mother and you at the moment. It's a repetition of a painting for Theo, Women picking olives. For this past fortnight I've worked hard continuously.'[36]

Then, on 4 January 1890, from Saint-Rémy-de-Provence, he wrote: 'Yesterday I sent some paintings to Paris – and the one of the women picking olives I designated for you and Mother. You'll see, I think, that in a white frame it takes on quite a soft colour effect, the opposition of the pink and the green. Soon I'll send a few more that are drying at the moment, some more mountains, and a view of the garden here with tall pines.'[37] The paintings Vincent described here are *Women Picking Olives*, *Ravine* and *Pine Trees with Setting Sun*. He seemed especially confident about the *Women Picking Olives*, writing to Wil nearly a month later: 'I hope that the painting of the women in the olive trees will be a little to your taste – I sent the drawing of it to Gauguin just recently and he told me that he thought it good, and he knows my work well, and he isn't embarrassed to say so when it isn't right. You would naturally be quite free to take another of them in its place if you wished, but in the long run I almost dare believe that you'd return to this one.'[38]

Wil's reaction to all these paintings and Vincent's instructions for displaying them will never be known, as her responses to Vincent of course no longer exist. *Women Picking Olives* was one of several works by Vincent to be shown at the exhibition of Les Vingt in Brussels in 1890. It was also one of the very few paintings he sold in his lifetime: it was bought by the Belgian painter Anna Boch, whose brother was also a painter and a good friend of Vincent's.[39]

Vincent is only known to have mentioned paintings for Anna and Lies once, in February 1890, when he asked Wil to let them choose something from the paintings he had sent her. 'If our other sisters would also like to have canvases, you can ask Theo for more and you can choose them according to your taste.'[40] This aside, he appears to have shown little interest in Anna and Lies. His mother and Wil he did miss, however. From Saint-Rémy-de-Provence, 'while the canvases [were] drying in the sun,' he told his mother and Wil that they were often in his thoughts. 'I hope you're well and Mother too; I think of you both very often. I could scarcely foresee when I left Nuenen for Antwerp that the tide of circumstance would take me so far and keep me away for so long.'[41] On 13 June 1890, just over a month before his death, he wrote to Wil from Auvers-sur-Oise, saying, 'I very much hope to paint your portrait one day.'[42] Yet he had consciously avoided meeting his youngest sister during her visits to Paris, and painting her portrait was a dream he would never fulfil.

CHAPTER 13

Oh Mother,
He Was So Truly My Brother

Paris, Leiden, 1890–1893

In the spring of 1889, Vincent was admitted to a psychiatric institution in Saint-Rémy. Wil was worried about this, as can be inferred from a letter that her friend Margaretha Meijboom sent her: 'Find an institution but not too unpleasant, Wil! I know from a lady who works there that the patients calm down almost as soon as they are admitted. It does them all good to get proper nursing.'[1] In January 1890, Vincent seemed to be recovering and Theo was seeking alternative accommodation for him. He considered various options, weighing up the interests of safeguarding his brother's health while not restricting his freedom to paint. In the end, after speaking with *père* Camille Pissarro, a fellow painter living there, he concluded that it would be best for Vincent to go to Auvers-sur-Oise, to the northwest of Paris, for treatment under the supervision of the homeopathic physician Paul Gachet.[2] Vincent agreed to Theo's suggestion and on 16 May took the night train to Paris, where Theo met him at the station. Vincent stayed with his brother, his sister-in-law Jo and their newborn son Vincent Willem for three days. Though he was smitten with his little nephew, Vincent found Paris too frenetic, and was relieved to move to the peaceful village of Auvers-sur-Oise.[3] While in Saint-Rémy Vincent had painted the *Almond Blossom*, a subject probably inspired by Japanese prints, to mark the birth of his godson, and he gave the canvas to Theo and Jo during this stay. The almond comes into bloom in February, soon after the child's birthday, heralding spring and better times.[4]

Shortly after his arrival in Auvers, Vincent met Dr Gachet, who helped him find lodgings. Rooms could be rented at the auberge run by Arthur-Gustave Ravoux, and one happened to be available. No sooner

163

had he moved in than Vincent started painting in and around Auvers. He was not the only artist to do so: at various times Cézanne, Corot, Daubigny and Pissarro also found inspiration in the rich natural diversity of the region. On 8 June, Theo and Jo came to visit Vincent and Dr Gachet, bringing the baby. They spent a pleasant day together.[5] In fact, that summer was a good time for Vincent. He was unusually productive, painting such works as the *Portrait of Dr Gachet*[6] and the *Church in Auvers*.[7] The one jarring note was news from Theo that little Vincent had been ill; Theo told his brother that the child's frequent crying had been caused by the poor quality of the milk on sale in Paris. Poison, he called it. The boy had recovered as soon as he was put on donkey milk and was doing well. Mother and child were asleep as he wrote, which was much needed too, as Jo was worn out from the stress of the past few days.[8]

It was a trying time for Theo. He was constantly worried about his son's health, but his own was a cause for concern as well. Furthermore, his future with Boussod, Valadon & Co. was uncertain. As he was so often at odds with his superiors he was contemplating starting a gallery of his own, a risky endeavour.[9] Vincent, dismayed by the news of his nephew's illness, decided to visit his brother and sister-in-law and took the train to Paris on 6 July. Little is known about the visit, but years later Jo remembered it as a day 'filled with anxiety and stress'.[10] Vincent had a violent quarrel with Theo, stormed out of the apartment and returned to the tranquillity of Auvers. Jo wrote to him, hoping to smooth things over. He had taken it all too much to heart, she said, and shouldn't have left so abruptly.[11]

That summer, after returning from her second visit to Paris, Wil took up a position as a probationary apprentice nurse at the Hôpital Wallon in Leiden, which served the Protestant community. She worked there from 4 May to 16 June 1890.[12] On 5 June Vincent wrote to Wil, saying he was pleased to hear that she was working at the hospital, and spoke of the valuable skills that her vocation demanded: 'As for me, I regret knowing nothing, anyway not enough, about all that.'[13] In another letter to his mother and youngest sister, which he must have written between 10 and 14 July, Vincent returned to the matter of Wil's employment, evidently not knowing that by then Wil had already left the post: 'Very good that Wil has started working at the hospital and that she says the operations weren't as bad as she expected, because she appreciates the means of alleviating pain and the many doctors who endeavour to do what has to be done, quietly, skilfully and with kindness – well, that's what I call the right approach and – faith.'[14]

The Hôpital Wallon was founded by the descendants of Protestant refugees from Wallonia, the French-speaking region in the south of Belgium and in France, who had fled Catholic persecution in the late sixteenth century. A second group of émigrés followed a century later, after King Louis XIV revoked the Edict of Nantes (1598), stripping the Huguenots of all civil and religious rights in France. The newcomers formed a close-knit community and established their own churches, schools, libraries, orphanages and, in 1886, Leiden's first Protestant hospital at 12 Rapenburg in the historic centre of Leiden.[15] Wil's home was within walking distance of the hospital, on a route that took her straight through the old centre of Leiden. Though her employment there lasted only six weeks, she was generally enthusiastic about her workplace and occupation. Not squeamish by nature, she was comfortable assisting in surgery, and found the operations fascinating. In June 1890, she wrote to Theo: 'One can learn a great deal about people there because you see people as they are. Actually, they are almost exclusively patients of Professor Itterson and Professor Treub who come for surgery and then leave when they are cured. Attending an operation is most extraordinary. I have always been able to remain at my post. The truth is, it was so interesting that I forgot to find it nasty.'[16]

Even so, Wil lost interest quickly. The Hôpital Wallon wanted her to stay on 'but,' she wrote, 'that is obviously out of the question'.[17] That summer she had struggled with her mental state, and was contemplating giving her life a new direction, following a path more similar to that chosen by her grandfather, father and Vincent: she intended to become a teacher of scripture. In a long letter to Jo, dated 26 June 1890, she explained that she had decided to leave the Hôpital Wallon to devote her energy instead to young people and inspire them 'to do good': 'I needed some solid ground, a better understanding of the things a person needs to have before they can give. That study paved the way for me to acquire a basic knowledge and, having the opportunity, I decided to take advantage of it.' In that difficult period, she said, she 'needed the support her work gave her'; without it, she 'wouldn't have held out.'[18]

Wil was excited by her new career prospects, and the future looked promising, but a terrible tragedy awaited the family. Though first-hand accounts differ on a few minor points, there can be little doubt as to what happened in Auvers on the night of Sunday 27 July 1890. That evening, Vincent took his easel and painting materials and made his way to the wheat field where he often painted. There he shot himself in the chest with a revolver. After staggering back to his room at the auberge, he collapsed onto his bed. He was discovered hours later by his landlord Ravoux, who summoned the local physician, Dr Mazery, and alerted Dr Gachet. The two men decided not to try to remove the bullet, and Dr Gachet sent an express letter to Theo that same night. As he did not know Theo's home address, he posted the letter to the gallery where Theo was employed.[19] Because of the delay, Theo only arrived in Auvers the following afternoon, to find that Vincent was dying.[20]

Theo was constantly at Vincent's side in the last hours of his life. Vincent's beloved brother and devoted friend held him in his arms as he spoke his last words: 'This is how I wanted to go.'[21] Reconciled to his fate, Vincent died at half past one in the morning of 29 July 1890.

The news of his death reached Leiden by post the next day. At first, Theo said nothing to Jo, who was spending time with her family in Amsterdam. He wanted his brother-in-law, Joan van Houten, to break the news to his mother and Wil first; Anna was at the time staying with her daughters at the Dennenoord Hotel in Ginneken, near Breda. Joan kept it to himself the night that he received the letter, saying only that Vincent wasn't well. But the following day, in the living room of the house on Herengracht he told Wil what had happened. When Wil went to her mother's room with tears in her eyes, Moe exclaimed, without a moment's hesitation, 'Oh is Joan here? Is Vincent dead?'[22] Moe wrote to Jo that same day, 31 July. 'What a blessing that his dear brother, our Theo, was with him to attend him to the end. Theo wrote what had happened, how gently he passed on, and now he is at rest from that tireless striving and struggling and suffering.'[23]

The family was distraught, unable to accept that this parting was for ever. As Theo had stayed in Auvers to make arrangements for the funeral, we know from the letters he received how they felt. Joan van Houten wrote to his brother-in-law on 31 July: 'Dear Theo, Yesterday afternoon I received your letter with the sad news of Vincent's death. I can imagine how shocked you must be. You were always so close and committed to him and therefore knew him better than anyone else. It must be a great comfort to you to know that he did not suffer at the end and that you managed to get there in time; I am truly pleased for you... you were more than a brother to him and for that you will miss him twice as much. Please accept my heartfelt sympathy in your bereavement and may you find comfort in the knowledge that he has found peace at the end of a troubled life. Yesterday evening, I told Moe and Mien [Willemien] that you had received bad news from Auvers again and this morning I told them the whole story. They are inconsolable, needless to say. It nevertheless came as a shock, too sudden for them to grasp the idea, for how many times did Vincent not recover after similar lapses, thanks to his strong constitution. I left Moe calm and reconciled to it, consoled by the thought that he has found peace at last. It will undoubtedly leave a great void in your life; fortunately your wife and child shall endeavour to fill it. I was delighted to hear from Amsterdam that the boy is growing nicely and that Jo is recovering her strength.'[24]

Moe wrote to her son later that day. 'Dear beloved Theo, We are upset by the distressing news! Joan prepared us and when I saw Wil with tears in her eyes, I said, is he dead? Thank you my dear Theo, for all you did for him. Your love and solicitude made his life worthwhile. The good Lord witnessed it and ordained that you be rewarded that you by seeing him close his eyes and laying him to rest. This was the reward of which the greatest love found you worthy. In all these terribly unexpected events I am thankful that he was in calm, good surroundings, that he could still talk to you and that, according to your letter, he departed without undue suffering to that land where turmoil and suffering shall be no more. I shall let you read his letter from a fortnight ago, saying how he felt. He also wrote that he often longed to see us again. How good that your abiding love was near him to the end. Blessings, Theo, from all of us, and may the good Lord bless you and Jo and little Vincent. May he be the joy of your life. A grateful kiss with thanks from your loving Moe.'[25]

Willemien wrote to Theo as well. 'I can hardly believe and cannot yet imagine that he is no more. We should not begrudge him his peace, but how hard it will be for you. Wonderful that you were with him, loyal brother, you deserved it. And that he passed away peacefully is the greatest blessing possible. What a strange coincidence, the cause that events took, that he had his wish to be and to live like ordinary people, and was now so near to you. He was certainly happier like this as he himself said, incidentally in his last letter. How glad you must be that Jo still managed to see him – who would have supposed then it would be for the last time; and that he also saw little Vincent. Poor fellow, not having your wife with you. Come to Holland soon, we long so much for you. Could you manage next week?' In a postscript, Wil asked Theo to 'thank Dr Gachet on our behalf.'[26]

The following day, the Van Goghs were back at their writing desks. Anna, still in Ginneken, wrote to her sister-in-law Jo. 'Dear Jo, I was most upset by the news of Vincent's unexpected death. You and Theo, who saw him so recently, must be devastated. How fortunate for the two brothers to have been together to the end; it will be a great comfort to Moe, that Theo was with him and able to help him. He will surely have welcomed the peace, as things have always been hard for him. Luckily, he was finding a lot of satisfaction in his work of late, and he also got to see his little namesake. You must be missing Theo more than ever. How lonely he must have felt in those unhappy days. Is he coming tomorrow? This morning I heard from Moe that the little one is fine and it is going well with the bottles [of milk formula]. I recently saw a child who was brought up on it but that gave one confidence. I am sure he enjoys being outdoors, especially in this pleasant weather. Are you feeling a bit stronger? I do hope so, before you go back to Paris. You must be missing Theo terribly, because even in one's parents' home, being separated is not ideal. That is how I feel too, and I am longing to see Jo[an] again. At the moment, being outdoors does not do as much good as we would wish, but luckily the fever has subsided. We wish our girls were somewhat stronger; we worry all the time, especially about An. And now I must conclude. Please give my regards to your family and give the little one a big kiss from me and the girls. I remain as always, your loving Anna.'27

After receiving the news of Vincent's death on 1 August 1890 in a letter from her mother and Willemien, Lies travelled from Soesterberg to Leiden to be with them. From there she wrote a long letter to her brother and sister-in-law the following day. 'What upsetting news I received on Friday! Never could I have imagined that Vincent's life would be cut short so abruptly, especially as it was just starting to take on a more agreeable aspect; but on re-reading the letter from mother and Wil telling me all they knew so far about his passing, and when I thought about his life as a whole – then it seemed to me that God himself had gently laid him to rest, after comforting and soothing him. What a change, both charming and invigorating, from a hospital environment to the midst of beautiful nature, which gave him all the novelty of a region different from the one to which he had grown accustomed. And on top of it, Paris nearby, the two of you within reach, and seeing his godchild, for whom I am sure he had high expectations, perhaps even saw in him a budding little artist. He experienced all those pleasant little rays of sunshine, up to now his condition did not affect his ability to work, but would that have been the case in the long run? He did not see a decline, not like someone maimed: he went down in a blaze of glory, Theo at his side, not alone on foreign soil. I remember the time he walked from Etten to Zundert and visited Aarsen [an old family friend].28 He arrived moments before he passed away and when he returned he said, "When I die, I hope to die like this". It made a lasting impression on him. When Pa died and Mrs Poots wanted to see him, Vincent stood with her and said, "Yes, Mrs Poots, it's hard to die, but even harder to live." I do not have to tell you, Theo, that we talk about you often and would very much like to know more. We are also worried about you because you shall be so terribly distressed, and it shall not be easy to cope with so much grief, physically or mentally. I am so deeply sorry that I cannot see you right now. But I could not do anything other than come here at once and could not wait until you were here. So I shall not be able to come right away, but you know why. Mother and Wil are being brave; it is good being together, talking about it all, and we shall be happy when Jo and you are together again. No one but your wife shall be able to comfort you now, and the little one, even though he cannot put it into words yet. I found the little paintings here, which I now cherish all the more. I am going to grow very attached to the landscape in particular; I look forward to seeing it hanging in my room. I have also got his tower in Nuenen in the snow, which is absolutely lovely! And, for now, adieu dear Theo and Jo; may spending time quietly at home do you good. With an affectionate kiss for you and little Vincent, who has now become even more of a kind of legacy from *Him* to us all.'[29] In a remark at the very end of her letter there is mention of a letter from her to Vincent. She asks Theo if it has been passed on to him together with her message, and thanks Theo for a book far too beautiful and expensive.[30]

Theo replied to Lies from Paris. 'To say we must be grateful that he is at peace – I still find it difficult to do so. I think it might be one of the greatest cruelties of life on this earth and perhaps he should be counted among the martyrs who have died with a smile on their face. He did not want to go on living and was at peace with himself because he had always fought for what he believed in, and that he had measured against the best and noblest of those who had gone before him. His love for his father, for the gospel, for the poor and the wretched, for the great men of literature and painting bears witness to this. In the last letter he wrote me, about four days before his passing, he said, "I'm trying to do as well as some of the painters I have greatly loved and admired." People should know that he was a great artist, which is often the same as being a great human being. One day they shall realize this and many shall regret that he left us so soon. He himself wanted to die. When I sat with him and said we would try to get him better and then hope he would be spared this despair again, he said, "La tristesse durera toujours." I understood what he meant....Soon afterwards, he had trouble breathing and a moment later closed his eyes. A great peace came over him and he never regained consciousness. The people of that beautiful village were very fond of him; everyone said he was loved and many of them carried him to his grave, where a stone will tell passers-by his name. I want to try and organize an exhibition of his work in Paris in a few months' time. I would like to be able to show you all of it together some time; it is easier to understand, if you see a lot of work side by side. People will also write about him. If I can get a room, the exhibition will be held in the month of October or early November. The Parisians are in town then. He shall certainly not be forgotten.'[31] This was the promise Theo made to Lies at the end of his letter of 5 August.

Vincent was denied a burial in the Catholic churchyard in Auvers: taking one's own life was considered a mortal sin and, moreover, Vincent was born a Protestant.[32] Instead, Theo bought a plot in the new, almost empty cemetery set among the wheat fields on a plateau above the village. The funeral took place on 30 July 1890. Vincent's mother, sisters and sister-in-law could not attend, but heard about it from Theo. Vincent's close friend, the painter Émile Bernard, wrote an eye-witness account of the occasion, but it was never to reach them. This account was written at the request of the art critic, poet and painter Gustave-Albert Aurier, who in January of that year had published a favourable review of Vincent's work in the prestigious magazine *Mercure de France*. Aurier used Bernard's piece as the basis for a second article on Vincent, which helped to spread Vincent's reputation. Bernard described the events of that day in great detail:

The coffin was already closed, I arrived there too late to see him again, he who had held such high expectations of every kind three years ago, when I parted from him....All of his last canvases were tacked to the walls of the room where the body was laid out. They hung like a halo around him and the brilliance, the genius they bespoke made his death even more distressing for the artists who were there. A simple white sheet covered the coffin, which was heaped with flowers, the sunflowers he adored, yellow dahlias, yellow flowers everywhere....His easel, his field stool and his paintbrushes were near him on the floor beside the coffin.[33]

Many people came, mainly artists...people from these parts who knew him to some degree, who had seen him once or twice and liked him because he was so kind, so human....At three o'clock the coffin was borne away, friends of his carried it to the hearse. People were in tears. Théodore van Gogh, who was devoted to his brother and had always encouraged him in his efforts to make a living from his art, sobbed incessantly....We reached the cemetery, a small

*cemetery with a scattering of new gravestones. It is up on the hill
overlooking the wheat fields under a wide blue sky that he might
still perhaps have loved.*

*Then he was lowered into the grave....Anyone would have been
moved to tears at that moment. The day was so perfect for him that
one imagined he was still alive and enjoying it.*

*Dr Gachet (a great art lover who possesses one of the finest
collections of contemporary Impressionists)...had wanted to say
a few words about Vincent and his life, but he too was choked with
tears and managed only to stammer a confused farewell....He had
been an honest man and a great artist, he said, who had only two
aims in life, humanity and art. He would live on through the art
he aspired to above all else.*

*Afterwards, we turned back. Théodore van Gogh was broken-
hearted and everyone present was deeply moved. Some returned to
the countryside, others made for the station. Laval and I went back
to Ravoux and talked about him'*[34]

After the tragedy of 29 July 1890, Vincent's mother was plagued by
a thought that no parent would readily admit to: that her son might be
better off dead. She had been mulling this over a year and a half earlier,
writing to Theo: 'Oh, Theo, how shall it turn out, what shall become
of him. I am almost tempted to say, if he were to fall ill, it would end.
But he is ill enough, you shall say, as bad as one can imagine. What
comforts me is that he is a child of our Heavenly Father and He shall
not abandon or forsake him. If it were up to me, I would ask, Take him
unto you, but we have to accept what God has given.'[35] After the funeral
Theo returned to Paris. In a heartrending letter to his mother, he broke
down: 'Oh, mother, he was so truly my brother.'[36]

Vincent's death brought Lies and Anna back to their mother's home
in Leiden. There, all together, they missed Theo, who had said he would
be coming, and their youngest brother Cor, who had emigrated to South
Africa. A poor correspondent at the best of times, indeed 'a hopeless
case,' as he himself confessed,[37] Cor only responded to the news of

Vincent's death two months after the event, though he was just as upset as his siblings. In this letter, Cor reminisced about Vincent, but wrote mainly about his own life and experiences in Johannesburg.[38]

The dramatic events of 1890 – the birth of Vincent Willem, illness that plagued the family and the death of Vincent – inevitably had a lasting impact on the family. For some time afterwards, the sisters continued to write about this period of shared intimacy. The scars left by Vincent's suffering and death took a long time to heal, as Anna recalled later in life.

Influenced by Romanticism in the last decade of the nineteenth century, letters of condolence became more personal and direct. This was the case for many of the letters the family received after Vincent's death. Whether short notes or lengthy epistles, more often than not these missives included personal reminiscences and observations. Among them are a few true gems. Paul Gauguin, with whom Vincent had a turbulent relationship, ended his succinct note with the words, 'As for me, with my eyes and with my heart I shall continue to see him in his work.'[39] Theo

Cor van Gogh, 1888. Photographed by Caleb C. Smith.

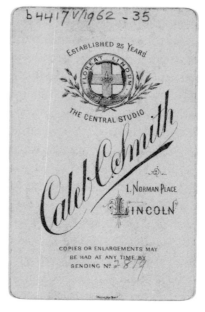

received written condolences from Claude Monet, Armand Guillaumin and Henri de Toulouse-Lautrec. Though Camille Pissarro was unable to attend the funeral personally, he sent his son Lucien to represent him.

Vincent's death drew the attention of Dutch artists too. The painter Anthon van Rappard, a firm friend of Vincent's since they had met in Brussels in October 1880, sent a letter to Moe. It was not easy, he said, to be friends with this man who demanded so much of himself, but of whom he had many fond memories, referencing a visit to the Van Goghs' home in Etten.[40] The Dutch Impressionist Isaac Israëls wrote to Theo to express his sorrow at Vincent's untimely death. He regretted never having met Vincent or having had the opportunity to paint with him.[41] George Hendrik Breitner, Israëls's friend and likewise an Impressionist painter from Amsterdam, also conveyed his sympathy to Theo, as did Isaac Meijer de Haan, who had once shared Theo's flat in Paris but never met Vincent.[42]

No communication between Theo and Degas on the matter of Vincent's death is known. Some time that year, however, in tribute to Vincent, Degas exchanged his *Two Sketches of Dancers* with art dealer Ambroise Vollard for Vincent's *Two Sunflowers* (1887) and a still life.[43]

For a while Theo's declining health was overshadowed by the birth of his son Vincent Willem and the death of his brother Vincent. Theo himself had a hand in this, having feigned a harmless cough to cover up a far more serious illness. But soon after his brother's death Theo's symptoms became more severe and harder to hide; he began to hallucinate, and became insulting, megalomanic and offensive at work. According to his doctor, he was in a far worse state than his brother had ever been. He had contracted syphilis, a venereal disease that was often fatal, and had failed to get proper treatment. For this he paid the ultimate price. As the disease was already at an advanced stage, Jo had Theo admitted to a clinic in Paris. Later, on the advice of a close friend, the psychiatrist, family doctor and writer Frederik van Eeden, she decided to have her husband transferred to the Arntz Clinic in Utrecht. But it was too late. Theo died in Utrecht on 25 January 1891, less than six months after his brother, aged thirty-three. He was buried at the Soesterberg cemetery in Utrecht on 29 January.[44] When, in 1905, the rights to Vincent's grave in Auvers expired, Jo started making the necessary arrangements to reunite the brothers. Her efforts were finally rewarded in 1914, when Theo was buried beside Vincent in Auvers. The two graves are covered with ivy grown from cuttings that Jo obtained from Dr Gachet's garden.[45]

The year 1891 must have been very difficult for Moe and the sisters, who were mourning the loss of both Vincent and Theo. Even so, there was cause for celebration at the end of 1891. After Mrs Du Quesne van Willis succumbed to her illness in 1889, Lies's clandestine relationship with her husband Jean Philippe du Quesne could finally be acknowledged and legitimized by marriage. Lies returned to her mother's home to prepare for the wedding, and the ceremony was held on 2 December 1891.[46] Joan van Houten acted as the couple's witness. Lies and Jean Philippe then returned to the Villa Eikenhorst in Soesterberg, the house in which Lies had nursed the first Mrs Du Quesne until her death. Few people knew that she and Jean Philippe already had a five-year-old child who was being raised a Catholic in Normandy.[47]

Hubertine at her first communion in Saint-Sauveur-le-Vicomte, 18 July 1897. Photographer unknown.

The family also found that Vincent's works were generating interest, at home and abroad. Vincent had been starting to gain recognition as a talented artist at the end of his lifetime. He managed to sell a few of his paintings and had benefited from Aurier's favourable review in the *Mercure de France*.[48] A growing arts scene in and around Leiden, where his mother and Wil and his sister Anna and her family were living, saw the onset of an innovative, almost avant-garde period in art led by a group of Amsterdam painters known as the Eighties Generation, including Willem Witsen, Jan Veth and Antoon Derkinderen. Along with the writers and poets of the 1880s (among them André Kloos,

Richard Roland Holst, front page of the catalogue for the exhibition at the Kunstzaal Panorama in Amsterdam, December 1892.

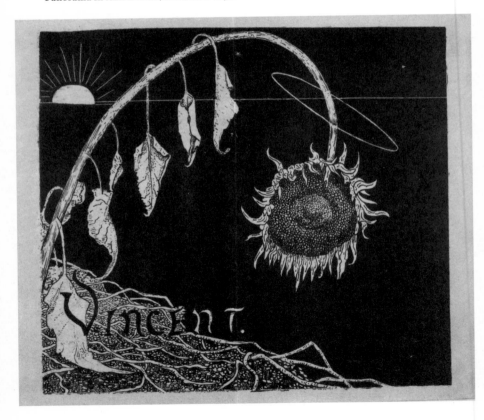

Frederik van Eeden, Albert Verwey, Lodewijk van Deyssel and, in his brief life, Jacques Perk), they formed a new movement under the credo *l'art pour l'art*: art for art's sake. The Leiden painter Floris Verster, one of the greatest artists of his time, also attracted attention, as did his brother-in-law, Menso Kamerlingh Onnes. Verster's brother, Cees, was an honorary curator at the Lakenhal, the municipal museum of Leiden, founded in 1874.[49]

The year 1890 was important for this circle of artists and intellectuals based in Leiden. The Lakenhal Museum marked the opening of a new gallery with an exhibition of contemporary Dutch paintings. Besides artists of the Hague School and the Amsterdam Impressionists, it featured works by Kamerlingh Onnes and Verster, including Verster's portrait of his sister, Jenny Kamerlingh Onnes, in a white dress. Verster and Kamerlingh Onnes aligned themselves with the Amsterdam Impressionists and the Eighties Generation. The poet Albert Verwey had meanwhile moved to the nearby resort of Noordwijk and befriended Verster. In addition, the famous painter Jan Toorop had moved to Katwijk, with a number of talented artists from different countries following in his wake. Toorop was one of the most important visual artists at the turn of the twentieth century. He initially painted in an Impressionist style, but developed via Pointillism into a Symbolist. Leiden also had its own Pointillist movement, represented by artists like Jan Vijlbrief, Jan Aarts and Charles Heykoop. Exponents of this revolutionary new technique used distinct dots of colour to create an image. However, they continued to paint conventional subjects: land-scapes and still lifes.

After Theo's death, Jo moved to Bussum and devoted herself to pro-moting her brother-in-law's oeuvre. This led to Vincent's first exhibition in The Hague, in May 1892. On the initiative of Jo's artist friend Jan Toorop, the show was staged at the Kunstkring rather than the more prestigious Pulchri Studio, which Jo preferred. Another exhibition followed later that year, at the Kunstzaal Panorama in Amsterdam. Richard Roland Holst – a painter, draughtsman, lithographer, book-cover designer, etcher, wood engraver, stained-glass artist and writer – was the driving force behind the event. The Roland Holst family had once

Emilie Knappert, 1878. Photographer unknown.

owned a country estate in the village of Zundert and knew the Van Gogh family from their time at the parsonage.[50]

Jo often visited her mother- and sisters-in-law in Leiden. An exhibition of Vincent's works was held there too, in the Lakenhal Museum's Hartevelt Gallery. Vincent's drawings were hung on four panels in the centre of the room, directly opposite Lucas van Leyden's famous *Last Judgment* and other seventeenth-century paintings. Cees Verster had persuaded his fellow members of the management board of the Lakenhal Museum to hold the exhibition, which ran for a fortnight but drew little attention from the national press. However, Verster published an article in the local newspaper, the *Leidsch Dagblad* (Leiden Daily), citing two influential writers, Frederik van Eeden and Richard Roland Holst, both staunch admirers of Van Gogh. Verster's steadfast endorsement of Vincent's work resulted in the third exhibition, in 1893.[51] 'The Drawings by Vincent van Gogh', a presentation of approximately sixty sheets, opened at the Lakenhal Museum on 25 April. It was the first major retrospective of Vincent's drawings to be held in a museum in the Netherlands.[52] Although there is no reliable evidence of the fact, Jo and Vincent's mother and sisters probably attended the opening. Emilie Knappert, friend and confidante of Willemien, organized at least five exhibitions of drawings by Vincent at the Volkshuis cultural centre in Leiden, in 1904, 1909, 1910 and 1913. Emilie advocated the edifying influence of art in all its forms, and was committed to making it accessible to ordinary people. She approached Jo for help in this endeavour, in 1904 asking Jo to loan several of Vincent's paintings to the shows.[53] These exhibitions ran for a week at most, and were open during the day and in the evening.[54]

These shows greatly enhanced Vincent's reputation. A prestigious exhibition at the Stedelijk Museum (Municipal Museum) in Amsterdam in 1905 took him to even greater heights. Many of the works on display came from Jo van Gogh-Bonger's collection. Vincent's mother went to the opening, but left before seeing any of his works: after breaking her leg in 1884 she was unable to climb stairs, and refused to take the goods lift to the exhibition on the first floor.[55] Anna and Joan van Houten also intended to see the exhibition, and went to the Stedelijk Museum sometime later, only to find that it had already closed. Nonetheless, it must have been gratifying for Vincent's mother and sisters to see that Theo had been right about Vincent's talent, and that their artist brother was indeed gaining recognition through the help of others. But their loss remained painful: the prospect of a future without Vincent and Theo was bleak.

CHAPTER 14

The Poison of Impropriety

Nijmegen, The Hague, 1893–1898

On 17 September 1890, Wil took and passed the entrance exam for a course in theology education at a training college in Utrecht. She had found her studies difficult, especially while coping with the death of her two beloved brothers, yet she persevered and qualified as a scripture teacher in 1893. After successfully finishing her degree, the thirty-year-old Wil left for the city of Nijmegen in the east of the Netherlands on 8 February 1893. There she took up a position as a substitute Bible teacher. Wil stayed in Nijmegen for over eight months, before moving to The Hague on 25 October. She found an apartment on the Prins Hendrikstraat, at number 25, and her mother moved in with her; the reason for this renewed cohabitation isn't mentioned in any of the family letters or other documents.[1] A woman called Margaretha Gallé lived in the same building. She would become an instigator of the first wave of feminism in the Netherlands a few years later – as would Wil.[2]

In The Hague Wil became a member of the Dameslees Museum (Library Museum for Ladies), a library and meeting place for well-to-do women. She first visited this institution in 1894 with her old friend Margaretha Meijboom, who was a member of the board. Margaretha was one of the twelve women involved in the founding of the museum earlier that year, inspired by a similar initiative in Amsterdam that had existed since 1877. The library, located at 15 Noordeinde, started out with 146 members and 494 books. It established itself as a place where women could read and discuss books in peace. Besides literary fiction, Margaretha wielded her considerable influence to make sure that books that dealt with socio-economic issues were included in the collection, next to a plethora of newspaper and magazine subscriptions. The Library

Margaretha Meijboom, *c.* 1900. Photographer unknown.

Museum for Ladies also functioned as a sort of 'gentlemen's club' for women. One could meet other members and friends for lunch, and even stay the night. It was a place to network and to talk about current affairs. Margaretha made sure that a couple of ladies who could not afford the annual fee were included as well. Wil did not get involved in the Library's board or any of its committees, but this was the place that would lead her to engage as a more active member of the women's rights movement.[5]

Some half-century earlier, it had seemed that things were changing for women. The subject of equal rights for the sexes moved into the public discourse and women's rights organizations gained a political presence, first in the United States, and later in other countries as well. The most pressing issues were the right to vote, the right to education, and the right to work – and, to a lesser degree, to equal pay. The movement also demanded the improvement of working conditions. As a result of the Industrial Revolution, there was a growing population of female labourers, often working in dismal conditions in the factories that were sprouting up in and around cities.

The increasing public attention for women's issues was short lived, however. After 1848, when violent revolutions broke out in several European capitals, the imposition of order and discipline became a top priority for governments, and this included reinforcing a strictly defined role for women as managers – and at the same time prisoners – of the domestic sphere. Only in the 1860s was the women's rights movement able to establish a firm presence in the national consciousness once again. Women's emancipation gained particular visibility in the Netherlands in 1870, with the circulation of magazines such as *Ons Streven* (Our Aspirations) and *Onze Roeping* (Our Calling). The founding of these magazines is often cited as the beginning of the women's rights movement in the country.[4] Simultaneously, men became less suspicious of women who were involved in the public act of writing, and the right to education became a less contentious issue. It was at this time that female writers like A.L.G. Toussaint and Elisabeth Hasebroek started publishing their work – and more importantly, their work was being read. In Hasebroek's novels the 'suffering woman' takes centre stage. Toussaint, conversely, generally depicted independent women, women who dream of and work towards becoming an individual. *Majoor Frans*, published in 1874, exemplifies this strain in Toussaint's writing. The eponymous protagonist rebels against the many oppressive conventions that women of her time were subjected to, distinguishing herself from them in both her manner of speech and her dress. The book also addressed the important issue of financial dependence within marriage; Majoor Frans rejects a wedding proposal once she finds out that the gist of the matter is money, not love. Yet curiously, Toussaint never explicitly aligned her work with the women's rights movement, in contrast to other writers who instrumentalized their prose for this effort.[5]

An interest in subjects that had typically been perceived as 'feminine' was also growing, particularly in the Naturalist novels that started appearing in the 1880s – mainly written by men. In these texts representations of the feminine were mostly sombre; strong,

Isaac Israëls, *Aletta Jacobs*, 1919. Oil on canvas, 101 × 71 cm (39¾ × 28 in.).

independent women like Majoor Frans were eschewed in favour of weak and nervous creatures, such as Frederik van Eeden's Hedwig Marga de Fontayne in *Van de koele meren des doods* (translated as 'The Deeps of Deliverance or Hedwig's Journey', literally 'Of the cold lakes of death'), Mathilde de Stuwe from *Een liefde* ('A love') by Lodewijk van Deyssel, and Louis Couperus' eponymous *Eline Vere*. The emptiness of the protagonist's life is at the centre of all these stories; these writers were not motivated by edifying or idealistic intentions. One characteristic, however, unites the work of both male and female writers: women and men were regarded as distinctly different. Women were presented as emotional and men rational, and this was considered a natural disparity between the sexes.

In 1870, relatively few women in the Netherlands – compared with their European neighbours – were working outside of the home or pursuing higher education. Aletta Jacobs became the first female student of medicine as late as 1871, when she started her studies at the University of Groningen after attending the local school in her birthplace, the town of Sappemeer. Middle-class women busied themselves with creative endeavours such as writing stories, poems, and letters, knitting or other forms of homecraft, or charity work.[6] In 1870 'Tesselschade Arbeid Adelt' (TAA) was founded in order to promote financial independence among middle-class ladies by teaching them to commercialize these 'feminine skills'. The organization considered a modest income generated by a woman herself to be the first step towards independence, yet the restricted legal status of women meant that many obstacles stood in the way of them developing a business of their own.[7]

The coronation of Queen Wilhelmina in 1898 was an additional opportunity for the TAA to establish a public presence. After her three half-brothers died, she was the only heir of the House of Orange eligible to take the throne after the death of Willem III. Thus on 6 September, the eighteen-year-old princess became the first reigning queen of the Netherlands. This development spurred on the women's movement: if a young woman like princess Wilhelmina could become the head of state, other important functions could arguably also be shouldered by women. Wilhelmina's coronation legitimized the call for an increased

E. Fuchs, *Emilie Knappert at an Older Age*, date unknown.
Pencil on paper, 56 × 42.8 cm (22 × 16⅞ in.).

equality between men and women, from the highest office of the state
down to washerwomen and weavers.[8]

The Van Gogh family members never directly addressed the subject
of the advancement of women's causes in their letters. Lies was the only
sister who ever explicitly talked about something like a career or about
earning money.[9] It is clear, however, that the importance of achieving
a certain independence was impressed upon the girls from a young
age. They had also been given opportunities to develop their skills
and prospects by their parents, such as Wil's training as a teacher of

scripture. Through this, she became involved in charitable enterprises. One of her tutors, the liberal Protestant professor Henricus Oort, who also taught theology at the universities of Leiden and Amsterdam, was empathetic and committed to a social ministry; he believed firmly that young people should be primed to fulfil the Church's mission outside the institution itself. Oort even turned out to be a member of the Dutch Bond for the Women's Right to Vote in Leiden.[10] Another of Oort's pupils, Emilie Knappert, was already involved in several social work projects in Leiden when Wil met her. She was mainly concerned with the alleviation of the poverty suffered by working-class families, and attended to the needs of women and children in particular, with a view to enabling them to develop their potential. Under the auspices of the Dutch Protestant Association she established a community centre in a working-class neighbourhood in 1894, and in 1901 she founded a working men's club in the centre of the city. Though these initiatives were faith-inspired, promoting religion was not necessarily an important part of their mission.[11]

Emilie and Wil often wrote about each other in letters to their families and friends. They came from similar backgrounds, and felt united by their common goals. Emilie urged Wil to persevere and complete her studies to qualify as a scripture teacher – as indeed she did in 1893. The friendship was of crucial importance to Wil, especially in her final year of training. Wil reflected that Emilie was 'the only person who does me good by never being too soft on me. Don't get me wrong: we would not be friends if we were not confident of each other's warm affection. But she understands that I need her stern side at the moment and gentleness almost does me harm.'[12]

In The Hague, Willemien became involved in the fight for the common good herself. Together with Margaretha Gallé, the woman who rented an apartment in her building, and Margaretha Meijboom, she joined the organization committee of the Nationale Tentoonstelling van Vrouwenarbeid (National Exhibition of Women's Labour), which was partially organized by the TAA, in cooperation with the Algemeene vrouwenvereeniging Tesselschade (Tesselschade General Association of Women). This new initiative was an opportunity to put the ideals these progressively minded women had been fostering – advocating for an increased accessibility to education, effective social work, and a reform of the role of religion in everyday life – into practice. The goal of the exhibition was to readjust the image of what women were able to contribute to the labour market, and to illustrate that women might even make better employees than men. They presented women as more accurate, swift and flexible, and – not to be underestimated – less prone to drinking than many men. A continuous circuit of lectures was central to the programme, in addition to the display of products made by women and by the machines operated by women. Special attention was given to the poor working conditions under which a lot of women laboured, and the meagre compensation they received for it. There still was a lot to fight for.[13]

The pioneering female physician Aletta Jacobs supported this effort, delivering several lectures. Emilie Knappert also contributed. During the course of the exhibition, which took place between 9 July and 21 September 1898, she chaired multiple conferences on social work

Committee of the National Exhibition of Women's Labour, with Willemien standing at the right, 1898. Photographed by Charlotte Polkijn.

and vocational training for women.[14] Knappert, however, refused to call herself a feminist. She was convinced that men and women needed to work together towards a new distribution of power, labour and domestic work. In her view, fighting for the betterment of women meant fighting for everyone.[15] Knappert's aims were notably more holistic than those of other feminists. After completing her degree in theology education, she decided to teach at schools located in the poorer neighbourhoods of Leiden. There she was struck by the terrible poverty in which her pupils, but also women and the elderly, were forced to live. Knappert considered it vital to provide the disadvantaged with the skills and opportunities to work themselves out of this sort of poverty.[16]

Joining one of the first feminist associations of the Netherlands was not necessarily a self-evident continuation of the course of Willemien's life so far, having been raised in a traditional Christian Reformed household. Yet she took to the cause enthusiastically and with dedication. Two of her other friends also joined, Marie Jungius and Marie Mensing. Together with some other women, they formed the 'regelingscommissie' (organization committee) of the exhibition, which was tasked with managing the day-to-day practicalities of the TAA. Wil's role was substantial: she was responsible for the exhibition's postal affairs, the decoration of the different stands, and the administration of the staff. She proved herself well-organized and pragmatic, and an effective decision-maker.[17]

The exhibition was held at the Scheveningseweg in The Hague, in a building especially constructed for the occasion and funded by Adriaan Goekoop, a prominent local entrepreneur who was a key developer of the new neighbourhoods arising around the city. This included the Statenkwartier, which is now famous for its Art Nouveau architecture. He was married to Cécile de Jong van Beek en Donk, the chair of the exhibition, who had become a public figure after the publication of her novel *Hilda van Suylenburg* in 1897. Jo's artist friend Jan Toorop designed the poster for the accompanying lottery of the exhibition, with the grand prize being a piece of jewelry worth 1,000 guilders. The TAA also asked the public to send in designs for the exhibition's lead poster. This competition was won by a Suze Fokker, who sent in a Jugendstil-inspired drawing of a beehive, symbolizing the industriousness of women's labour (pl. xxi).[18] The exhibition lasted for two and a half months and attracted 90,000 visitors. It even turned a considerable profit, which was used in 1901 to found the National Bureau of Women's Labour, an organization whose objective was to understand, improve, and broaden the labour market for women.[19]

The National Exhibition of Women's Labour was the beginning of a closer cooperation within the women's movement in the Netherlands, and a decisive step towards further emancipation. The women's movement gained momentum through public events like the exhibition, causing unrest among certain strata of society, particularly the conservative Christian movement. The Reformed women's magazine *Bethesda* was appalled by the exhibition: 'In the heart of many young man and woman a poisonous impropriety is injected which will have a who knows what sort of disastrous effect. No, a "congress" like this should not be attended by any man or woman considering themselves to be a good Christian.' How Wil experienced this tumultuous period is mostly unknown, as no letters from this time have survived. It seems, however, that she felt right at home. Her work ethic and the meticulous care with which she carried out her new duties are a testament to this; she assumed control of the 'regelingscommissie' with apparent ease. At the exhibition's closing ceremony, she gave a speech in front of the support staff – the cleaners, male guardians, police officers, and caretakers – thanking them for their hard work, and earning their applause.[20] She had become the person in charge.

But the strong impression that Wil made on her colleagues in the women's movement during the exhibition did not last, as her mental state deteriorated shortly afterwards. Her friends and her sisters began to worry about her, and this was only the start of the troubles to come.

CHAPTER 15

Such Momentous Times!

Leiden, Dieren, Baarn, Ermelo-Veldwijk, 1900–1920

The loss of Theo and Vincent overshadowed much of the 1890s for Moe and the sisters Van Gogh, and the beginning of the twentieth century did not signal an end to the family's misfortunes. Another tragedy was to occur in 1900: the youngest brother, Cor, would perish in the Second Boer War (1899–1902).

Cor took a ship to Johannesburg from Southampton in August 1889 in order to work at a gold mine, eventually moving on to a job making technical drawings for the Netherlands–South-African Railway Company (Nederlandsch-Zuid-Afrikaansche Spoorweg Maatschappij, NZASM) in Pretoria. He married the German-born and Roman Catholic-raised Anna Eva Catherina Fuchs on 16 February 1898 in Pretoria. But this marriage was not even to last a year: after only eight months, Anna left him, taking most of their possessions with her.[1]

Perhaps motivated by heartbreak, or simply by the great sympathy many Dutchmen felt for the Boers, Cor decided to join a special 'Foreigners Battalion', fighting against the English. During the first few months of the war, Cor worked as an overseer at an NZASM workshop that was manufacturing ambulances, guns, cannons and bullets, instead of the usual trains. Real danger only arrived when Cor, along with 2,000 of his countrymen, entered the battlefield. While their enthusiasm was appreciated by the Boers, they were considered relatively incapable equestrians, bad at handling guns, and not suited to the extreme climate and bare landscapes of the Transvaal. Cor's contribution to the war ended when he was admitted to the Red Cross hospital of Brandfort, a little town in the recently conquered Orange Free State, early in April 1900. He was plagued by fever; most probably it was his Boer companions who had delivered him here, as the English would not arrive in Brandfort until 3 May.[2]

Cor's prospects looked grim; most Dutch doctors and nurses had just been evacuated from the area. Medical supplies were running out quickly, and the makeshift hospital – which was housed in an old school building – was well above its maximum capacity. Cor was struck by a heavy fever, and his morale was at an all-time low.[3]

Throughout his convalescence, Cor remained, curiously, in possession of his gun. One day, perhaps accidentally, he aimed it at himself

Cor van Gogh, 1889. Photographed by Charles H. Schouten.

and the gun fired. The thirty-two-year-old Cor died in his hospital bed on 12 April 1900.[4] The death of Vincent inevitably comes to mind.

A year later, on 22 April 1901, Wil wrote to Jo: 'These days, I imagine our thoughts wandering in the same regions at times, those terrible memories of Cor. I am, however, grateful he is not in pain anymore.'[5] Around this time Moe had also written to her daughter-in-law: 'You probably are thinking of Cor as well, last year we received the news that he had not been on earth with us for fourteen days already. Such momentous times! Jo, you wouldn't believe how good Vincent's paintings look on our wall. Wil has cleaned the big one and they look perfect against the bright walls, catching all the best light. Did I understand correctly that they are being taken to Amsterdam again.'[6] Moe was perhaps under the impression that Cor died in combat, writing later that year: 'Jo, you undoubtedly often think of our beloved Cor as well...it is impossible to forget him, with all these young people still dying in battle. So many sweet faces, I always think of him, always searching for his likeness.'[7]

After the National Exhibition came to an end, Wil returned to teaching religion in The Hague. Two years after the death of Cor, she was making plans to visit Copenhagen with Margaretha Meijboom who, aside from her work on several women's organizations, was also a translator of Scandinavian literature. She was familiar with the place they were intending to stay, a pension with a homely atmosphere. Wil even started learning Danish and passed her exam, and she indeed visited Denmark in July, though it is unknown whether Margaretha accompanied her.[8] But Wil was struggling with both her mental and physical health, which had quickly deteriorated, reminding her of the last few months when Theo was still alive in Utrecht. At that time, to protect herself, she had to take the painful decision to withdraw herself and leave Jo alone with the patient as she herself had collapsed over the situation, as she later described in a letter to Jo.[9]

For a time Willemien managed to prevent the situation from worsening by continuing her work and by studying, but she was eventually taken to the Medical Institute for the Insane in the Oude Haagweg in The Hague. She was forty years old at the time.[10] Later that year, on 4 December 1902, she was transferred to the Veldwijk psychiatric hospital in Ermelo. In the referral letter her doctor in The Hague reported: 'Is still angry and acts wild often. She screams, bites, scratches, and throws punches. At other times she is quiet and seems unaware of her environment...she refuses to eat, and hallucinates.'[11] Wil herself had theorized why she, along with her brothers Vincent and Theo, had often battled with melancholy: during their upbringing they were not taught to withstand the world that they were going to live in and moreover lacked the light-heartedness to put things in perspective.

In the 1880s, Dorus had already noticed some alarming signals and started worrying about Wil's, and also Lies's, mental health – on top of the usual worries he had for Vincent. It was he who sent Wil to Middelharnis in 1884, away from the stressful environment that Vincent's presence had created in Nuenen. Pa often sent her on holidays like this, believing that these outings provided her with a necessary reprieve. Not long, however, after Wil spent a few weeks in Noordwijk with Anna in 1884, Dorus wrote to Theo: 'Wil is tired again and she seems not well'.[12]

In February 1889, after the death of their father and their move to Breda, Wil confided her internal struggles to Jo: 'And then there is that awful swarm of everything mixed up in one's head, it is frightening. You must know what I mean by "clean up one's head", it is what I did last week, in complete solitude. I am better now and I hope it will stay this way.'[13] It was not the first time that she had expressed her concern over her mental well-being to someone outside the immediate family circle. Since 1887 she had regularly discussed her troubles with her best friend Margaretha Meijboom. The arrival of Jo provided her with an additional confidante; the two women seemed to understand each other. Jo not only visited her often, but also exchanged many letters with her.

Moments of a mind invaded by an 'awful swarm of everything mixed up' occurred more and more in the following years. In order to recover, Will would retreat from the world, sometimes withdrawing for months at a time. In these periods she would lose touch with her friends and colleagues, and no one knew exactly what she was doing during her absence.

The Veldwijk hospital in Ermelo was sited on an estate that had passed through the hands of several members of the nobility and was taken over by the Chevallier family in 1866. Lady Chevallier replaced one of the farmer's cottages with a large country house. Her son, Mathilde Jacques Chevallier, was one of the founders of the Christian Association of Mental and Nervous Maladies, and saw that the house and grounds might suitably serve as a mental institution. He sold the estate to the Association in 1884, and the asylum opened on 28 January 1886. For the first three months, only thirty patients resided here.[14]

M.J. Chevallier wielded a considerable influence in the region, and even succeeded in getting a train station constructed nearby – a significant achievement at a time when the railways were relatively new. The station connected the asylum to the outside world, enabling residents to receive visitors with far greater ease. The Association transformed the estate to better suit its new purpose, following the 'pavilion plan' (advocated by Florence Nightingale) that had become common for hospitals but was progressive for mental institutions. Several pavilions were constructed around the property, all specially equipped to treat the 'mentally insane'. The doctors tried to provide patients with a routine that resembled their lives outside the walls of the estate, albeit under strict supervision, and so the institution had a more intimate and friendly environment than the usual psychiatric hospital. This was in line with the growing conviction that people suffering from mental ill health should be treated almost as family members rather than patients.[15] Such a philosophy informed the treatment at the mental institution of Geel, close to Turnhout in Belgium, where most patients lived relatively free lives within the walls of the hospital. Dorus had considered sending Vincent to Geel for treatment.[16] Earlier approaches had mostly focused on bed rest and medication, essentially sedating the patients, whereas at Veldwijk their schedule resembled normal day-to-day life, and included tasks that bordered on regular work. The institute quickly expanded, and different villas and chalets were built on the property, along with several homes nearby where patients were hosted by a regular family.

The Villa Parkzicht (Park View) was opened on the site in 1888. At this new facility the wealthy received individualized care in their own private apartments. It was also known as 'the Gilded Cage'. Wil was not interned here, however, and was instead assigned a room in Sparrenheuvel (Spruce Hill), another recent addition. Upon Wil's arrival at Veldwijk she became uncommunicative; her doctors reported that she spoke 'only softly and unintelligibly', or else uttered dark threats – 'you will be the reason of my eternal condemnation if you don't watch out' – or spoke of suicide.[17] She refused to eat, and had to be force-fed. Her doctors had trouble settling on a diagnosis, describing her as 'ravaged by dementia' – a term commonly applied to people who suffered from hallucinations and other psychiatric symptoms.[18]

Willemien would live at Veldwijk until her death, spending almost half her life at the facility. Throughout the years, she showed no signs of improvement: 'the condition of this long-term mental patient does not show noticeable signs of change...she is very solitary-minded, never speaks spontaneously, and barely responds to questions addressed to her. For whole days she is gone, she just sits on the same chair at the same place for the whole day, can't focus on anything, is not aware of her surroundings.'[19] In 1938, thirty-six years after she arrived, she remained silent and solitary: 'Every afternoon she knits by herself and interacts with no one.'[20]

Anna, Lies and Jo visited Wil, and kept each other updated on her condition. Anna wrote to Jo on 30 January 1905: 'Last week I received a letter from Dr. Van Dalen telling me that Wil was more present, more level headed. Tomorrow I will visit her with Margreet [Margaretha] Meijboom, and I hope she is in the right state to receive visitors. The doctor did not mind us coming at least. I will let you know in what condition we find her.'[21] Lies wrote to Jo later that year: 'Last time, Wil gave me the impression she was doing better, although not much seems to change around her, what a pity!'[22] From the letters it becomes clear that Anna visited Wil most regularly, while Moe never once went to Veldwijk.

After the loss of her first child, all three of her adult sons and her husband, the hospitalization and deterioration of Wil was probably too much for Moe to handle. She had dedicated her life to serving her family as a faithful wife and mother. Her marriage to a minister put additional responsibilities on her plate, including tending to the sick and visiting the poor. In her limited spare time she enjoyed knitting, a skill she taught to her daughters and parishioners, but only decades after her death was it discovered that she had another creative outlet: a family album recovered in 1956 contained some of her sketches and

The Sparrenheuvel pavilion at Veldwijk, Ermelo. Date and photographer unknown.

Anna van Gogh-Carbentus crocheting, between 1895 and 1905.
Photographer unknown.

watercolours (pl. 1). Moe died on 29 April 1907 in Leiden, having left
The Hague in 1905. The obituary made notice of a 'long-lasting suffering'.[23] On 2 May she was buried at Groenesteeg cemetery in Leiden: a
modest headstone is all that commemorates the mother of the six Van
Gogh children.

Lies wrote to Jo five days after Moe's funeral: 'Dear Jo, now the
endless days are behind us again, since we saw our dear mother depart.
I don't know what touched me more on that day, witnessing the dead
body, or being surrounded by the living. There is so much our hearts
never speak of, beautiful as the pearls, the solidified tears of the deep
sea. The world provides distraction however and I was happy to return
home, where the kids were in a bad mood....If I could only go to Wil,
but I've been so tired recently that I would get sick if I'll have that heart-
breaking meeting with her now. I consider these meetings to be essential,
but their impact is considerable. Luckily she is able to go outside more
often at the moment, because while it rains, the outside air is delicious.'[24]
On 26 June, 1907 she wrote again to Jo about the loss of her mother:
'I just cannot get it into my head that she is not here anymore, she was
such an important part of everyone's lives and now we all have trouble

realizing she is dead.'[25] A year later she wrote to Jo once more: 'I miss Mother so dearly, she was always so lovingly involved and I cherish the few words she spoke to me during my last visits, they are like golden nuggets.'[26] In the same letter, Lies wrote about her oldest brother: 'It is wonderful that Vincent's paintings enjoy such great success. He never doubted himself, and never seriously acknowledged the monetary sacrifices Father and Theo made, it was just a temporary loan to him!'[27]

Vincent's success, spearheaded by Jo, had an unforeseen result. Anna wrote to Jo on 22 November 1909: 'Dear Jo! Thanks for the letter and the news of the sale of Wil's painting. I remember the room and when Wil got the painting from Vincent, but what a figure! Who would have thought that Vincent would contribute to Wil's upkeep in this way? Theo has always claimed it would happen, but what an unforeseen turn of events, such surprising outcomes. You have to know that during the division of the paintings, when I received the one with the orchard, Jo said "the proceeds will go into your pocket". You'll understand what a windfall, what unexpected wealth this f. 600 is for me!'[28] Anna wanted to spend the money on Wil, continuing: 'If it isn't too difficult for you, you should join me on my next visit. It probably won't do you any good, nor Wil, but I find it very difficult that you might think we are not doing everything in our power to provide for Wil. The only book she sometimes reads is *Aurora Leigh* and the rest of times she just sits and sews for the nurses. If you come across a book you think she might like, please send it to her. Treats are well received, she shares it with the other patients, she eats well and sleeps comfortably in her own little room. In the morning she sits on the porch feeding the birds, but if a nurse then tries to go for a little walk in the garden with her, she refuses.'[29] Wil rarely left her room or went for walks – that much-loved family pastime in Brabant – around the estate, and Anna thought that her shoes – insufficiently warm – or her slippers – too small – might be the problem, so she bought her 'comfortable shoes with a woollen lining' and 'soft, leather slippers'.[30] Wil, however, refused to wear them, and this drove Anna to desperation: 'I try all sorts of things and I keep hoping something will get through to her and that it does her well not to be forgotten by us. She is never unpleasant to me.'[31]

Jean Philippe du Quesne and Lies du Quesne-van Gogh,
probably 1916. Photographed by Anton Cornelis Thomann.

Wil's condition worsened throughout the years, prompting many upset letters between Lies, Anna and Jo. Anna wrote on 25 March 1910: 'Dear Jo! We just received some news from Ermelo, Wil is in bad shape. Oh, let's hope this is the beginning of the end, maybe her suffering will finally stop, how grateful we would be to God. I keep thinking so ardently about her case, and her life is one big "nothing", like she described recently. The news came in an unexpected letter from Dr Van Dale, so her case must be serious, otherwise I would not have sent you this letter.'[32] Lies, writing to Jo a few weeks later, was more temperate: 'Dear sister, here the latest news regarding Wil. There is no immediate danger, but her sad life will not go on for much longer, of this I am convinced. Visiting her would not make a difference at the moment, when she is in a state like this, they don't admit visitors anyway.'[33]

During these years, Lies had her own troubles, as it became clear that her husband Jean Philippe du Quesne was also dealing with some mental problems. When she married him in 1891 she had no idea what was in store for her. In that year, Lies and Jean Philippe returned to the Villa Eikenhorst in Soesterberg not as employer and employee, but as husband and wife. Their first son, Theo, was born on 20 November 1892,[34] six years after the birth of their illegitimate daughter Hubertine, who still lived in Normandy. Barely a year later they moved to a smaller house in Baarn, the Villa Edzardina at 10 Dalweg, only a few miles north of Soesterberg.

For Lies, this move offered a fresh start. Her affair with Jean Philippe had after all begun in Eikenhorst, while she tended to his sick wife. In the following six years, they had three more children: Jeannette Adrienne Angeline in 1895,[35] Rose Wilhelmine (Mien) in 1897[36] and Felix in 1899.[37] Lies was forty years old when she gave birth to her youngest.[38]

Following her parents' example, Lies wanted to prepare her children for an entry into 'proper society',[39] but she was not in possession of the resources to do so. The early years of her married life were defined by financial instability. Jean Philippe held a position as a deputy cantonal judge in the nearby town of Amersfoort, but a permanent position was never offered to him and he resigned from the post in 1897. He started his own legal practice in Baarn, but he represented so many clients pro bono that he could not make a financial success of it. A steady income from his stock portfolio kept the family afloat, but this wealth evaporated during the crash of the global stock market after the Russian Revolution.[40] Jean Philippe retired from his practice in 1916, and the family became reliant on interest earned on capital. The sale of precious family

Villa Edzardina, 10 Dalweg, Baarn. Date and photographer unknown.

possessions, including the increasingly valuable paintings by Vincent, was inevitable.

On 13 December 1917, Lies sold *Path to the Cemetery* to the art dealership J.H. Bois in Haarlem, which had formerly been headed by Uncle Cor, for 2,000 guilders,[41] and in 1926 she sold, among others, an unidentified work by Vincent through Frederik Muller & Co. in Amsterdam, from whom she was to receive a reproduction of the painting.[42] The family sold glassware, silver and tableware. Even Lies' pearls were taken to a jeweler in Utrecht.[43] She also explored the possibility of leasing out a vast estate that had been in the possession of the Du Quesne family for decades, Cillaershoek, in Hoekse Waard, though it had always been Jean Philippe's wish that this estate would stay in the hands of the family. But needs must. Lies needed the money, and sold off Cillaershoek in parts from 1922.[44] Despite their financial troubles, Lies and Jean Philippe sent all of their children to good schools and even, with the exception of the youngest daughter Mien, to university. Theo attended an agricultural

Jean Philippe and Lies du Quesne-van Gogh at their silver wedding anniversary in 1916, seated in the middle with Rose Wilhelmine (Mien) at left and Jeannette at right. Photographer unknown.

ABOVE Felix and Theodore du Quesne van Bruchem, *c.* 1905. ABOVE RIGHT Jeannette and Rose Wilhelmine du Quesne van Bruchem, *c.* 1905. Both photographed by Adr. Boer Baarn.

Rose Wilhelmine (Mien) du Quesne van Bruchem. Date and photographer unknown.

college in Wageningen, Felix studied economics in Rotterdam, and Jeannette completed a law degree in Utrecht. Mien chose a different path. After boarding at a 'home economics school' in Utrecht, she returned home to help her mother run the household.[45]

Perhaps in part due to the ever-present financial strain on his family, Jean Philippe du Quesne's mental health crumbled. He stayed awake through the night, and was in the habit of loudly praying to God and Christ while seated in front of a picture of a young girl – most likely Hubertine. Lies had her own picture of Hubertine, which she once or twice showed to her children, though without telling them that she was in

Jean Philippe du Quesne van Bruchem, *c*. 1916. Photographer unknown.

fact their oldest sister. Lies was sick with worry about her husband, as were the children; on 29 December 1919 Jeannette contacted one of her half-brothers, who was a doctor, about their father's condition. He considered the situation to be so dire that Du Quesne was no longer qualified to take care of his family or finances; in 1920 the family was granted power of attorney.[46] On 19 November 1920 Mien wrote to Jeannette: 'It is relatively peaceful at home at the moment. Last week was terrible, due to Father. His malicious mood has more or less retreated and now he just mumbles harmlessly. He cries a lot, convinced that his mother died this week and he keeps wanting to go out to order a headstone for her.'[47] Despite his behaviour, Lies did not want to hospitalize her husband. Her granddaughter, An Weenink, who wrote *Mijn Oma* (My Grandmother) in 2003, suspected Lies was afraid their secret might come out once Du Quesne was out of her sight. The spectre of her sister in Veldwijk must also have played its part. Lies's life would change drastically when Jean Philippe died on Christmas day in 1921.[48]

Lies wrote long letters about her own health to Jo and Anna: sometimes she was 'asthmatic' or was plagued by 'muscle contractions';[49] sometimes she was unable to attend doctor's appointments in Amsterdam due to the difficulties of travelling, particularly during the night; sometimes the change of season had disastrous effects on her. Yet she never wrote about Jean Philippe. Sometimes she stated: 'My husband is his usual self',[50] or 'My husband's throat is negatively affected by the chilly weather. Let's hope this is where his health problems stop',[51] but she did not elaborate on his troubles or their financial worries. Despite the toll the family's struggles must have taken on her, she instead devoted her energies to another important goal in her life: realizing her literary ambitions.

CHAPTER 16

Poetry as Clear as a Brook

Baarn, Ermelo-Veldwijk, 1920–1936

While she raised her children, Lies never lost her ambition to become
a writer: 'Ever since I was young, I've been writing letters to my father
and best-loved brother Theodoor under the pseudonym Theodora. I made
up little fairy tales and nursery rhymes for my children, which were
included in a children's magazine....I did everything in my capacity to
keep writing my poems. A successful family life was most important
to me, including lots of fresh air and a flourishing garden...all the while
I've never let it get in the way of my writing. Every day I shut myself off
in my room for at least an hour.'[1] So she wrote in an autobiographical
account commissioned by a municipal archivist in The Hague in 1932.
In this five-page report she emphasized her success as a poet, though
this may not have matched her actual standing in the literary community; at this time her fame was largely dependent on the growing
admiration for Vincent.[2] Increasingly, though, she was recognized as
a talent in her own right, and around 1935 was included in a selection
of the most important Dutch poets by the Society of Dutch Literature
(Genootschap ter bevordering van de Letterkunde).[3]

In 1906, Lies published a collection of Breton folk songs she had
translated into French and adapted for a modern public. An illustrated
edition followed six years later.[4] Lies also wrote poetry of her own.
Her influences included the Loveling sisters: two writers, Rosalie and
Virginie, who were born and raised in the East-Flemish village of Nevele.
From the 1870s, they garnered a reputation for their perceptive Realist
poems, with a touch of sentimentality, as well as their novellas and
stories about both small-town life and modern city living. 'Aren't the
verses of the Flemish sisters Loveling equal to the song of a one year

old nightingale sitting in a recently pruned, fragrant birch?' Lies wrote in the introduction to her first published poetry collection, *Gedichten I* (Poems I), in 1907.[5] She published the works under the name E. H. du Quesne-van Gogh, which she would use for the rest of her career. The publisher was a small enterprise called J.F. van de Ven based in Baarn, where Lies had lived since leaving the Villa Eikenhorst in 1893. She also cited as her inspiration famous Dutch poets including Vondel, Gezelle and Van Deyssel.[6]

Carl Scharten, writer and critic for the famous Dutch literary magazine *De Gids*, was one of the few who reviewed the work, and responding to the influences that Lies referenced in her introduction he wrote that 'this student has only partially absorbed the lessons of our biggest masters', brutally designating her works 'little poems of Gezelle's most retarded student.'[7] Lies was able to partially deflect this harsh criticism of her work, writing to Jo in the spring of 1909: 'My poems are at least not being ignored, even though the responses are ridiculously divergent. That is exactly the reason why they sell well. They are preparing a second printing for Sinterklaas and they are going to pay me to have my portrait included, in order to add something new to this edition.'[8]

On 28 July 1914 the First World War erupted, radically changing the European landscape. Belgium would be defeated by German forces on their way to France, and many Belgians fled to the neutral Netherlands. Eventually one million Belgians would cross the border into the Netherlands over the course of the war. The civil refugees were housed in special camps, but there were also many soldiers who had left their vanquished country. They were sent to barracks spread across the Netherlands, which quickly reached maximum capacity. Extra camps, consisting of haphazard, wooden buildings, were hastily constructed, one of them at the edge of Soesterberg: Camp Zeist.

Lies corresponded with a number of Belgian refugees, including interned soldiers in a camp in Harderwijk and civilians living in Nunspeet. Her daughters Jeannette and Mien were involved in the care of refugee children. The Belgian sculptor-painter and former soldier Rik Wouters was housed in Camp Zeist, and Lies contacted him, sending him her poetry collections. Her granddaughter, An Weenink, wrote

Rik Wouters and his wife Hélène (Nel) Duerinckx, at the artist's
home in 1908. Photographer unknown.

in *Mijn oma* (My Grandmother) that Wouters read Lies's poems to his
fellow soldiers 'while the sun set on the heath'. In March 1915 Wouters
fell ill. His chondrosarcoma had spread to his eye, and together with
his wife Nel Deurinckx he was transferred to Amsterdam for treatment.
Lies wrote him a letter: 'My family and I wish you a speedy recovery.
When peace comes and you return to your country, you'll have to visit
us here again. It is so close. We so dearly wish peace would come!...We
will send you some newspapers; tell us when you get back to Zeist.'[9]
Wouters did not respond. He died in Amsterdam on 11 July 1916, when
he was just thirty-three years old.

The devastations of war and the fate of the hundreds of thousands of refugees left a deep impression on Lies. In 1915 she published a collection called *Oorlogsgedichten* (War Poems), which was distributed among the soldiers on the front line in order to 'support and motivate them'.[10] According to Lies, the poems were warmly received and widely read among the soldiers in the trenches: 'My biggest triumph is that the unsophisticated are moved by my poems: poetry has to be clear as a brook in order to quench the thirst of men, is what I always say.'[11] Lies also wrote passionately about the protection of a Flemish homeland.

In later years she published six more collections, some supported by a publisher, others self-published: *Kerstrozen* (Christmas Roses) in 1915; *Gedichten II* (Poems II) in 1919; *Wingerdbladeren* (Grapevine Leaves) in 1921; *Latelingen* (Latecomers) in 1926; *Latelingen II* (Latecomers II) in 1932; and *Tijdlozen* (The Timeless) in 1932. She also wrote a poem called 'Eerste Lach' (First Laugh) after the birth of her first grandson Felix. Until deep into her old age, she wrote a monthly poem for Baarn's local Sunday newspaper, *De Baarnsche Courant*. These were mostly inspired by local landscapes, only occasionally touching upon her feelings and moods.[12]

She read many of her contemporaries. According to a newspaper interview in honour of her seventy-fifth birthday on 15 May 1934, she was reading *De waterman* (Aquarius) by Arthur van Schendel. She was a big admirer of him and of Aart van der Leeuw.[13] Lies also occupied herself with the new language and spelling reforms of Dutch Minister for Education Henri Marchant in 1934, determined to master them as quickly as possible. Quite a few redundant grammatical cases were retired from the Dutch language; whenever possible double o's and e's became single letters, and the ending 'sch' was replaced by 's' in most cases. This new Dutch orthography was officially ratified on 1 September 1934.[14]

While Lies's poetry collections did not garner her a lot of attention, her book *Vincent van Gogh: Personal memories regarding an artist*, published in 1910 and soon thereafter translated into German, English and French, was a commercial success. In it she wrote with great empathy about her brother: 'His genius was not always easily controlled, did not thrive in a constrained environment subjected to everyday routines, his genius rejected this.'[15]

Lies wrote from her memory; it seems she had not saved Vincent's letters, and as a consequence she had to rely entirely on her own recollection of events. She mixed up dates, occasions and locations, and the other Van Goghs had certain reservations about the contents of the book.[16] Jo in particular took issue with the way that Lies had decided to tell Vince nt's story. The book was also criticized for minimizing Vincent's mental health issues. Yet this seems not to have been deliberate; Lies was simply convinced that Vincent's life revolved around one passion: art. In interviews she stated that her own personal experiences with Vincent were unimportant in light of this consuming passion. She repeated this claim in the extended and revised edition of the autobiography that appeared in 1923, this time under a new title and with the same difficulty: Lies had not been a witness of Vincent's entire life.[17]

Lies did not, however, suspend all judgment. Vincent was a humble person, she said, but he, like many other great men, possessed little sense of decency, little sense of civilization. He turned away from his family and his eccentric behaviour caused his parents a lot of grief. Friends, neighbours and acquaintances also complained to Lies about Vincent's reclusiveness, his maladjustment, and his tendency to make fun of people he disagreed with: 'Who would have expected that from a boy who was always praised by his teachers! And how sad for his family members, who only ever hoped for the best for him.' Lies, who hadn't seen Vincent in the last five years of his life, ended the book with a letter from Theo – in her own words her favourite brother – in which he described the last hours of Vincent's life, the misery his death caused, and his funeral.[18]

The book caused a serious rift between Lies and Jo. Jo was dismayed that Lies would publish the memoir just before her own publication of Vincent's letters, which were to be accompanied by a short biography of his life. Lies, for her part, had objections to the manner in which Jo had decided to publish Vincent's letters. The fact that only Vincent's letters to Theo were included, and not Theo's replies, made the narrative too one-sided, according to Lies, not to mention her fear that too many family secrets were revealed. The formerly intimate friendship devolved into a frosty silence. The animosity between the two was only heightened when, in 1914, Jo finally published *Brieven aan zijn broeder* (Letters to his brother) and Lies found that all references to herself had been removed from Vincent's correspondence. The literary alliance that had taken off between the two women in 1885 had definitively come to an end.[19]

In a letter dated 26 October 1927 to a certain J. Verwiel, one of the founders of a monument for Vincent (made by Hildo Krop) in Nuenen, Lies returned to her conflict with Jo: 'Regarding the publication of the letters by Mrs. Cohen Gosschalk [the new name of the remarried Jo Bonger], widow of Th. van Gogh, it was all about money. They have simply been sold to the highest bidder. I have withdrawn my approval, as none of my brothers, humble and reclusive when it came to their art as they were, would have agreed to make their heartfelt letters public if they were still alive.'[20] In 1934, in an interview for the newspaper *Algemeen Handelsblad* (General Commercial Newspaper), she would also state: 'His letters? Yes, he wrote many, copying some of them three times over, mother would keep the copies away from father. The publication of the letters to Theo, filled to the brim with intimate details, have always been a cause of grief for us. Vincent and Theo would have loathed it; a careful selection would have been so much better. If the goal was an increased understanding of his art, a publication of the letters addressed to his former boss at the art dealership, Tersteeg, would have been more beneficial. When Tersteeg moved from The Hague to Baarn, he had a chiffonier whose drawers were stuffed full of letters. All of those have been destroyed.'[21] Only years later, after Lies had died, would Vincent Willem van Gogh, son of Jo and Theo, share with Lies's children that his mother had always regretted the way her relationship with Lies went awry.[22]

In 1923 the second edition of Lies's book was issued, this time with the title *Herinneringen aan haar broeder* (Memories of her brother). This new edition included illustrations by Vincent, including a self-portrait, as well as a poem that Lies had written after visiting an exhibition of his work in Utrecht. The poem is called 'Aan mijn broeder' (To my brother)[23] and ends with the following stanza:

Celebrate what was hers, her son, the day of birth
Who was first to offer her your most perfect Love,
And then died, coming down from above
Where I offered you my sisterly salute,
All the way to your furrow;
Brother,
Slumber in peace

The publisher's catalogue listed the price of the book (1.75 guilders for a softcover, 2.60 guilders for a hardcover),[24] as well as a few press clippings: 'With great affection, Ms. Du Quesne paints a picture of the life of her brother!' (*De Nederlander*); 'Written by a delicate talent!' (*Amersfoorts Dagblad*).[25]

The new edition also included an introduction by Van Gogh scholar Benno J. Stokvis. Thirty years after Vincent's death, Stokvis declared him to be the greatest painter after Rembrandt, and even went so far as to call him a prophet, whose body was weak but whose spirit possessed 'the diabolical power of someone drunk on life'.[26] He even used the word 'madness' to refer to Vincent, and called his suicide 'an act of fearless liberation, saving himself from the hellish pains of his own demise.'[27] Stokvis considered Lies's book, together with Jo's collection of letters, a document fundamental to the endeavour of understanding Vincent, and wrote that Lies had written down her memories like a 'refined artist'.[28]

In July 1929 Lies published a new collection of prose poems, imaginatively called *Proza* (Prose). The apparently personal story 'Every Family has its Secrets' stood out: 'As soon as I enter the strange house, secrets silently ambush me from all sides.'[29] It is possible that Lies was referring to her own home, haunted by the memories of her secret relationship, her illegitimate child in Normandy, the mental health of her husband and her financial troubles. She touched upon these subjects elsewhere in this collection, though never explicitly furnished the details of her personal life.

The publisher Emil Wegelin, based in Bussum, printed the collections *Latecomers II* and *The Timeless* in 1932. Lies distributed the latter herself, approaching several libraries personally. By this time her writing career seemed in decline. Shortly after reading her poems on the national radio in 1931, she was told there was too little airtime available to facilitate further appearances.[30] Yet in 1934 Lies received 100 guilders in funding from the Willem Kloos Foundation for the Support of Dutch Literature and its Writers.[31] She also received considerable press attention on her seventy-fifth birthday. Several newspapers mentioned this special anniversary. In one of the associated interviews Lies claimed to be too tired to talk for long. This does not mean, though, that life no longer had anything to offer her. Her ambitions still got her out of bed every morning, and she spent these early hours writing. She continued to publish a poem in *De Baarnsche Courant* every month, and was working on her seventh poetry collection up to her death in 1936.[32]

She also made the effort to visit her sister Willemien, still confined to the Veldwijk institution, even when her own health began to fail her; at the end of 1934 she suffered increasingly serious heart problems. Nonetheless, she made a recovery and visited Wil in the new year. It had been a long time. Lies's granddaughter, An Weenink, writes the following about her visit: 'Curiously, Wil, who normally is unresponsive, called out this fact [Lies's long absence].'[33] The family evidently appreciated her effort, however – Joan van Houten wrote to her daughter Jeannette after Lies's death: 'Your mother was so diligent in her visits to Wil in Ermelo, even when they started weighing more and more heavily on her.'[34]

Lies's financial situation had become increasingly desperate in her final years. She sold the family house in Baarn, but the proceeds were not enough to cover the mortgage and her children had to step in to save her from debt.[35] She would never live independently again, moving from boarding house to boarding house. Her daughter Mien wrote to her sister Jeannette on 22 December 1930: 'Mother was more sprightly than usual, but she is slowly wasting away and looks very pale. She barely eats, I believe. Her restless mind dominates her body, forces her to stay alive.'[36] In 1933, Lies appeared 'without making any arrangements...at the Kapelweg in Amersfoort with a fully loaded moving van, ready to move into her daughter Mien's house.'[37] Her granddaughter An remarked how pleasant it was, after the initial shock of finding her so malnourished, to have her grandmother this close: 'We prepared a room

Lies du Quesne-van Gogh, 9 May 1934. Photographer unknown.

to her liking; a bit messy and busy....She has the tendency to meddle with all sorts of family affairs...but after establishing some clear rules, this was curtailed. She enjoyed having her grandchildren close. In the morning, she would always take me for a walk to the post office.'[38] An's older sister, Lenie, remembered their grandmother 'as an eccentric, strict little lady, like a grandmother with beautiful white hair, someone who demanded respect.'[39]

This cohabitation lasted only four months. At the end of June 1933 Lies moved into a room in another neighbourhood of Amersfoort. Money was still tight, particularly after the global economic crash of 1929, when the value of her stocks and shares plummeted. It was her son

Felix, who was living in Canada, and her stepson Nico who supported her financially during this time, each without knowing of the other's interventions.[40] Nico wrote to Lies on 6 October 1931: 'I have wanted to ask you before if I could do something for you, because I understand very well that you, sustaining yourself by capital income, are in trouble, like everyone, in these terrible times.'[41] Apparently Lies had declined an earlier offer of help, as Nico stated: 'I know very well that you will do everything possible to reject my offer, I know you well, but please don't. You have always been a force of good in our lives and for this I am grateful, I want to help you if I can and if you need it. I know others would like to do the same for you, but are not in the position to do so at the moment. No one knows about it and no one will know about it.'[42] Appealing to her pride, Nico persuaded her to accept his help.

For the lion's share of her adult life Lies had not been particularly interested in Vincent, but as he got more famous, this began to change. She began to introduce herself as the sister of the famous painter and a representative of the Van Gogh family. In addition to her memoir about her artist brother, she wrote an article in 1924 for the Dutch newspaper *De Telegraaf* about a new Van Gogh exhibition in Amsterdam.[43] A year later she was present at the unveiling of a marble commemorative plaque installed on the house of Jean-Baptiste Denis in the village of Wasmes in the Borinage, where Vincent had attempted to launch his career as an evangelist.[44]

In 1930, the year of Anna's death, Lies unveiled another commemorative plaque on the 40th anniversary of Vincent's death, this one placed on the wall of Vincent's workshop in the garden of the parsonage in Nuenen.[45] The following year an art society in the city of Eindhoven, who had commissioned the plaque in Nuenen, invited her to give a lecture about her brother. She became a member of the society and in 1932 she was once again present at the unveiling of a monument on Nuenen's market square. This monument was a granite column standing about 2 metres (6½ feet) high with a shining sun on top of it, symbolizing Vincent's art. During the speech she gave for the occasion, Lies called the work of her brother 'a splendour without joy'.[46] A concert by the local brass band concluded the day.

On 11 June 1933 Lies wrote a message for her niece on the cardboard cover of a drawing by Wil: 'Dear Annie, you and Saar sent me the sweetest package on 16 May that I felt like returning the favour. Hereby, a little keepsake I hold dear, but not dearly enough not to part with it. It was originally drawn by Vincent, very finely done. Then, Wil did a solid job copying it. It might please you to have this, as you already have the old parsonage in Nuenen.'[47] She was referring to the drawing of the parsonage in Etten, not Nuenen, that Wil had copied from an original made by Vincent in 1876. Throughout the years, several unconnected parties have claimed that the gift Lies gave to her nieces was actually Vincent's original drawing. The letter clearly stated that this is not the case, describing how Wil sometimes copied his work. Yet it has taken time for it to be recognized that Wil, besides being a model for the aspiring artist, also enjoyed drawing.

For the occasion of her seventy-fifth birthday on 16 May 1934 Lies was described in a local newspaper article 'as an old lady with a friendly

Lies du Quesne-van Gogh and her daughter Jeannette, unveiling a memorial stone at the parsonage in Nuenen, 1930. Photographer unknown.

LEFT Lies du Quesne-van Gogh at her house in Baarn, 1930s. Photographer unknown. Detail RIGHT.

face, framed by silvery grey, curly hair'.[48] She was living in a room at 6 Cantonlaan in Baarn. Above her door she hung the last remaining work of Vincent that was still in her possession: a drawing of their childhood home in Nuenen.[49] At five o'clock in the morning on 30 November 1936 Lies van Gogh passed away in a boarding house in Baarn. She was seventy-seven years old. She was most likely wearing the same cross around her neck that her mother used to wear. Three days later she was buried at the New General Cemetery (Nieuwe Algemene Begraafplaats) in Baarn, at one in the afternoon. The eulogy was recited by her son-in-law Jan Kooiman. Kooiman thanked everyone present for their great support during the last months of Lies's life.[50] The local newspaper reported that Vincent van Gogh's last surviving sister had died, apparently unaware of the existence of Willemien, who was still living in Veldwijk.[51]

CHAPTER 17

The Last Years

Leiden, Baarn, Dieren, Ermelo-Veldwijk,

1925–1941

Anna, Joan and their daughters had been living in Leiden since 1890. They moved frequently within the city: three years after arriving at 19 Plantsoen, a house looking out on the park that stretches along the Zoeterwoudse Singel, they found a new property at 72 Breestraat. Then something peculiar happened: Anna moved to Bussum with her daughters on 25 April 1896, while Joan moved in the same street in Leiden, to 156a Breestraat. A year later he moved again, still alone, to 1 Breestraat.[1]

Not until 2 May 1898, when Joan moved to 17 Nieuwe Rijn, did his wife and daughters join him again. The reason for the married couple's many moves and their temporary separation – they did not get divorced – cannot be directly deduced from any of the Van Goghs' letters. But a letter that Anna wrote to Jo after Vincent's death, on 1 August 1890, may contain a hint. The health of her daughters, and particularly of her youngest, An, was fragile, and fresh countryside air was thought to be beneficial. An had always been a sickly child and her lungs were especially weak. It is not clear if her ailments persisted into her teenage years, but in her *Notes* Aunt Mietje also brings up the health of Anna's daughters as a reason for their restlessness. While Joan, as head of the lime kiln company, was tied to Leiden, it was perhaps considered best for Anna to take An to live among the green plains of Het Gooi. The health benefits of the Gooi countryside also attracted Jo, who had a summer house built there after Theo's death. The Villa Helma, located at the Koningslaan in Bussum, provided the child with healthy, fresh air: 'I have moved to Bussum, to pay for it I've set up a boarding-house.'[2]

215

Dat lief en luid nog eens een groet.
U Bruidspaar ! tegenruisch :
Wij doen het met een blij gemoed ,
Gedenk somtijds dit huis !
Ras juicht *Uw* huis U 't welkom toe ,
't Geluk blijve ongestoord :
En zingen we allen wel te moê :
Leef daar in vrede voort !

O, Bruidspaar ! ga zoo hand aan hand
En Zegen volg' uw paân ,
Waar gij ook zijt in stad of land ,
De reis vangt spoedig aan.
Houd liefde en vrede vroeg en spa —
Vergeet , vergeet ons niet !
En ruisch altijd de galm U na
Van ons welmeenend lied :

The lyric sheet for the marriage of Anna Theodora (An) van Houten on 15 February 1906, with an image of the Villa Cecilia at top. Photographer unknown.

Anna wrote evocatively about their countless moves – of the trials and excitements of settling into a new home, with a new garden to attend to; of packing and unpacking boxes; and of family members coming to visit. Her memories of the family's 'domestic travels' remained vivid even after they were settled in Leiden again. In April 1901 she wrote to Jo, who was about to move to a new house in Laren, as someone who could speak from experience: 'You are probably packing up at the moment. Separating oneself from one's house will bring up many memories and while tidying up you will continuously be transported to other times and circumstances.'[3] She also kept Jo up to speed with her domestic affairs: 'We are almost done cleaning here. Around mid-May we will go to Katwijk....Our little garden looks so lovely at the moment, the pear blossom has opened up and we see everything grow in front of our eyes. Saar will go out sewing at acquaintances' tomorrow, she and An are doing well, keeping themselves busy. An will probably go to the school of the ladies Van Bemmelen in Oosterbeek, from September to May; we have heard many good stories, particularly about the teaching of foreign languages and music. On Saturday I will go to The Hague and bring back Aunt Mietje with us, who will stay here for a week.'[4]

According to An, Anna was planning to move again in 1904. She wrote to her Aunt Jo in October: 'Mother longs to move to the outskirts of the city; we've been out to look at several houses but it is so hard to find something suitable. All these new houses barely have a garden, or none at all, and are very small in general.'[5] The twenty-one-year-old An also gave an impression of their household: 'Father is of course away for most of the day, Saar is busy with the house or with letter writing, and I occupy myself with bookkeeping. I am quite busy with it at the moment and this is also why I quit my piano lessons after a few months; I spent way too little time on it and then tried to compensate by studying really hard for a bit...I don't have time for a longer letter, I need to take it to the post before 9.'[6]

It did not take long for the family to find something. Anna wrote to Jo on 3 December 1904: 'Your house is so lovely and full of light. In the spring, we will move into a similar house, much smaller than the current one but with an oh so beautiful view on all sides, it is on the

Saar van Houten and Broer de Jong on the day of their marriage, 9 November 1905. Photographer unknown.

Zoeterwoudesingel. I think we will move in March, so we can enjoy the house once the weather starts to improve.'[7] Soon after, at the end of January 1905, there was more to tell: 'Some news, Saar will be engaged soon to Broer de Jong, who is writing his doctorate in theology. At the end of the week it will probably be made public. He is almost finished, he passed his "trial sermon" last week. He is Frisian, born in Makkum, and the two only know each other more intimately since May last year. He has spent the last few months in England, at Woodhook with Prof. Randle Harris. He has a very good reputation among the professors and is a simple, reliable man, a kindred spirit to Saar, not necessarily high spirited. We hope dearly that they will make each other happy.'[8]

In November 1905 the two were married in Leiden, and their wedding reception was held in the new house on the Zoeterwoudesingel. When Broer, who had recently been made a Dutch Reformed minister, was called to duty, the couple moved to Helenaveen, a village close to Deurne,

Villa Cecilia, the Van Houten-van Gogh residence at the corner of Zoeterwoudesingel and De Laat de Kanterstraat, 1905. Photographer unknown.

in North Brabant. Thus Pa and Moe van Gogh's eldest granddaughter ended up in Brabant through a similar route as they had followed. Saar and Broer would have five children together.

Saar wrote to her Aunt Jo about a number of books she had borrowed from her, among them *The Life of Charlotte Brontë*, *Middlemarch* and *À la recherche du bonheur*. She also told Jo about a short visit from her mother, and her worries about her grandmother: 'It was lovely to have mother over, even if it was only for a few hours. It was completely

Anna van Gogh-Carbentus ('Moe'), *c.* 1905. Photographed by Antonius Joannes van der Stok.

unexpected. Mother had to leave the same day, it must have been a tiring day for her, especially with that pain in her leg. She also had to stay up the following night because grandmother was in a bad state. Poor, dear grandmother; she has been suffering for so long.'[9] Five days after Saar sent this letter, Moe van Gogh died. Yet new life was also being brought into the world: 'It is hard to imagine that in 5 weeks the "little stranger" will be here. I am still not ready for him, but the time is approaching fast. Have you seen a photo of An's baby yet?'[10] Four generations of Van Gogh women are brought together in this letter.

Saar's younger sister An married Johan Paul Scholte, also a minister, in Leiden in 1906. The wedding festivities also took place at the Van Houten family house at Zoeterwoudesingel. The newlyweds moved to a village called Dwingeloo in Drenthe. They would have four children, Frederika Antonia, Anna Cornelia Theodora, Joan Marius, also named Job, and Johanna Paulina, nicknamed Pautje.

Decades later, in a letter dated 24 March 1926, An wrote to her cousin Vincent Willem. Jo Bonger, his mother, had died the year before, and the estate of their famous Uncle Vincent was to be distributed among

Jo Bonger in the living room of her house at 77 Koninginneweg, Amsterdam, 1915.
Photographed by Bernard Eilers.

the cousins. An wrote to him: 'How grateful [we are] for this generous gift you offer us in the name of your Mother. When Father told us, it came as a total surprise...we appreciate that you have taken such care in settling the matters: we agree that it would be better to put it in the name of the children and that you give a part of it to Father, who will transfer it to us....It will be delightful to worry less about money, definitely now that the children are getting older.'[11]

After their daughters had moved out and Moe had died, there were few reasons, apart from Joan's business, for Anna and her husband to stay in Leiden. On 25 March 1909 they moved to Dieren in Gelderland, the region where Joan had spent most of his youth. In 1920 they moved within Dieren from Villa Rustoord to Villa Oldegaard.[12] Anna was sick a great deal of the time, and often felt cut off from the world, and particularly from the young student population of Leiden. She returned to Leiden often and regularly visited Aunt Mietje, whose later years resembled Moe's. Anna also visited the Hôpital Wallon, where Wil had briefly worked in her youth, to get her leg treated. And when Mietje died in 1911 she was buried at Groenesteeg cemetery, as was Moe van Gogh.

Anna van Houten-van Gogh on the balcony, with her daughters Saar and An beside her at Villa Oldegaerde, 1924. Photographer unknown.

Anna van Houten-van Gogh (middle, in a black dress) and her daughters, Saar and An (both in white), beside her, at An's engagement party, Leiden, 12 May 1905. Photographer unknown.

Maria Johanna (Aunt Mietje) van Gogh in the garden,
before 1911. Photographer unknown.

Jo, Vincent Willem and Anna attended her funeral.[13] But for Anna, Dieren
was a place of calm, where she could enjoy peace in nature and in her
big garden. Leiden slowly turned into a memory, into a place that had
been and was now gradually fading away.[14]

An acquaintance from Velsen, H.J. Calkoen, wrote in *Weekblad van
de Nederlandse Protestanten Bond* (The Dutch Protestant League Weekly)
that he and his wife had regularly visited Anna and Joan in the Villa
Oldegaarde in the 1920s.[15] He described the several works by Vincent
that hung on their wall: an early painting of the chapel of Nuenen, a
still life of red geraniums in a vase ('I can still recall the twinkling,
thickly laid on colour'[16]), a pen drawing of marsh landscape with reed
and waterlilies, and a small study for *The Potato Eaters*, 'very richly
drawn'.[17] Of all of them, the Calkoens favoured a big pen drawing in

Anna and Joan Marius van Houten-van Gogh in Dieren,
1908. Photographer unknown.

Anna van Houten-van Gogh holding Pautje, her granddaughter, in the garden
of Villa Rustoord, Dieren, 1915. Photographer unknown.

brown ink of a spring landscape full of birches. Calkoen wrote about the shadow that Vincent's life still cast over the rest of the Van Gogh family, and how it had lingered throughout the decades. 'Only after our conversations did we understand the impact of Van Gogh's genius and the tragic course it took on the peaceful minister's family. It was like we were insiders to the recurrent disappointments, the worries and the struggle and the endless difficulties caused by Vincent's "otherness"…. Until long after his death, the tragedy of his life and the way it ended has left the family scarred, despite a growing recognition of his work and his posthumous fame.'[18]

According to Calkoen, Anna resembled Vincent not only physically, but also in temperament: her interest in religion, her love for nature, her determined personality, and the great warmth and love for humanity in its entirety that she exuded. Anna let the couple read some of Vincent's unpublished letters. Calkoen also mentioned a photo album that Anna had gifted him, in 'an endearingly ugly brown cover' with 'scraps' written on it in golden lettering. It contained about forty etchings, engravings, and lithographs that Vincent had collected during his stay in Paris, by a

range of artists.[19] To Calkoen's great surprise, Joan also sent him the pen drawing of the birches.[20]

On 20 September 1930, at the age of seventy-five, Anna van Houten-van Gogh died in Dieren after a short illness.[21] Her widower Joan van Houten subsequently moved to Binnenweg 49 in Ellecom, close to Dieren, where a lady called Klazes Bijlsma took care of him. For years, Joan had been the legal guardian of Willemien and he had also been responsible for her finances, a task

Anna van Houten-van Gogh, 1929.
Photographer unknown.

XIII
Vincent van Gogh,
Rue Lepic Paris – View from Theo's Apartment, 1887
Oil on canvas,
45.9 × 38.1 cm (18⅛ × 15 in.)

XIV
Vincent van Gogh,
Blossoming Almond Branch in a Glass with a Book, 1888
Oil on canvas,
24 × 19 cm (9½ × 7½ in.)

XV
Vincent van Gogh,
Orchard Bordered by Cypresses, 1888
Oil on canvas,
32.5 × 40 cm (12¾ × 15¾ in.)

XVI ABOVE
Vincent van Gogh,
Women Picking Olives, 1889
Oil on canvas,
72.7 × 91.4 cm (28⅝ × 36 in.)

XVII OPPOSITE, ABOVE
Edgar Degas,
Les Danseuses Bleues, 1890
Oil on canvas,
85.3 × 75.3 cm (33⅝ × 29⅝ in.)

XVIII OPPOSITE, BELOW
Business card of Edgar Degas,
with inscription to Theo van Gogh.

XIX
Vincent van Gogh,
Self-Portrait, 1887
Oil on cardboard,
19 × 14.1 cm (7½ × 5½ in.)

XX
Vincent van Gogh,
Self-Portrait or Portrait of Theo van Gogh, 1887
Oil on cardboard,
19 × 14.1 cm (7½ × 5½ in.)

XXI
Suze Fokker's competition-winning
poster for the National Exhibition
of Women's Labour, 1898

he would eventually transfer to his nephew, Vincent Willem.[22]

Vincent Willem would assume responsibility over the division of his painter uncle's estate after the death of his mother in 1925, to find that the picture was somewhat complicated by the existence of a previously unknown heir. Anna and Lies's children were witness to the growing national and international fame of their uncle, whom they had never met. Most of this generation were unaware that there was another Van Gogh descendant: Hubertine. Lies had told her daughter Jeannette about her half-sister about three months after the death of her father, but the rest of the Du Quesne children only discovered

Rose Wilhelmine (Mien) du Quesne van Bruchem, 1922. Photographer unknown.

the story three years later. Theo stated that he had never heard his parents speak about Hubertine. The youngest daughter, Mien, had a hunch that the two shared a secret: she saw a connection between their mailbox, which was always locked (so the children would not be able to accidentally intercept a letter from France) and the hushed arguments between her mother and father late at night.[23]

Lies had in fact travelled down to Normandy shortly after the death of her husband. In the spring of 1922 she took a sleeper train to Saint-Sauveur-le-Vicomte together with her daughter Jeannette. They stayed at the Hôtel de la Victoire, where Lies had given birth to her first daughter more than thirty-five years before. She hoped that she could take her back to the Netherlands as a sort of lady-in-waiting, disguising her true identity, but she hadn't counted on the intimate relationship between Hubertine and her stepmother, Madame Balley. Hubertine had no interest whatsoever in engaging with these 'strange ladies' from the Netherlands, and stayed in

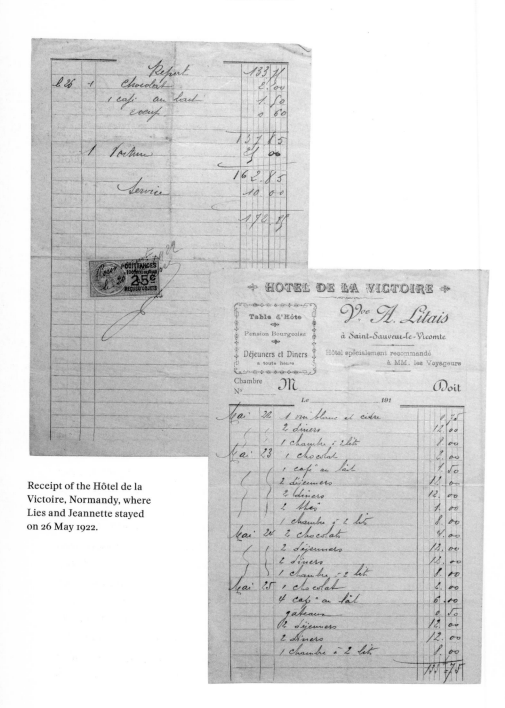

Receipt of the Hôtel de la
Victoire, Normandy, where
Lies and Jeannette stayed
on 26 May 1922.

Saint-Sauveur-le-Vicomte.[24] After visiting the graves of Vincent and Theo in Auvers-sur-Oise with Jeannette, Lies returned home. The failure of the trip greatly pained her. Years later, in January 1936, she wrote in a letter to Jeannette: 'I often think of you know who during the turn of the year. Do you ever hear from her? Do you know how she is doing? I would like to know more.' She noted, with clear disappointment, later on: 'She is so reclusive. We approached her gently and with love, but she is like a rock.'[25]

Far past her childhood Hubertine lived with her foster mother, the widow Frédéric Balley, who had raised her as if she were her own. Balley received a regular allowance from Jean Philippe du Quesne; at the turn of the century he also, without notifying his wife, provided her with an IOU for 1,000 guilders. Dr Bellet, to whom he entrusted this document, died in 1905. It is not known whether Balley ever profited from this gesture.

Hubertine and Balley remained in close contact even when Hubertine, a daily churchgoer, moved to an abbey. Here she wrote poems and learned how to play a church organ, supporting the local parish with this newly acquired skill. Hubertine was the first Catholic in the Van Gogh family and the only Catholic among the grandchildren of Moe and Pa van Gogh. In her later years she became, like her Aunt Willemien, a theology teacher to the children of her parish. In education she seemed to have found her calling in life. She pursued this interest with great zest, and received her official licence in Caen. She taught in Paris, then Lyon; but her career took an unexpected turn when a heavy bout of flu permanently damaged her hearing and left her with chronic fatigue. She had returned to live with Balley during her recuperation, but when her stepmother died in 1922, Hubertine was left all alone.[26] She departed for Paris once more, this time to work as a sales associate at a general trade office, but the work proved too demanding and she was forced to move back to the south of France, where she worked in Marseille as a colporteur. This was quite a setback for someone with her education. She went door-to-door, hawking candy, writing supplies and calendars, sometimes with images of her Uncle Vincent's paintings. Later on, she moved to Lourdes to do the same.[27]

Jeannette cared about her half-sister's future. Just before her marriage to Jan Kooiman, on 16 October 1923, she decided to visit Hubertine to

Hubertine van Gogh, *c.* 1930. Photographed by E. Vaslot.

give her a part of her inheritance, as some sort of compensation for her parents' abandonment. While Hubertine appreciated the gesture, she declined Jeannette's offer, saying that she would prefer that Jeannette save the money for her own future children.[28]

Thereafter, Hubertine did not have contact with anyone from the Van Gogh family until Lies's death; but in her letter of condolence she asked for the address of the person who was with Lies in her last moments on earth. A year after their mother's death, a meeting between the sisters Jeannette, Mien and Hubertine took place. The three met in Paris, where Hubertine was teaching once again.[29] Though they tried to keep in touch afterwards, they eventually lost contact, likely in part due to the outbreak of the Second World War. Almost fifteen years later Hubertine, by then sixty-five years old, met her cousin Vincent Willem at an exhibition of Vincent's work in Arles, which had been set up by Vincent Willem himself. The show centred around the work that Vincent made in and around Arles and Saint-Rémy. An Weenink writes: 'Standing right in front of him, this small, rather shabby woman who, full of pride regarding her kinship to this great artist, announced to him: "Je suis Hubertine, votre cousine".'[30]

The cousins had never laid eyes on each other before, and this first meeting was a little awkward. For both of them it was difficult to relate to one another; they were family, but without a shared history. Vincent Willem made an effort nonetheless. He took Hubertine to dinner in Arles and ensured that she got a private tour of the exhibition before it officially opened. His wife also lent her an outfit so that she would make a good impression at the opening. Vincent Willem helped her pick out and paid for an expensive hearing aid. He dropped her off at her boarding house before he made his way back to the Netherlands. Few people at the time knew that Vincent Willem had also agreed to provide her with a monthly allowance of 400 francs, which he would later increase to 600 francs.[31] She would receive this support from her Dutch family until the day she died. At last, Hubertine was able to enjoy a piece of the wealth generated by her uncle's fame and work. This delay, and the tragedy of poverty preceding it, had a simple but far-reaching cause: Jean Philippe du Quesne had been unable to legally recognize her as his child at her birth because he was still married to Catharina van Willis. Years later, once Lies and Jean Philippe had married, they

Lies du Quesne van Bruchem-van Gogh, 1920s.
Photographer unknown.

229

could have amended this, but apparently no one in the family dared to face the social stigma of having an 'illegitimate' child, even after it became a public secret. It was because of this that Hubertine could make no legal claim to any sort of inheritance. Like her husband, Lies had tried to balance the inequality between her oldest daughter and the rest of her children; in an appendix to her will she granted 1,000 guilders to Hubertine. Yet Lies did not set this sum aside, instead urging her children to generate it from their own inheritances.[32] As with Jean Philippe's IOU, it is not clear if this 'declaration of intent' was carried out.

Hubertine's story was made public in the 1960s. The wife of a journalist in Marseille told her husband that she had bought a Van Gogh calendar on the street from a woman who claimed to be his niece. The journalist went in search of her, and wrote about their meeting in his column in February 1965. Her poverty relative to her uncle's fame – she owned only the bare essentials, lived in a cramped attic room, and was in poor health – gave him his angle.[33] A year later the story was picked up in the Netherlands, in an article called 'The honorary doctor and the black sheep' ('De eredoctor en het zwarte schaap') in the magazine *Panorama*.[34] The worst of Hubertine's poverty was alleviated by the monthly allowance organized by Vincent Willem, but she was never fully taken into the Van Gogh family – and was therefore never fully

Willemien van Gogh's tombstone at the Veldwijk cemetery.

able to enjoy the riches of Vincent's inheritance – and spent her remaining years in a string of shabby boarding houses. On 6 August 1969 she passed away in Des Lourdes, a village close to the pilgrimage site of Lourdes, just three days after her eighty-third birthday.

After Anna and Lies's deaths Wil was the only surviving Van Gogh sister. She remained in the Veldwijk psychiatric hospital until her death on 17 May 1941, the birthday of her younger brother Cor. She had spent the last thirty-eight years of her life at the institution, seeing very few people besides her family, doctors and nurses. With each passing year, the number of visitors decreased; it is unclear whether Willemien was aware that her family was slowly dying. Of her generation, her brother-in-law Joan would hold out the longest. After her death, the ninety-year-old Joan took care of her funeral and other practical matters. She was buried in the hospital grounds, and her gravestone can be found there to this day. Joan himself died on 10 January 1945.

Nothing is known about Wil's funeral. The inventory of her room in Veldwijk was sent to her nephew Vincent Willem by Joan van Houten. The letter asks him if he wants to come into possession of her meagre belongings:

12 cups and saucers f 2,50
7 plates f 1,50
Prayer book with golden lock f 16,-
Writing gear and box f 1,50
2 brooches, 1 cameo (gold) f 18,-
1 bracelet (idem) f 30,-
2 rings (idem) f 10,-
Old silver: buckle, bracelet, band, napkin ring, watch, 2 brooches f 7,50
2 boxes, 1 pot, 2 copper bowls f 4,-
4 moulds, 1 serving tray, 1 cover f 2,50
Pen drawing Vincent van Gogh and Japanese prints f 250,-
Little table, half-moon shape f 50,-
2 copper bowls, taken to the metal collection service.[35]

This was all that remained of her life.

Epilogue

As for me, I shall see him with my eyes
and with my heart in his works.[1]

With Willemien's death in May 1941, the last remaining member of the Van Gogh-Carbentus pastoral family had passed away. The three brothers, Vincent, Theo and Cor, had died young, and all within the last decade of the nineteenth century; the three sisters lived into old age, all seeing the twentieth century. Neither Vincent's brothers, nor his parents, would live to see his art and name achieve international recognition; only his sisters – including his worldly sister-in-law, Jo van Gogh-Bonger – would ever know that his deepest desire, to become a truly great painter, would be fulfilled.

None of Anna and Lies's descendants ever met Vincent, and of course they are not named Van Gogh. Nevertheless, from an early age they would have known that they were part of a family tree with a remarkable branch – endowed with certain values and made up of reverends, art dealers, booksellers and, most notably, that one, world-famous painter.

When Vincent died, the vast majority of his letters, drawings and paintings were inherited by Theo. Anna and her husband Joan, Lies and Wil agreed this amongst themselves, and informed him so in a letter from Leiden in August 1890.[2] After Theo's death, which of course followed Vincent's by just half a year, his widow Jo looked after the artworks and correspondence in her husband's possession. As is now well known, it was Jo – Vincent's literary-minded sister-in-law from Amsterdam, with her connections in the art world – who became the greatest advocate of Vincent's work (both his written and visual record), rather than Anna, Lies and Wil – his own sisters. They appeared somewhat distant when it came to Vincent's oeuvre. On rare occasions they mentioned it in their letters, mostly uncertain what to think of it.

Although Anna and Vincent, the two eldest Van Gogh siblings, had bonded through visiting museums together and discussing art during their years in England, Anna often struggled to know what to make of his work.[3] She was open to explanation, and would receive that shortly after moving to Dieren in 1909, from a reverend who aspired to become a painter, Jakob Nieweg. They both worshipped at the Protestant Association, where Nieweg delivered sermons as a minister and Anna attended as a believer. He would teach her how to truly see Vincent's work and help her understand its deeper meanings.[4] That guidance was extremely valuable to her. As a gesture of thanks, Anna wanted to give him a painting as a gift, but Nieweg was a modest man and refused. Later on, he did accept a drawing that Vincent had given to Anna, the size of a postcard, of Austin Friars that he had made when the siblings were both in London (see page 59). Nearly twenty-five years would pass after Vincent's death before Anna gave in to the need to know more about her famous brother's work. The several occasions that she received Nieweg at her home formed an important step in that direction.

Lies was of course much younger than Vincent, and as he left home at an early age, first for boarding school and then for work, they spent little time together during her childhood years. They shared a love for literature, though on that subject Vincent wrote more often to Willemien and, above all, to Theo. Lies wrote about books to Jo, with whom she began to correspond in the 1880s.[5] Lies loved Theo dearly, but often complained about her difficult relationship with Vincent. Vincent reserved his thoughts on literature and, moreover, on art for Theo and Wil – first during his years in England but especially while living in France, long after he had broken contact with Anna and Lies. In particular, letters by Moe, Anna or Lies are mainly about daily life, such as receiving visitors, travel, family matters, housekeeping, health and the weather. Rarely, if ever, did his mother or oldest sisters write about his art. It might seem that it was out of a lack of knowledge, or even interest, that the two elder Van Gogh sisters concerned themselves so little with Vincent's work. It is, then, also difficult to determine what they actually thought of it, though both Anna and Lies did keep a number of his drawings and paintings in their possession.

Of Vincent's three sisters, it was in Willemien, the youngest, that he found a kindred spirit. Wil, like Vincent, loved literature and art dearly, and not just passively; it appears from her correspondence with her friend Margaretha Meijboom that she drew and perhaps even painted, and she also sometimes mused about becoming a writer. The themes in her artwork were strongly influenced by Vincent.[6] In their letters, the two siblings also readily and openly addressed their susceptibility to mental health problems, as Wil also did with Margaretha (the latter would sometimes read Vincent's letters when Wil included them in her correspondence, out of admiration or inspiration).[7] A number of the works she and her brother discussed, and that Vincent had intended for Willemien, would find their way into the collection that Wil kept while still living in the family home – mainly small pieces.[8] After Wil's hospitalization at Veldwijk, Jo Bonger looked after these works, together with the paintings that Theo had inherited from his brother.

When Jo died in 1925, her son, Vincent Willem, inherited both his father's and Willemien's collections. Just like his mother, he would care for it with attention and prudence. He sometimes sold pieces on his aunts' behalf. Wil's paintings were sold only when necessary for her upkeep in Veldwijk. The portion kept by his other two aunts, however, shrank quickly: Anna occasionally gave away a painting or drawing by Vincent, and Lies was often forced to sell a piece due to her worsening financial circumstances in later life. That must have pained her deeply. During this period, she nonetheless positioned herself more and more as *the* sister of the now famous painter, though she was far from well-off and, among other things, had to sell her eldest brother's work in order to keep herself afloat. In a letter to her sister Jeannette in 1917, Lies's daughter Mien called it a 'slave's life', adding: 'it hurts me to see her dirty little hands.'[9] Lies's books and activities regarding an increasingly famous Vincent in the 1920s and 1930s no doubt brought her some regard and pleased her, but offered little in the way of lasting improvement to her financial situation. Still, after her death, Lies would surprise her family with a small amount of capital spread across diverse stocks, just as her father had done when the inventory was made after his death in May 1885 in Nuenen.[10]

Lies and Jean Philippe du Quesne van Bruchem's five children – Hubertine, Theo, Jeannette, Mien and Felix – never owned a single Van Gogh, and rarely concerned themselves with his oeuvre, most likely because their cousin Vincent Willem already did so.[11] It is true that they had never known Vincent, but he was also their uncle, their mother's brother, even though they are named Du Quesne van Bruchem – a pedigree family name, registered in the genealogical reference work *Nederlands Patriciaat* (The Netherlands's Patriciate, also known as the 'Blue Book') – and not Van Gogh. Saar and An, the two daughters of Anna and Joan van Houten-Van Gogh – the latter of whom also came from a prominent noble family – both married reverends, and in many ways continued the traditional way of life of their grandparents and great-grandparents. Saar and Broer de Jong-van Houten would have five children, three sons (John, Joan and Bram) and two daughters (An and Foekje). An van Houten, who married Johannes Paulus Scholte the following year, gave birth to Free, Anna Cornelia Theodora, Joan Marius (Job) and Pautje. Her youngest daughter would not live past the age of four. They would also lose their son Job, a medical student at the University of Groningen, to tuberculosis when he was just twenty years old.

Living in villages or small cities where the reverend and his wife were among the notables, it was social work, Christian values and norms, and caring for one's fellow human beings that were central to the rhythm of these nieces of Vincent and their husbands' lives. Just like their ancestors, they were highly regarded and had many opportunities, but were not outlandishly wealthy. They, too, were real Van Goghs, though they did not carry the name. Presumably, everything that went on regarding Uncle Vincent's oeuvre took place outside their field of vision, namely in Amsterdam and Het Gooi, where Vincent Willem worked at founding the Vincent van Gogh Foundation in 1960 and opening the Van Gogh Museum in 1973. While his mother Jo Bonger held together the collection of letters, drawings and paintings, Vincent Willem would ensure they found a home under one roof, were visible to the public and were accessible to scholars. Vincent Willem worked together with three of his children and his second wife, Nelly van der Goot.[12] Later generations would continue this collaboration.

And thus grew Vincent's name and fame during the twentieth century, first with steadily rising prices, books, exhibitions and eventually films about his life and work, and thereafter with record prices for his paintings in the latter half of the century. It was Jo van Gogh-Bonger and her son Vincent Willem who, with their artistic and business insight and perseverance, built up Vincent van Gogh's reputation and lifted him to great heights; however, it was his parents, brothers and sisters who gave Vincent this: love, background, family values, concern for his fellow human beings, passion for nature, art and literature, and, above all, the conviction to follow his heart. And not only to Vincent; Lies and Wil would also make modern and independent choices in art and poetry, and Wil campaigned for social change.

This is how the Van Gogh sisters will be remembered in the collective memory: Anna the pious, obedient one, with whom Vincent seemed to bond at a young age, but who ultimately caused him to go abroad and never return; Lies the eccentric poet and writer with a big secret, who presented herself as 'the sister of' the famous painter but never truly bonded with her brother or his art; and Wil, Vincent's favourite sister, to whom he dedicated many paintings – the little sister who, like him, was 'different', and with whom he shared a love of art and literature above everything else.

RIGHT
Anna Scholte-van Houten's children
Anna, Free and Job Scholte, 1922.
Photographer unknown.

BELOW
Anna Theodora Scholte-van Houten
with her son Job, 1915. Photographer
unknown.

RIGHT
Saar and Broer de Jong-van Houten
and their five children: John, An,
Joan, Foekje and Bram. Date and
photographer unknown.

ABOVE
Saar de Jong-van Houten sitting on
a couch with daughter Foekje, 1915.
Photographer unknown.

RIGHT
Lies du Quesne-van Gogh with eldest
son Theo and daughter Jeannette,
c. 1930. Photographer unknown.

Lies du Quesne-van Gogh (right),
Rose Wilhelmine Riem Vis-du
Quesne, Jeannette Kooijman-du
Quesne, probably Huis de Wiel (left).
Date and photographer unknown.

RIGHT
An van Houten and Jan Paul
Scholte and their children, Anna
Cornelia Theodora, Frederica
Antonia and Joan Marius (Johanna
Paulina in a frame), after 1919.
Photographer unknown.

LEFT
Josina van Gogh-Wibaut and Vincent
Willem van Gogh, in the living room
at 77 Koninginneweg, Amsterdam,
1915. Photographer unknown.

Vincent van Gogh (1789–1874) — Elisabeth Huberta Vrijdag (1790–1857)
1811

Johanna Wilhelmina (Antje) van Gogh (1812–1883)	Hendrik Vincent van Gogh (1814–1877) — Johanna Samuelle de Geus (1818–1839) 1837	Dorothea Maria (Doortje) van Gogh (1815–1882)	Johannes (Jan) van Gogh (1817–1885) — Wilhelmina Hermana Elisabeth (Eliza) Bruyns (1819–1864) 1843	Willem Daniel van Gogh (1818–1872) — Magdalena Suzanna (Lena) van Stockum (1828–1903) 1855	Vincent (Cent) van Gogh (1820–1888) — Cornelia (Cornelie) Carbentus (1829–1913) 1850
	2nd marriage: Maria Boon (1819–1885) 1 daughter		1 daughter 3 sons	2 daughters 2 sons	

Vincent van Gogh (1852–1852)	Vincent Willem van Gogh (1853–1890)	Anna Cornelia (Anna) van Gogh (1855–1930) — Joan Marius van Houten (1850–1945) 1878	Theodorus (Theo) van Gogh (1857–1891) — Johanna Gezina (Jo) Bonger (1860–1925) 1889	Elisabeth Huberta (Lies) van Gogh (1859–1936) — Jean Philippe Theodore du Quesne van Bruchem (1840–1921) 1891	Willemien Jacoba (Wil) van Gogh (1862–1941)

Sara Maria (Saar) van Houten (1880–1977) — Broer de Jong (1881–1957) 1905	Anna Theodora (An) van Houten (1883–1969) — Johannes (Jan) Paulus Scholte (1879–1963) 1906	Vincent Willem van Gogh (1890–1978) — Josina Wibaut (1890–1933) 1915	Hubertina Marie Normance van Gogh (1886–1969)	Theodore Louis Gilles du Quesne van Bruchem (1892–1939) — Arnolda Cornelia Idzerda (1900–1975) 1920
		2nd marriage Nelly van der Goot (1897–1967)		

John Rendel de Jong (1907–1994) Anna Cornelia (An) de Jong (1909–1997) Joan Marius de Jong (1912–2001) Foekje de Jong (1914–2004) Abraham (Bram) de Jong (1916–1978)	Frederica Antonia (1907–2002) Anna Cornelia Theodora (1909–1998) Joan Marius (Job) Scholte (1911–1932) Johanna Paulina (Pautje) (1915–1919)	Theo van Gogh (1920–1945) Johan van Gogh (1922–2019) Florentius Marius van Gogh (1925–1999) Mathilde Johanna van Gogh (1929–2008)		Lies du Quesne van Bruchem (1921–1982) Miene du Quesne van Bruchem (1922–2020) Nicolaas Frederik du Quesne van Bruchem (1923–2018)

Theodorus (Dorus) van Gogh (1822–1885) — Anna Cornelia Carbentus (1819–1907) 1851	Elisabeth Huberta (Bertha) van Gogh (1823–1895) — Abraham Pompe (1835–1856) 1867	Cornelis Marinus (Cor) van Gogh (1824–1908) — Phoebe Elisabeth Reinhold (1855–1856) 1855 .... 2nd marriage Johanna (Jans) Franken (1836–1919) 1 daughter 2 sons	Geertruida Johanna (Truitje) van Gogh (1826–1891) — Abraham Anthonie 's Graeuwen (1824–1903) 1858	Willem Frederik van Gogh (1828–1829)	Maria Johanna (Mietje) van Gogh (1831–1911)

Cornelis Vincent (Cor) van Gogh (1867–1900) — Anna Catharine Fuchs (1877–1944) 1898			Francina (Fanny) 's Graeuwen (1859–1935)	Elisabetha Hubertha (Betje) 's Graeuwen (1862–1898)	Abraham Anthonie (Bram) 's Graeuwen (1868–1913) — Elisabeth Zonneveld 1898

Jeannette Adrienne Angeline du Quesne van Bruchem (1895–1952) — Jan Kooiman (1873–1939) 1923	Rose Wilhelmine (Mien) du Quesne van Bruchem (1897–1972) — Joseph Leendert Arie Riem Vis (1900–1975) 1922	Felix Jean Philippe du Quesne van Bruchem (1899–1993) — Arnolda Anna Cornelia Verhoef (1903–?) 1923

Annie Kooiman (1916–2008) Angeline Hubertina (Tineke) Kooiman (1924–1998) Vincent Willem Kooiman (1927–?) Hendrik (1932–?) Wilhelmina Kooiman (1935–?) Annie Kooiman (1936–?)	Helena (Lenie) Thwosora Riem Vis (1922–2019) Felix Riem Vis (1924–2004) Anna Cornelia (Annetje) Riem Vis (1927–2011)	Nicolaas du Quesne van Bruchem (1934–1995) Vincent du Quesne van Bruchem (adopted) (?–?) Felix du Quesne van Bruchem (?–?)

NOTES

In the notes that follow I give the date and location of letters sent to, by or about the Van Gogh sisters. I have read about 170 letters from and to Willemien van Gogh; over 200 letters and postcards from and to Lies van Gogh; and about 90 letters from and to Anna van Gogh. At the time of writing, these were (and probably still are) all of the known letters written or received by the sisters. I also read a number of letters about Dorus, Moe, Theo, Cor and other family members, written by Aunt Mietje, Jo Bonger and other relatives and friends. I found these letters in various libraries and museums, in literature, on the internet, and in the course of my communication with descendants of the Van Gogh family. Many of the letters referenced here, including the correspondence between Margaretha Meijboom and Willemien van Gogh, have seldom (or never) been read by a wider audience, and most probably only by family members, and myself.

All letters written or received by Vincent van Gogh can be found on www.vangoghletters.org, the official website of the Van Gogh Museum in Amsterdam. *Vincent van Gogh – The Letters*, the six-volume edition published by the Van Gogh Museum and Amsterdam University Press/Thames & Hudson in 2009, is also a useful resource. Letters that are not by Vincent require a little more patience to track down, but some of them can be found, in dozens of places. The majority are in the possession of the Van Gogh Museum, whose helpful staff offered much support and insight as I pieced together the story of the sisters.

The family's letters of mourning after the death of Vincent, however, can be found in Ronald Pickvance's *'A Great Artist is Dead': Letters of Condolence on Vincent van Gogh's Death, Edited by Sjaar van Heugten and Fieke Pabst*. The correspondence between Theo van Gogh and his wife Jo Bonger can be found in H. van Crimpen, *et al.*, *Brief Happiness: The Correspondence of Theo van Gogh and Jo Bonger* (Amsterdam/Zwolle 1999). The important role Jo Bonger had in the family, as well as the reception of Vincent's work after his death, comes to life at the website www.bongerdiaries.org, especially in the letters.

CHAPTER 1

1 Johannes van Gogh to Mietje van Gogh, Nuenen, 28 March 1885.
2 *Ibid.*

3 Vincent van Gogh to Anthon van Rappard, Nuenen, on or about 13 March 1884.
4 Beek, N.A. van, *De Aantekeningen van tante Mietje van Gogh*, The Hague 2010, p. 74.
5 Willemien van Gogh to Line Kruysse, Breda, 26 August 1886.
6 Margaretha Meijboom to Willemien van Gogh, The Hague, 14 July 1887; Margaretha Meijboom to Willemien van Gogh, Assen, 27 September 1887.
7 Willemien van Gogh to Line Kruysse, Breda, 26 August 1886. Line Kruysse was deputy director of the Buitengasthuis hospital in Amsterdam, an institution for patients with mental health problems, and introduced new methods of nursing, using the English model as an example.
8 Vincent van Gogh to Theo van Gogh, The Hague, 29 December 1881.
9 *Ibid.*
10 Vincent van Gogh to Theo van Gogh, Nuenen, 6 April 1885.
11 *Ibid.*
12 *Ibid.*
13 Vincent van Gogh to Theo van Gogh, Nuenen, 2 June 1885.
14 *Ibid.*
15 Vincent van Gogh to Theo van Gogh, Nuenen, 6 April 1885; 'The summer that...suffered so much': Anna van Gogh wrote in a memoir of her sister Lies van Gogh, probably in 1923.
16 Vincent van Gogh to Willemien van Gogh, Paris, end of October 1887.
17 Vincent van Gogh to Theo van Gogh, Nuenen, on or about 17 November 1885.
18 Gogh-Bonger, J. van, *Brieven aan zijn Broeder*, Amsterdam 1923, p. xliv.

CHAPTER 2

1 Beek, N.A. van, *Het geslacht Carbentus*, The Hague 2011, pp. 5, 10, 15; Naifeh, S. and G. White Smith, *Vincent van Gogh, De Biografie*, Amsterdam 2011, p. 33.
2 Naifeh, S. and G. White Smith, *Vincent van Gogh, De Biografie*, Amsterdam 2011, pp. 31–34; Beek, N.A. van, *Het geslacht Carbentus*, The Hague 2011, pp. 29–30.
3 Beek, N.A. van, *Het geslacht Carbentus*, The Hague 2011, pp. 24–25; Naifeh, S. and G. White

Smith, *Vincent van Gogh, De Biografie*, Amsterdam 2011, p. 34; *Carbentus-kroniek*, p. 12.

4 Anna van Gogh-Carbentus to Theo van Gogh, Breda, 29 December 1888, after Vincent's death (see p. 172, this volume); Naifeh, S. and G. White Smith, *Vincent van Gogh, De Biografie*, Amsterdam 2011, p. 34.

5 Naifeh, S. and G. White Smith, *Vincent van Gogh, De Biografie*, Amsterdam 2011, p. 35; Beek, N.A. van, *Het geslacht Carbentus*, The Hague 2011, p. 31.

6 Naifeh, S. and G. White Smith, *Vincent van Gogh, De Biografie*, Amsterdam 2011, p. 35.

7 *Ibid.*, p. 34.

8 Beek, N.A. van, *De Aantekeningen van tante Mietje van Gogh*, The Hague 2010, pp. 17-18.

9 *Ibid.*, pp. 7-19.

10 *Ibid.*, p. 104.

11 Uitert, E. van, *Van Gogh in Brabant. Schilderijen en tekeningen uit Etten en Nuenen*, Zwolle 1987, pp. 77-78; Beek, N.A. van, *De Aanteekeningen van Tante Mietje van Gogh*, The Hague 2010, pp. 45-46.

12 Naifeh, S. and G. White Smith, *Vincent van Gogh, De Biografie*, Amsterdam 2011, pp. 83-85; Beek, N.A. van, *De Aanteekeningen van Tante Mietje van Gogh*, The Hague 2010, p. 45.

13 Hamoen, G. and J. van Dijk, *Maatschappij van welstand: 175 jaar steun aan kleine protestantse gemeenten*, Bekking Amersfoort 1997, pp. 33-34.

14 Kools, F., *Vincent van Gogh en zijn geboorteplaats. Als een boer van Zundert*, Zutphen 1990, pp. 10-11; Beek, N.A. van, *De Aanteekeningen van Tante Mietje van Gogh*, The Hague 2010, p. 27; Vries, W., *150 Jaar Welstand. De Maatschappij tot Bevordering van Welstand, voornamelijk onder landlieden, 1822-1972. Bijdragen tot de Geschiedenis van het Zuiden van Nederland*, XXIII, Tilburg 1972, pp. 217-18.

15 Beek, N.A. van, *De Aanteekeningen van Tante Mietje van Gogh*, The Hague 2010, p. 107.

16 *Ibid.*, p. 108.

17 Kools, F., *Vincent van Gogh en zijn geboorteplaats. Als een boer van Zundert*, Zutphen 1990, pp. 11-14; Beek, N.A. van, *De Aanteekeningen van Tante Mietje van Gogh*, The Hague 2010, pp. 45-46, 107-8.

18 Beek, N.A. van, *De Aanteekeningen van Tante Mietje van Gogh*, The Hague 2010, p. 46.

19 Naifeh, S. and G. White Smith, *Vincent van Gogh, De Biografie*, Amsterdam 2011, pp. 36-37; Beek, N.A. van, *De Aanteekeningen van Tante Mietje van Gogh*, The Hague 2010, p. 46.

20 Anna Cornelia van Gogh-Carbentus, diary entries (manuscript), Zundert, 20 March 1852, collection Vincent van Gogh Huis, Zundert.

21 *Ibid.*

22 *Ibid.*

23 Poppel, F. van, *Trouwen in Nederland. Een historisch-demografische studie van de 19e en vroeg-20e eeuw*, Wageningen 1992.

24 Anna Cornelia van Gogh-Carbentus, diary entries (manuscript), Zundert, 20 March 1852, collection Vincent van Gogh Huis, Zundert.

25 *Ibid.*

26 *Ibid.*

27 *Ibid.*; Beek, N.A. van, *De Aanteekeningen van Tante Mietje van Gogh*, The Hague 2010, pp. 47, 109; Naifeh, S. and G. White Smith, *Vincent van Gogh, De Biografie*, Amsterdam 2011, pp. 36-37.

28 Du Quesne-van Gogh, E.H., *Vincent van Gogh. Persoonlijke herinneringen aangaande een kunstenaar*, Baarn 1910, p. 37.

29 *Ibid.*, pp. 35-37.

CHAPTER 3

1 Kools, F., *Vincent van Gogh en zijn geboorteplaats. Als een boer van Zundert*, Zutphen 1990, p. 26.

2 Beek, N.A. van, *De Aanteekeningen van Tante Mietje van Gogh*, The Hague 2010, p. 109.

3 Uitert, E. van, *Van Gogh in Brabant. Schilderijen en tekeningen uit Etten en Nuenen*, Zwolle 1987, p. 7.

4 Vincent van Gogh to Hermanus Gijsbertus Tersteeg, Amsterdam, 3 August 1877; F. Kools, *Vincent van Gogh. Als een boer van Zundert*, Zutphen 1990, p. 27.

5 Naifeh, S. and G. White Smith, *Vincent van Gogh, De Biografie*, Amsterdam 2011, p. 35.

6 Vincent van Gogh to Theo van Gogh, Amsterdam, 27 August 1877; E. van Uitert, *Van Gogh in Brabant. Schilderijen en tekeningen uit Etten en Nuenen*, Zwolle 1987, pp. 59-60.

7 Kools, F., *Vincent van Gogh en zijn geboorteplaats. Als een boer van Zundert*, Zutphen 1990, pp. 16-20.

8 Naifeh, S. and G. White Smith, *Vincent van Gogh, De Biografie*, Amsterdam 2011, p. 35.

9 *Ibid.*

10 Du Quesne-Van Gogh, E.H., *Vincent van Gogh, Herinneringen aan haar broeder*, Baarn 1923, p. 16.

11 Kools, F., *Vincent van Gogh en zijn geboorteplaats. Als een boer van Zundert*, Zutphen 1990, pp. 39-40.

12 Beek, N.A. van, *De Aanteekeningen van Tante Mietje van Gogh*, The Hague 2010, pp. 108-9.

13 Berkelmans, F.A., 'Vincent van Gogh en Zundert', in *Jaarboek der Oranjeboom* (1953), p. 55, though note that mayor Van de Wall (1890-1925) is incorrectly given for mayor Gaspar van Beckhoven (1840-1888).

14 Kools, F., *Vincent van Gogh en zijn geboorteplaats. Als een boer van Zundert*, Zutphen 1990, pp. 46-47.

15 *Ibid.*, pp. 39-40.
16 Druick, D.W. and P. Kort Zegers, *Van Gogh en Gauguin. Het atelier van het zuiden*, Zwolle 2002, pp. 11-12.
17 Vincent van Gogh to Theo van Gogh, Welwyn, 17 June 1876.
18 Kools, F., *Vincent van Gogh en zijn geboorteplaats. Als een boer van Zundert*, Zutphen 1990, pp. 93-94.
19 *Ibid.*, p. 98.
20 *Ibid.*, pp. 96-97.
21 *Ibid.*, p. 102.
22 Vincent van Gogh to Theo van Gogh, Isleworth, 3 October 1876.
23 Vincent van Gogh to Theo van Gogh, Arles, 22 January 1889.
24 Du Quesne-van Gogh, E.H., *Vincent van Gogh. Persoonlijke herinneringen aangaande een kunstenaar*, Baarn 1910, pp. 15-17.

CHAPTER 4

1 Kools, F., *Vincent van Gogh en zijn geboorteplaats. Als een boer van Zundert*, Zutphen 1990, pp. 117-20; Smulders, H., 'Van Gogh in Helvoirt', *De Kleine Meijerij*, 41 (1990: 1), p. 8; Uitert, E. van, *Van Gogh in Brabant. Schilderijen en tekeningen uit Etten en Nuenen*, Zwolle 1987, pp. 79-82.
2 Mast, M. van der and Ch. Dumas, *Van Gogh en Den Haag*, Zwolle 1990, pp. 10-11.
3 Beek, N.A. van, *De Aanteekeningen van Tante Mietje van Gogh*, The Hague 2010, p. 110.
4 Vincent van Gogh to Theo van Gogh, The Hague, 29 September 1872; Vincent van Gogh to Theo van Gogh, The Hague, 13 December 1872.
5 Smulders, H., 'Van Gogh in Helvoirt', *De Kleine Meijerij*, 41 (1990: 1), p. 10; De Noo, H. and W. Slingerland, *Helvoirt, De Protestantse Gemeente en de Oude Sint Nikolaaskerk*, Helvoirt-Haaren 2007, p. 43; Wuisman, P.J.M., 'Mariënhof te Helvoirt', *De Kleine Meijerij*, 23 (1972: 1), p. 4.
6 Beek, N.A. van, *De Aanteekeningen van Tante Mietje van Gogh*, The Hague 2010, p. 72.
7 Smulders, H., 'Van Gogh in Helvoirt', *De Kleine Meijerij*, 41 (1990: 1), p. 2; Anna van Gogh-Carbentus to Theo van Gogh, Helvoirt, 10 July 1874.
8 Smulders, H., 'Van Gogh in Helvoirt', *De Kleine Meijerij*, 41 (1990: 1), p. 12.
9 *Helvertse schetsen: geïllustreerde beschrijvingen van historische en monumentale gebouwen*, Helvoirt 1985, p. 8; Smulders, H., 'Van Gogh in Helvoirt', *De Kleine Meijerij*, 41 (1990: 1), pp. 11-13 ; Uitert, E. van, *Van Gogh in Brabant. Schilderijen en tekeningen uit Etten en Nuenen*, Zwolle 1987, p. 80; De Noo,

H. and W. Slingerland, *Helvoirt, De Protestantse Gemeente en de Oude Sint Nikolaaskerk*, Helvoirt-Haaren 2007, pp. 53-55.
10 Smulders, H., 'Van Gogh in Helvoirt', *De Kleine Meijerij*, 41 (1990: 1), p. 13; De Noo, H. and W. Slingerland, *Helvoirt, De Protestantse Gemeente en de Oude Sint Nikolaaskerk*, Helvoirt-Haaren 2007, p. 44.
11 Anna van Gogh, register of the French Day and Boarding School for Young Mistresses (1855-*c.* 1874), Historisch Centrum Leeuwarden, acc. 1312, inv. no. 612.
12 Boekholt, P.Th.F.M. and E.P. De Booy, *Geschiedenis van de School in Nederland, vanaf de Middeleeuwen tot aan de huidige tijd*, Assen/Maastricht 1987, p. 130: 'For women it was not appropriate to choose a social occupation in the civic society later in life.... The purpose of the French Day and Boarding School for Young Mistresses might have been to prepare them for their most ideal future destination (marriage), some women found in this very entourage – few out of many – a social profession as a teacher.'
13 Anna van Gogh to Theo van Gogh, Leeuwarden, 6 January 1874.
14 Anna van Gogh, register of the French Day and Boarding School for Young Mistresses (1855-*c.* 1874), Historisch Centrum Leeuwarden, acc. 1312, inv. no. 612: the doctor Nicolaas Johannes Bartelomeus Landman (1815-1902) gave Anna the vaccination against cowpox in Helvoirt, February 1871, and wrote her a vaccination certificate.
15 In this case for receiving a vaccination against cowpox.
16 Rebecca Plaat (1828-1905), principal of the French Day and Boarding School for Young Mistresses at Leeuwarden and a history teacher between 1859 and 1894 (from 1875 at the Middle School for Girls).
17 Dorus van Gogh to Theo van Gogh, Helvoirt, 18 November 1874.
18 Boekholt, P.Th.F.M. and E.P. De Booy, *Geschiedenis van de School in Nederland, vanaf de Middeleeuwen tot aan de huidige tijd*, Assen/Maastricht 1987, p. 130.
19 Anna van Gogh to Theo van Gogh, Leeuwarden, 4 February 1873.
20 *Ibid.*
21 *Ibid.*
22 Anna van Gogh to Theo van Gogh, Leeuwarden, 6 January 1874.
23 *Ibid.*
24 Uitert, E. van, *Van Gogh in Brabant. Schilderijen en tekeningen uit Etten en Nuenen*, Zwolle 1987, p. 80.

25 Anna van Gogh to Theo van Gogh, Leeuwarden, 24 February 1874; Anna van Gogh to Theo van Gogh, Leeuwarden, 6 January 1874.

26 Anna van Gogh to Theo van Gogh, Leeuwarden, 20 January 1874.

27 Beek, N.A. van, *De Aanteekeningen van Tante Mietje van Gogh*, The Hague 2010, pp. 67, 111, 115.

28 Lies van Gogh to Theo van Gogh, Breda, [undated] 1873.

29 Lies van Gogh to Theo van Gogh, Helvoirt, [undated] 1873.

30 Lies van Gogh to Theo van Gogh, Helvoirt, 20 June 1873.

31 Lies van Gogh, register of the French Day and Boarding School for Young Mistresses (1855–*c.* 1874), Historisch Centrum Leeuwarden, acc. 1312, inv. no. 612.

32 Lies van Gogh to Theo van Gogh, Leeuwarden, 18 October 1874.

33 Anna van Gogh to Theo van Gogh, Leeuwarden, [undated] 1873.

34 Lies van Gogh to Theo van Gogh, Leeuwarden, 11 April 1875.

35 Lies van Gogh to Theo van Gogh, Leeuwarden, 26 April 1875.

36 Lies van Gogh to Theo van Gogh, Tiel, 26 September 1875.

37 Lies van Gogh to Theo van Gogh, Leeuwarden, 11 April 1875; Lies van Gogh to Theo van Gogh, Leeuwarden, 26 April 1875.

38 Lies van Gogh to Theo van Gogh, Tiel, 15 August 1875; Tilborgh, L. van and F. Pabst, 'Notes on a donation: the poetry albums for Elisabeth Huberta van Gogh', *Van Gogh Museum Journal* 1995, p. 89.

39 Lies van Gogh to Theo van Gogh, Leeuwarden, 11 April 1875.

40 *Ibid.*

41 *Ibid.*

42 Anna van Gogh-Carbentus to Theo van Gogh, Helvoirt, 9 April 1875.

43 Smulders, H., 'Van Gogh in Helvoirt', *De Kleine Meijerij*, 41 (1990: 1), p. 9; Dorus van Gogh to the Mayor of Helvoirt, BHIC 's-Hertogenbosch, 19 July 1873.

44 *Ibid.*; Uitert, E. van, *Van Gogh in Brabant. Schilderijen en tekeningen uit Etten en Nuenen*, Zwolle 1987, p. 80.

45 Beek, N.A. van, *De Aanteekeningen van Tante Mietje van Gogh*, The Hague 2010, pp. 66–67, 110.

46 *Ibid.*, p. 111.

47 Dorus van Gogh to Theo van Gogh, Helvoirt, 29 April 1875.

48 Hoffman, W., 'De tantes: wederwaardigheden van een paar "van Goghjes"', *Noord-Brabant: tweemaandelijks magazine voor de provincie*, March/April 1987, pp. 61–64.

49 Lies van Gogh to Theo van Gogh, Helvoirt, about 1 May 1873.

50 *Ibid.*

51 Willemien van Gogh to Theo van Gogh, Helvoirt, end of April 1874.

52 Dorus van Gogh to Theo van Gogh, Helvoirt, 11 May 1873.

53 Vincent van Gogh to Theo van Gogh, Isleworth, 26 August 1876.

54 Lies van Gogh to Theo van Gogh, Tiel, 26 September 1875.

55 Dorus van Gogh to Theo van Gogh, Helvoirt, 11 August 1875.

CHAPTER 5

1 Beers, J. van, *Levensbeelden: Poezij...*, Amsterdam/Antwerp 1858, p. 99; Vincent van Gogh to Caroline and Willem van Stockum-Haanebeek, London, 2 July 1873.

2 Reverend Cornelis van Schaick (1808–1874) was a minister in Holland and in Paramaribo, Suriname, as well as a poet and writer of prose.

3 Vincent van Gogh to Theo van Gogh, The Hague, 9 May 1873.

4 Vincent van Gogh to Theo van Gogh, London, 20 July 1873.

5 Groenhart, K. and W.-J. Verlinden, *Hoe ik van Londen houd. Wandelen door het Londen van Vincent van Gogh*, Amsterdam 2013, pp. 18–19.

6 *Ibid.*, pp. 59–60.

7 Anna van Gogh to Theo van Gogh, Leeuwarden, 24 February 1874.

8 Vincent van Gogh to Caroline and Willem van Stockum-Haanebeek, London, 3 March 1874.

9 Vincent van Gogh to Theo van Gogh, London, 31 July 1874.

10 Beek, N.A. van, *De Aanteekeningen van Tante Mietje van Gogh*, The Hague 2010, pp. 23, 64.

11 Oosterwijk, B., 'Vincent van Gogh en Rotterdam', *Rotterdams Jaarboekje* (1994), pp. 329–89.

12 Vincent van Gogh to Betsy Tersteeg, Helvoirt, 7 July 1874; Bruin, G., *Van Gogh en de Schetsboekjes voor Betsy Tersteeg*, graduation thesis, University of Leiden 2014, p. 28.

13 Anna van Gogh-Carbentus to Theo van Gogh, Etten, 17 February 1876. Moe was having doubts about Vincent's interest in education; he didn't study for his exams while in Holland. But it was

important to her that he make his own choices, and go his own way.

14 Vincent van Gogh to Dorus and Anna van Gogh-Carbentus, Ramsgate, 17 April 1876.

15 Vincent van Gogh to Theo van Gogh, London, 31 July 1874.

16 Dorus van Gogh to Theo van Gogh, Helvoirt, 4 August 1874.

17 Anna van Gogh to Theo van Gogh, London, 30 July 1874.

18 Moe van Gogh to Theo van Gogh, Helvoirt, 15 August 1874.

19 Vincent van Gogh to Theo van Gogh, London, 31 July 1874.

20 Anna van Gogh to Theo van Gogh, Welwyn, 28 April 1875.

21 Anna van Gogh to Theo van Gogh, Welwyn, 28 April 1875; Vincent van Gogh to Theo van Gogh, Etten, 7 April 1877.

22 Anna van Gogh to Theo van Gogh, Welwyn, 28 April 1875.

23 *Ibid.*

24 Anna van Gogh to Theo van Gogh, Welwyn, 28 April 1875; Vincent van Gogh to Theo van Gogh, Etten, 8 April 1877.

25 Anna van Gogh to Theo van Gogh, Welwyn, 28 April 1875.

26 *Ibid.*

27 *Ibid.*; Vincent van Gogh to Theo van Gogh, Etten, 8 April 1877.

28 Vincent van Gogh to Theo van Gogh, Paris, 13 August 1875.

29 Dorus van Gogh to Theo van Gogh, Helvoirt, 11 August 1875.

30 *Ibid.*

31 *Ibid.*

32 Moe van Gogh to Theo van Gogh, Etten, 17 February 1876.

33 Vincent van Gogh to Theo van Gogh, Ramsgate, 26 April 1876. G.H.M. stands for General Holding Mail.

34 Vincent van Gogh to Theo van Gogh, Ramsgate, 28 April 1876.

35 *Ibid.*

36 *Ibid.*

37 Vincent van Gogh to Theo van Gogh, Ramsgate, 6 May 1876.

38 Anna van Gogh to Theo van Gogh, Welwyn, 17 June 1876.

39 Vincent van Gogh to Theo van Gogh, Welwyn, 17 June 1876.

40 Anna van Gogh to Theo van Gogh, Ivy Cottage, Welwyn, 12 October 1876.

CHAPTER 6

1 Willemien van Gogh to Theo van Gogh, Helvoirt, 11 August 1875.

2 Moe van Gogh to Theo van Gogh, Helvoirt, 13 March 1875; Rozemeyer, J.A. (ed.), *Van Gogh in Etten*, Etten-Leur 1990, p. 31; Smulders, H., 'Van Gogh in Helvoirt', *De Kleine Meijerij*, 41 (1990: 1), p. 12; Beek, N.A. van, *De Aanteekeningen van Tante Mietje van Gogh*, The Hague 2010, pp. 67, 111.

3 Moe van Gogh to Theo van Gogh, Helvoirt, 13 March 1875; Rozemeyer, J.A. (ed.), *Van Gogh in Etten*, Etten-Leur 1990, p. 31; Smulders, H., 'Van Gogh in Helvoirt', *De Kleine Meijerij*, 41 (1990: 1), p. 12; Beek, N.A. van, *De Aanteekeningen van Tante Mietje van Gogh*, The Hague 2010, pp. 67, 111.

4 Dorus van Gogh to Theo van Gogh, Helvoirt, 30 July 1875.

5 Dorus van Gogh to the consistory of Etten, Helvoirt, 31 July 1875; Rozemeyer, J.A. (ed.), *Van Gogh in Etten*, Etten-Leur 1990, p. 31.

6 Rozemeyer, J.A. (ed.), *Van Gogh in Etten*, Etten-Leur 1990, pp. 30-31.

7 75 guilders in 1876 was equivalent to €803.95, or £736.95, annually.

8 Rozemeyer, J.A. (ed.), *Van Gogh in Etten*, Etten-Leur 1990, p. 29; 'Voor u is...veel voor heeft.' Dorus van Gogh to Theo van Gogh, Helvoirt, 30 July 1875.

9 Lies van Gogh to Theo van Gogh, Tiel, 15 August 1875; Lies van Gogh to Theo van Gogh, Tiel, 26 September 1875.

10 Lies van Gogh to Theo van Gogh, Tiel, 15 August 1875.

11 Lies van Gogh to Theo van Gogh, Tiel, 26 September 1875.

12 Rozemeyer, J.A. (ed.), *Van Gogh in Etten*, Etten-Leur 1990, pp. 30-31, 33; Uitert, E. van, *Van Gogh in Brabant. Schilderijen en tekeningen uit Etten en Nuenen*, Zwolle 1987, p. 82.

13 Beek, N.A. van, *De Aanteekeningen van Tante Mietje van Gogh*, The Hague 2010, p. 111.

14 Rozemeyer, J.A. (ed.), *Van Gogh in Etten*, Etten-Leur 1990, p. 31.

15 Vincent van Gogh to Theo van Gogh, Etten, 22 July 1878.

16 Rozemeyer, J.A. (ed.), *Van Gogh in Etten*, Etten-Leur 1990, p. 29.

17 *Ibid.*, p. 26.

18 Moe van Gogh to Theo van Gogh, Etten, 6 March 1876.

19 Rozemeyer, J.A. (ed.), *Van Gogh in Etten*, Etten-Leur 1990, pp. 33-34.

20 Willemien van Gogh and Anna van Gogh to Theo van Gogh, Welwyn, 30 January 1876.

21 *Ibid.*
22 Willemien van Gogh to Theo van Gogh, Welwyn, [undated] April 1876.
23 Beek, N.A. van, *De Aanteekeningen van Tante Mietje van Gogh*, The Hague 2010, p. 111.
24 Council reports and printed minutes of the local council of Leeuwarden 1875, with appendices, Historisch Centrum Leeuwarden, acc. 1002, inv. no. 288, pp. 2–3.
25 *Report of the municipal committee on education*, Tiel, February 1872, pp. 5–12.
26 Nelemans, R., *Van Gogh en Brabant*, Schiedam 2012, p. 27, n. 24.
27 *Report of the municipal committee on education*, Tiel, February 1872, p. 7.
28 Lies van Gogh to Theo van Gogh, Tiel, 13 January 1878.
29 Lies van Gogh to Theo van Gogh, Tiel, 7 December 1877.
30 Dorus and Anna van Gogh-Carbentus to Theo van Gogh, Etten, 5 December 1877.
31 Lies van Gogh to Theo van Gogh, Tiel, 7 December 1877.
32 Lies van Gogh to Theo van Gogh, Tiel, 23 September 1877.
33 *Ibid.*
34 Dorus van Gogh to Theo van Gogh, Etten, 10 May 1878; Dorus van Gogh to Theo van Gogh, Etten, 12 May 1878.
35 Lies van Gogh to Theo van Gogh, Tiel, 23 September 1878.
36 *Ibid.*
37 *Ibid.*
38 Lies van Gogh to Theo van Gogh, Dordrecht, 7 December 1878.
39 *Ibid.*
40 *Ibid.*
41 Anna van Gogh to Vincent van Gogh, Welwyn, 30 December 1875.
42 Lies van Gogh to Theo van Gogh, Dordrecht, 21 February 1879.
43 *Ibid.*
44 Anna van Gogh-Carbentus to Theo van Gogh, Etten, 18 April 1879.
45 Beek, N.A. van, *De Aanteekeningen van Tante Mietje van Gogh*, The Hague 2010, p. 112; Weenink-Riem Vis, A., *Mijn oma Elisabeth Huberta van Gogh (1859–1936)*, De Bilt 2003, p. 25.

CHAPTER 7
1 Willemien van Gogh to Vincent and Theo van Gogh, Welwyn, 19 December 1875.
2 Beek, N.A. van, *De Aanteekeningen van Tante*

Mietje van Gogh*, The Hague 2010, p. 111; Uitert, E. van, *Van Gogh in Brabant. Schilderijen en tekeningen uit Etten en Nuenen*, Zwolle 1987, p. 83.
3 Beek, N.A. van, *De Aanteekeningen van Tante Mietje van Gogh*, The Hague 2010, p. 111.
4 Vincent van Gogh to Dorus and Anna van Gogh-Carbentus, Ramsgate, 17 April 1876.
5 *Ibid.*; Vincent van Gogh to Theo van Gogh, Ramsgate, 17 April 1876.
6 Vincent van Gogh to Dorus and Anna van Gogh-Carbentus, Ramsgate, 17 April 1876.
7 Vincent van Gogh to Theo van Gogh, Isleworth, 25 November 1876.
8 Vincent van Gogh to Theo van Gogh, Isleworth, 7 and 8 October 1876.
9 Beek, N.A. van, *De Aanteekeningen van Tante Mietje van Gogh*, The Hague 2010, p. 111.
10 Dorus van Gogh to Theo van Gogh, Etten, 12 May 1876.
11 Vincent van Gogh to Theo van Gogh, Ramsgate, 12 May 1876; Janssen, H. and W. van Sinderen, *De Haagse School*, Zwolle 1997, pp. 88–93.
12 Rozemeyer, J.A. (ed.), *Van Gogh in Etten*, Etten-Leur 1990, p. 35; Kools, F., *Vincent van Gogh en zijn geboorteplaats – als een boer van Zundert*, De Walburg Pers 1990, pp. 121–22.
13 Vincent van Gogh to Theo van Gogh, Isleworth, 3 October 1876.
14 Vincent van Gogh to Theo van Gogh, Isleworth, 25 November 1876.
15 *Ibid.*
16 *Ibid.*
17 Willemien van Gogh to Theo van Gogh, Etten, *c.* 17 December 1876.
18 Vincent van Gogh to Theo van Gogh, Etten, 31 December 1876.
19 Anna van Gogh to Theo van Gogh, Welwyn, 12 October 1876.
20 Vincent van Gogh to Theo van Gogh, Etten, 31 December 1876.
21 Lies van Gogh to Theo van Gogh, Tiel, 18 August 1876.
22 Dorus van Gogh to Theo van Gogh, Etten, 19 February 1877.
23 Beek, N.A. van, *De Aanteekeningen van Tante Mietje van Gogh*, The Hague 2010, p. 112.
24 Dorus van Gogh to Theo van Gogh, Etten, 9 July 1877.
25 Vincent van Gogh to Theo van Gogh, Amsterdam, 15 July 1877.
26 Dorus van Gogh to Theo van Gogh, Etten, 9 July 1877.

27 Dorus van Gogh and Anna van Gogh-Carbentus to Theo van Gogh, Etten, 5 August 1878.
28 Vincent van Gogh to Theo van Gogh, Etten, 5 August 1878.
29 Dorus van Gogh to Theo van Gogh, Etten, 24 June 1878.
30 Dorus van Gogh and Anna van Gogh-Carbentus to Theo van Gogh, Etten, 5 August 1878.
31 Dorus van Gogh and Anna van Gogh-Carbentus to Theo van Gogh, Etten, 5 August 1878.
32 *Ibid.*
33 *Ibid.*
34 *Ibid.*
35 Dorus and Anna van Gogh-Carbentus to Theo van Gogh, Etten, 21 August 1878.
36 Joan van Houten to Theo van Gogh, Etten, 14 August 1878.
37 Anna van Gogh-Carbentus to Theo van Gogh, Etten, [undated] August 1878; Joan van Houten to Theo van Gogh, Etten, 14 August 1878.
38 Joan van Houten to Theo van Gogh, Etten, 14 August 1878.
39 Johannes Bernardus van Houten was born in Amsterdam on 21 October 1805, and died in Hengelo on 30 June 1878, less than two months before his son's marriage to Anna van Gogh in Etten on 22 August 1878.
40 Dorus van Gogh to Theo van Gogh, Etten, 15 August 1878.
41 Dorus and Anna van Gogh-Carbentus to Theo van Gogh, Etten, 21 August 1878.
42 *Ibid.*
43 Dorus van Gogh to Theo van Gogh, Etten, 24 August 1878.
44 Anna van Gogh-Carbentus to Theo van Gogh, Etten, 24 August 1878.
45 Beek, N.A. van, *De Aanteekeningen van Tante Mietje van Gogh*, The Hague 2010, p. 111.
46 *Ibid.*
47 Vincent van Gogh to Theo van Gogh, Amsterdam, 12 June 1877; Vincent van Gogh to Hermanus Tersteeg, Amsterdam, 3 August 1877.
48 Vincent van Gogh to Theo van Gogh, Amsterdam, 27 July 1877.
49 Vincent van Gogh to Theo van Gogh, Brussels, 15 October 1880.
50 Beek, N.A. van, *De Aanteekeningen van Tante Mietje van Gogh*, The Hague 2010, p. 112.
51 Rozemeyer, J.A. (ed.), *Van Gogh in Etten*, Etten-Leur 1990, p. 42.
52 Beek, N.A. van, *De Aanteekeningen van Tante Mietje van Gogh*, The Hague 2010, p. 112.
53 Uitert, E. van, *Van Gogh in Brabant. Schilderijen en tekeningen uit Etten en Nuenen*, Zwolle 1987, pp. 196–97; Nelemans, R. and R. Dirven, *De Zaaier, het begin van een carrière*, Vincent van Gogh in Etten, Uitgeverij Van Kemenade – Breda 2010, p. 110; Tilborgh, L. van, 'Letter from Willemien van Gogh', *Van Gogh Bulletin* 3 (1992–93), p. 21.
54 Lies van Gogh to Saar and An van Houten, 1920s.
55 Beek, N.A. van, *De Aanteekeningen van Tante Mietje van Gogh*, The Hague 2010, p. 112.
56 *Ibid.*; Vincent van Gogh to Theo van Gogh, Etten, end of June 1881.
57 Vincent van Gogh to Theo van Gogh, Etten, end of June 1881.
58 Beek, N.A. van, *De Aanteekeningen van Tante Mietje van Gogh*, The Hague 2010, p. 113.
59 Vincent van Gogh to Willemien van Gogh, Arles, 12 November 1888; Vincent van Gogh to Theo van Gogh, Arles, 1 December 1888.
60 Vincent van Gogh to Willemien van Gogh, Arles, 12 November 1888.
61 *Ibid.*
62 Vincent van Gogh to Theo van Gogh, Arles, 9 or 10 October 1888.

CHAPTER 8
1 Uitert, E. van, *Van Gogh in Brabant. Schilderijen en tekeningen uit Etten en Nuenen*, Zwolle 1987, p. 84.
2 *Ibid.*
3 Beek, N.A. van, *De Aanteekeningen van Tante Mietje van Gogh*, The Hague 2010, p. 70.
4 Uitert, E. van, *Van Gogh in Brabant. Schilderijen en tekeningen uit Etten en Nuenen*, Zwolle 1987, p. 84; Beek, N.A. van, *De Aanteekeningen van Tante Mietje van Gogh*, The Hague 2010, p. 113.
5 Dorus van Gogh to Theo van Gogh, Nuenen, 19 July 1884.
6 *Ibid.*
7 *Ibid.*
8 *Ibid.*
9 Uitert, E. van, *Van Gogh in Brabant. Schilderijen en tekeningen uit Etten en Nuenen*, Zwolle 1987, p. 84.
10 Beek, N.A. van, *De Aanteekeningen van Tante Mietje van Gogh*, The Hague 2010, p. 70.
11 Uitert, E. van, *Van Gogh in Brabant. Schilderijen en tekeningen uit Etten en Nuenen*, Zwolle 1987, pp. 102–27.
12 *Ibid.*
13 Vincent van Gogh to Theo van Gogh, Nuenen, 9 April 1885.
14 Vincent van Gogh to Theo van Gogh, Amsterdam, 28 May 1877; Margaretha Meijboom to Willemien van Gogh, location unknown, after 10 September 1889.

15 Margaretha Meijboom to Willemien van Gogh, The Hague, 6 March 1887.
16 *Ibid.*
17 Mietje van Gogh to Theo van Gogh, Nuenen, 12 February 1883.
18 *Ibid.*
19 Beek, N.A. van, *De Aanteekeningen van Tante Mietje van Gogh*, The Hague 2010, p. 113.
20 Lies van Gogh to Theo van Gogh, Nuenen, 9 December 1883.
21 Beek, N.A. van, *De Aanteekeningen van Tante Mietje van Gogh*, The Hague 2010, pp. 74–75, 113.
22 Vincent van Gogh to Theo van Gogh, Nuenen, 2 March 1884.
23 *Ibid.*
24 Beek, N.A van, *De Aanteekeningen van Tante Mietje van Gogh*, The Hague 2010, p. 113.
25 *Ibid.*
26 *Ibid.*, pp. 75, 113.
27 Dorus van Gogh to Theo van Gogh, Nuenen, 30 December 1884.
28 *Ibid.*
29 Anna van Gogh-Carbentus to Theo van Gogh, Nuenen, 21 January 1885.
30 Vincent van Gogh to Theo van Gogh, Nuenen, 2 July 1884.
31 Dorus van Gogh to Theo van Gogh, Nuenen, 19 July 1884.
32 Vincent van Gogh to Theo van Gogh, Nuenen, 3 February 1884.
33 Dorus van Gogh to Theo van Gogh, Nuenen, 30 December 1884.
34 *Ibid.*
35 Du Quesne-van Gogh, E.H., *Vincent van Gogh – persoonlijke herinneringen aangaande een kunstenaar*, Baarn 1910, pp. 75–76; Du Quesne-van Gogh, E.H., *Vincent van Gogh – herinneringen aan haar broeder*, Baarn 1923, p. 55.
36 Dorus van Gogh to Theo van Gogh, Nuenen, 19 February 1885.
37 Vincent van Gogh to Theo van Gogh, Nuenen, 30 April 1884.
38 Anna van Gogh-Carbentus to Theo van Gogh, Nuenen, [undated] September 1885.
39 Anna van Gogh-Carbentus and Willemien van Gogh to Theo van Gogh, Nuenen, 25 March 1885.
40 *Ibid.*
41 Du Quesne-van Gogh, E.H., *Vincent van Gogh. Persoonlijke herinneringen aangaande een kunstenaar*, Baarn 1910, p. 95; Du Quesne-van Gogh, E.H., *Vincent van Gogh, Herinneringen aan haar Broeder*, Baarn 1923, pp. 53–54.
42 Du Quesne-van Gogh, E.H., *Vincent van Gogh, Herinneringen aan haar Broeder*, Baarn 1923, pp. 39–40.
43 Willemien van Gogh to Line Kruysse, Nuenen, 26 August 1886.
44 Original document at RHC Eindhoven, coll. no. 10237; Notary Archives, Nuenen 1811–1898, inv. no. 95.
45 Testament of Theodorus van Gogh from 21 May 1851 at The Hague with Cornelis Johannes van de Watering; Uitert, E. van, *Van Gogh in Brabant. Schilderijen en tekeningen uit Etten en Nuenen*, Zwolle 1987, p. 89.
46 Uitert, E. van, *Van Gogh in Brabant. Schilderijen en tekeningen uit Etten en Nuenen*, Zwolle 1987, pp. 86–89.
47 *Ibid.*, p. 88.
48 Vincent van Gogh to Theo van Gogh, Antwerp, 29 January 1886.
49 *Ibid.*

CHAPTER 9

1 Lies van Gogh to Jo van Gogh-Bonger, Soesterberg, 17 November 1885.
2 Beek, N.A. van, *De Aanteekeningen van Tante Mietje van Gogh*, The Hague 2010, p. 112.
3 Jo Bonger to Lies van Gogh, Elburg, 13 October 1885.
4 Lies van Gogh to Jo Bonger, Soesterberg, 21 October 1885.
5 *Ibid.*
6 *Ibid.*
7 Lies van Gogh to Jo Bonger, Soesterberg, 6 November 1885.
8 Jo Bonger to Lies van Gogh, Elburg, 15 November 1885.
9 Lies van Gogh to Jo Bonger, Soesterberg, 17 November 1885.
10 Lies van Gogh to Jo Bonger, Soesterberg, 6 November 1885.
11 Lies van Gogh to Jo Bonger, Soesterberg, 17 November 1885.
12 Lies van Gogh to Jo Bonger, Soesterberg, 15 November 1885.
13 Jo Bonger to Lies van Gogh, Elburg, 13 October 1885.
14 Jo Bonger to Lies van Gogh, Elburg, 1 November 1885.
15 *Ibid.*
16 Lies van Gogh to Jo Bonger, Soesterberg, 6 November 1885.
17 Lies van Gogh to Jo Bonger, Soesterberg, 21 January 1886.

18 Jo Bonger to Lies van Gogh, Amsterdam,
21 February 1886.
19 Lies van Gogh to Jo Bonger, Soesterberg,
17 November 1885.
20 Lies van Gogh to Jo Bonger, Soesterberg,
21 October 1885.
21 Ibid.
22 Theo van Gogh to Lies van Gogh, Paris,
13 October 1885.
23 Jo Bonger to Lies van Gogh, Amsterdam,
1 November 1885.
24 Lies van Gogh to Jo Bonger, Soesterberg,
10 January 1886.
25 Jo Bonger to Lies van Gogh, Amsterdam,
19 January 1886.
26 Lies van Gogh to Jo Bonger, Soesterberg,
21 January 1886.
27 Jo Bonger to Lies van Gogh, Amsterdam,
21 February 1886.
28 Vincent van Gogh to Willemien van Gogh, Paris,
late October 1887.
29 Vincent van Gogh to Theo van Gogh, Ramsgate,
12 May 1876.
30 Vincent van Gogh to Theo van Gogh, Etten,
5 August 1881.
31 Vincent van Gogh to Theo van Gogh, Etten, on
or about 23 December 1881; Vincent van Gogh
to Theo van Gogh, The Hague, 16 May 1882.
The quote is from Eduard Douwes Dekker's
(Multatuli's) 'Prayer of an unbeliever. From the
diary of a madman', The Hague 1861.
32 Vincent van Gogh to Theo van Gogh. The Hague,
on or about 15 February 1883.
33 Vincent van Gogh to Theo van Gogh. The
Hague, on or about Monday, 11 December 1882;
Groenhart, K. and W.-J. Verlinden, Hoe ik van
Londen houd, Amsterdam 2013, pp. 34–36.
34 Vincent van Gogh to Willemien van Gogh, Arles,
between 28 April and 2 May 1889.
35 Vincent van Gogh to Willemien van Gogh, Saint-
Rémy-de-Provence, on or about 23 December
1889. The poem is 'Who is the maid?' by Thomas
Moore (1779–1852).
36 Vincent van Gogh to Willemien van Gogh, Arles,
on or about 26 August 1888.
37 Ibid.
38 Willemien van Gogh to Theo van Gogh,
Middelharnis, 19 October 1888.
39 Vincent van Gogh to Willemien van Gogh, Paris,
late October 1887.
40 Vincent van Gogh to Willemien van Gogh, Arles,
on or around 12 November 1888.
41 Lies van Gogh to Theo van Gogh, Tiel,
26 September 1875.

CHAPTER 10
1 Van Overbruggen, P. and J. Thielemans, Van
Domineeshuis tot van Goghhuis 1764–2014,
Protestantse Gemeente Nuenen 2014, p. 95.
2 Dirven, R. and K. Wouters, Verloren vondsten, het
mysterie van de Bredase kisten, Breda 2003, p. 12.
3 Ibid., pp. 14–15.
4 Ibid., pp. 15, 16; Beek, N.A. van, De Aanteekeningen
van Tante Mietje van Gogh, The Hague, 2010,
p. 83.
5 Theo van Gogh to Lies van Gogh, Paris,
13 October 1885.
6 Dirven, R. and K. Wouters, Verloren vondsten,
het mysterie van de Bredase kisten, Breda 2003,
p. 12; Beek, N.A. van, De Aanteekeningen van Tante
Mietje van Gogh, The Hague 2010, p. 110; Uitert, E.
van, Van Gogh in Brabant. Schilderijen en tekeningen
uit Etten en Nuenen, Zwolle 1987, p. 76.
7 Weenink-Riem Vis, A., Mijn oma Elisabeth Huberta
van Gogh (1859–1936), De Bilt 2003, pp. 22, 29.
8 Lies van Gogh to Moe, Cor and Willemien van
Gogh, Coutances, 8 July 1886.
9 Lies van Gogh to Moe, Cor and Willemien van
Gogh, Carteret, 30 July 1886.
10 Stokvis, B., Lijden zonder klagen. Het tragische
levenslot van Hubertina van Gogh, Baarn 1969,
pp. 5–11.
11 Du Quesne-van Gogh, E.H., Proza, Baarn 1929;
Weenink-Riem Vis, A., Mijn oma Elisabeth Huberta
van Gogh (1859–1936), De Bilt 2003, p. 50.
12 Weenink-Riem Vis, A., Mijn oma Elisabeth Huberta
van Gogh (1859–1936), De Bilt 2003, pp. 29–30.
13 Lies van Gogh to Moe van Gogh, La-Haye-du-
Puits, 7 August 1886; Weenink-Riem Vis, A.,
Mijn oma Elisabeth Huberta van Gogh (1859–1936),
De Bilt 2003, p. 29.
14 Anna van Gogh-Carbentus to Theo van Gogh,
Etten, [undated] August 1878.
15 Margaretha Meijboom to Willemien van Gogh,
The Hague, 28 April 1887.
16 Margaretha Meijboom to Willemien van Gogh,
after 28 April 1887.
17 Willemien van Gogh, De Hollandsche Lelie,
Weekblad voor Jonge Dames, September 1887 (1).
18 Margaretha Meijboom to Willemien van Gogh,
The Hague, 22 April 1887.
19 Dirven, R. and K. Wouters, Verloren vondsten, het
mysterie van de Bredase kisten, Breda 2003, p. 18.
20 Ibid., pp. 16–17.
21 Ibid.; Vincent van Gogh to Willemien van Gogh,
Arles, between 16 and 20 June 1888.
22 Margaretha Meijboom to Willemien van Gogh,
The Hague, 25 April 1888.

23 Dirven, R. and K. Wouters, *Verloren vondsten, het mysterie van de Bredase kisten*, Breda 2003, pp. 16–18.
24 Vincent van Gogh to Willemien van Gogh, Arles, between 16 and 20 June 1888.
25 Testament of Vincent van Gogh, copy by Mr. J.C.L. Esser, notary at Princenhage, 10 October 1889.
26 Dirven, R. and K. Wouters, *Verloren vondsten, het mysterie van de Bredase kisten*, Breda 2003, pp. 16–18.
27 Margaretha Meijboom to Willemien van Gogh, The Hague, 1 October 1889.
28 *Ibid.*
29 Willemien van Gogh to Theo van Gogh, Middelharnis, 19 October 1889.
30 Cor van der Slist also appears in Willemien's poetry album as the author of one of the rhymes.
31 Dirven, R. and K. Wouters, *Verloren vondsten, het mysterie van de Bredase kisten*, Breda 2003, p. 18; Anna van Gogh-Carbentus to Theo van Gogh, Breda, 25 October 1888.
32 Willemien van Gogh to Jo Bonger, Breda, 10 February 1889.
33 Theo van Gogh to Jo Bonger, Paris, 22 February 1889.

CHAPTER 11
1 Theo van Gogh to Lies and Willemien van Gogh, Paris, 24 January 1889.
2 Beek, N.A. van, *De Aanteekeningen van Tante Mietje van Gogh*, The Hague 2010, p. 93; Willemien van Gogh to Jo Bonger, Breda, 2 October 1889.
3 Willemien van Gogh to Theo van Gogh, Breda, 16 March 1889.
4 Lies van Gogh to Jo Bonger, Soesterberg, 21 January 1886.
5 Diary of Jo Bonger, Amsterdam, 25 July 1887.
6 *Ibid.*
7 There doesn't seem to be any direct communication between Theo van Gogh and his mother regarding his feelings towards Jo Bonger until the engagement party at her parents' house on 9 January 1889.
8 Druick, D.W. and P. Kort Zegers, *Van Gogh en Gauguin. Het atelier van het zuiden*, Zwolle 2002, p. 260.
9 Vincent van Gogh and Dr Félix Rey to Theo van Gogh, Arles, 2 January 1889.
10 Theo van Gogh and Jo Bonger posted Vincent a copy of their printed engagement announcement on 6 January 1889.
11 Willemien van Gogh to Theo van Gogh, Breda, 16 March 1889.

12 *Ibid.*
13 *Ibid.*
14 Beek, N.A. van, *De Aanteekeningen van Tante Mietje van Gogh*, The Hague 2010, p. 92.
15 Jo Bonger to Lies and Willemien van Gogh, Paris, 26 April 1889.
16 *Ibid.*
17 *Ibid.*
18 Naifeh, S. and G. White Smith, *Vincent van Gogh, De Biografie*, Amsterdam 2011, pp. 598–602; Stolwijk, C. and R. Thomson, *Theo van Gogh, 1857–1891. Kunsthandelaar, verzamelaar en broer van Vincent*, Zwolle 1999, pp. 39–40.
19 Vincent van Gogh to Willemien van Gogh, Arles, between 9 and 14 September 1888.
20 Vincent van Gogh to Willemien van Gogh, Arles, 21 or 22 August 1888.
21 Vincent van Gogh to Theo van Gogh, Arles, 3 September 1888.
22 Vincent van Gogh to Theo van Gogh, Arles, 3 April 1888. By 'Petit Boulevard' Vincent was referring to the Parisian neighbourhood around boulevard de Clichy and boulevard de Rochechouart in Montmartre, where the younger painters, like Seurat, Guillaumin, Gauguin, as also De Toulouse-Lautrec, Signac, Lucien Pissarro and himself worked and exhibited in the cafés; Homburg, C. *et al.*, *Vincent van Gogh and the Painters of the Petit Boulevard*, New York/Frankfurt 2001.
23 Vincent van Gogh to Willemien van Gogh, Arles, 30 March 1888. This painting was indeed in the possession of Willemien; see Stolwijk, C. and H. Veenenbos, *The Account Book of Theo van Gogh and Jo van Gogh-Bonger*, Amsterdam/Leiden 2002, p. 20, n. 33.
24 Stolwijk, C. and H. Veenenbos, *The Account Book of Theo van Gogh and Jo van Gogh-Bonger*, Amsterdam/Leiden 2002, p. 20, n. 33.
25 Vincent van Gogh to Willemien van Gogh, Arles, 30 March 1888.
26 Margaretha Meijboom to Willemien van Gogh, [date and location unknown] 1888.
27 Willemien van Gogh to Theo van Gogh, Middelharnis, autumn 1888.
28 Margaretha Meijboom to Willemien van Gogh, [location unknown], 19 October 1888.
29 Willemien van Gogh to Theo van Gogh and Jo Bonger, Middelharnis, 13 September 1889.
30 Willemien van Gogh to Jo Bonger, Breda, 2 October 1889; Dirven, R. and K. Wouters, *Verloren vondsten, het mysterie van de Bredase kisten*, Breda 2003, pp. 21–22.

31 Vincent van Gogh to Anna van Gogh-Carbentus, Saint-Rémy-de-Provence, 19 September 1889.

32 Anna van Gogh-Carbentus to Theo van Gogh and Jo Bonger, Leiden, between 26 and 29 November 1889.

33 U. Vroom, *Stoomwasserij en kalkbranderij*, Unieboek Bussum 1983, pp. 24–30.

34 Theo van Gogh to Willemien van Gogh, Paris, before 2 January 1890.

35 Jo Bonger to Vincent van Gogh, Paris, 5 July 1889.

36 Vincent van Gogh to Willemien van Gogh, Arles, 30 March 1889 and Vincent van Gogh to Willemien van Gogh, Arles, between 16 and 20 June 1888. Vincent states his position on the World Exhibition: 'Next year will be rather important. Just as the French are undeniably the masters in literature, so it is in painting too, in modern art history there are names like Delacroix, Millet, Corot, Courbet, Daumier, who dominate everything that was produced in other countries. Yet the clique of painters who currently stand at the head of the official art world is resting on the laurels won by those earlier men, and is in itself of much lesser calibre. So *they* can't do much at the forthcoming World Exhibition to help French art retain that importance it's had until now. Next year the attention, not of the public – who naturally look at everything without wondering about the history – but the attention of those who are well informed, will be attracted by the retrospective exhibition of the paintings of the great men who are already dead, and by the Impressionists.'

37 Vincent van Gogh to Willemien van Gogh, Arles, 30 March 1889.

38 Vincent van Gogh to Willemien van Gogh, Arles, 21 or 22 August 1888.

39 Vincent van Gogh to Willemien van Gogh, Saint-Rémy-de-Provence, 4 January 1890.

40 Vincent van Gogh to Willemien van Gogh, Arles, 20 January 1890.

41 *Ibid.*

42 Vincent van Gogh to Willemien van Gogh, Saint-Rémy-de-Provence, 4 January 1890.

43 *Ibid.*

44 *Ibid.*

45 *Ibid.*

46 Vincent van Gogh to Willemien van Gogh, Saint-Rémy-de-Provence, 19 February 1890.

47 Stolwijk, C. and R. Thomson, *Theo van Gogh, 1857–1891. Kunsthandelaar, verzamelaar en broer van Vincent*, Zwolle 1999, pp. 107–10.

48 Vincent van Gogh to Willemien van Gogh, Saint-Rémy-de-Provence, 19 February 1890; Stolwijk, C. and R. Thomson, *Theo van Gogh, 1857–1891. Kunsthandelaar, verzamelaar en broer van Vincent*, Zwolle 1999, pp. 107–10.

49 Theo van Gogh to Vincent van Gogh, Paris, 9 February 1890.

50 *Ibid.*

51 Stolwijk, C. and R. Thomson, *Theo van Gogh, 1857–1891. Kunsthandelaar, verzamelaar en broer van Vincent*, Zwolle 1999, pp. 108–9.

52 Beek, N.A. van, *De Aantekeningen van Tante Mietje van Gogh*, The Hague 2010, p. 93.

53 Theo van Gogh to Moe and Willemien van Gogh, Paris, 15 April 1890.

54 Anna van Houten-van Gogh to Jo Bonger, Dennenoord, 1 August 1890.

55 Theo van Gogh to Vincent van Gogh, Paris, 9 February 1890.

CHAPTER 12

1 Vincent van Gogh to Willemien van Gogh, Arles, 16 and 20 June 1888.

2 Anna van Gogh to Vincent van Gogh, Welwyn, 30 December 1875.

3 Vincent van Gogh to Theo van Gogh, Amsterdam, 4 September 1877.

4 Lies van Gogh to Theo van Gogh, Etten, 23 September 1877.

5 Vincent van Gogh to Willemien van Gogh, Paris, late October 1887.

6 *Ibid.*

7 Vincent van Gogh to Theo van Gogh, Nuenen, 2 June 1885.

8 Vincent van Gogh to Anthon van Rappard, Nuenen, 20 January 1884; Vincent van Gogh to Willemien van Gogh, Arles, between 28 April and 1 May 1889.

9 Vincent van Gogh to Willemien van Gogh, Arles, between 28 April and 2 May 1889.

10 Margaretha Meijboom to Willemien van Gogh, Assen, 27 September 1887.

11 Margaretha Meijboom to Willemien van Gogh, Assen, 14 November 1887.

12 Margaretha Meijboom to Willemien van Gogh, The Hague, [undated] 1888.

13 Margaretha Meijboom to Willemien van Gogh, Assen, 14 November 1887.

14 Vincent van Gogh to Willemien van Gogh, Paris, late October 1887; Margaretha Meijboom to Willemien van Gogh, Assen, 14 November 1887.

15 Vincent van Gogh to Willemien van Gogh, Arles, 31 July 1888.

16 Beek, N.A. van, *De Aanteekeningen van Tante Mietje van Gogh*, The Hague 2010, pp. 74, 113.

17 Vincent van Gogh to Willemien van Gogh, Arles, 28 April and 2 May 1889.

18 *Ibid.*

19 *Ibid.*; Charles Dickens, *Nicholas Nickleby*, Chapman & Hall, London, 1838, chapter 6, 'The Baron of Grogzwig', p. 80: 'And my advice to all men is, that if ever they become hipped and melancholy from similar causes (as very many men do), they look at both sides of the question, applying a magnifying glass to the best one; and if they still feel tempted to retire without leave, that they smoke a large pipe and drink a full bottle first, and profit by the laudable example of the Baron of Grogzwig.'

20 Vincent van Gogh to Willemien van Gogh, Saint-Rémy-de-Provence, 21 October 1889.

21 There is no explicit mention of Clara Carbentus (1817–1866) being epileptic in the *Carbentus-kroniek*.

22 Vincent van Gogh to Willemien van Gogh, Saint-Rémy-de-Provence, 20 January 1890.

23 Vincent van Gogh to Willemien van Gogh, Arles, between 16 and 20 June 1888.

24 *Ibid.*

25 Vincent van Gogh to Willemien van Gogh, Arles, 31 July 1888.

26 *Ibid.*

27 Vincent van Gogh to Willemien van Gogh, Arles, 30 March 1888.

28 Vincent van Gogh to Willemien van Gogh, Arles, 16 and 20 June 1888.

29 Vincent van Gogh to Willemien van Gogh, Saint-Rémy-de-Provence, 19 September 1889.

30 Stolwijk, C. and H. Veenenbos, *The Account Book of Theo van Gogh and Jo van Gogh-Bonger*, Leiden 2002, p. 20.

31 Vincent van Gogh to Willemien van Gogh, Saint-Rémy-de Provence, 21 October 1889.

32 *Ibid.*

33 Vincent van Gogh to Willemien van Gogh, Saint-Rémy-de Provence, 9 or 10 December 1889.

34 Vincent van Gogh to Theo van Gogh, Saint-Rémy-de-Provence, 19 December 1889; Vincent van Gogh to Theo van Gogh, Saint-Rémy-de-Provence, 28 September 1899; Vincent van Gogh to Theo van Gogh, Saint-Rémy-de-Provence, 4 January 1890.

35 Vincent van Gogh to Theo van Gogh, Saint-Rémy-de-Provence, 28 September 1899.

36 Vincent van Gogh to Willemien van Gogh, Saint-Rémy-de-Provence, 23 December 1889.

37 Vincent van Gogh to Willemien van Gogh, Saint-Rémy-de-Provence, 4 January 1890.

38 Vincent van Gogh to Willemien van Gogh, Saint-Rémy-de-Provence, 20 January 1890.

39 Vincent van Gogh to Theo van Gogh, Auvers-sur-Oise, 24 June 1890.

40 Vincent van Gogh to Willemien van Gogh, Saint-Rémy-de-Provence, 19 February 1890.

41 Vincent van Gogh to Willemien van Gogh, Saint-Remy-de-Provence, 16 June 1889.

42 Vincent van Gogh to Willemien van Gogh, Auvers-sur-Oise, 13 June 1890.

CHAPTER 13

1 Margaretha Meijboom to Willemien van Gogh, The Hague, 20 March 1889.

2 Theo van Gogh to Vincent van Gogh, Paris, 29 March 1890; Vincent van Gogh to Theo van Gogh, Saint-Rémy-de-Provence, 5 October 1889; Theo van Gogh to Vincent van Gogh, Paris, 4 October 1889. Theo points out that Camille Pissarro (1830–1903) is the link between him (later Vincent) and the doctor Paul-Ferdinand Gachet in Auvers-sur-Oise.

3 Vincent van Gogh to Theo van Gogh and Jo Bonger, Auvers-sur-Oise, 20 May 1890.

4 Vincent van Gogh to Anna van Gogh-Carbentus, Saint-Rémy-de-Provence, 19 February 1890; Vincent van Gogh to Willemien van Gogh, Saint-Rémy-de-Provence, 19 February 1890; Vincent van Gogh to Theo van Gogh, Saint-Rémy-de-Provence, 17 March 1890.

5 Vincent van Gogh to Theo van Gogh and Jo Bonger, Auvers-sur-Oise, 10 June 1890.

6 Vincent van Gogh to Theo van Gogh, Auvers-sur-Oise, 3 June 1890.

7 Vincent van Gogh to Willemien van Gogh, Auvers-sur-Oise, 5 June 1890.

8 Theo van Gogh to Vincent van Gogh, Paris, 30 June and 1 July 1890.

9 Druick, D.W. and P. Kort Zegers, *Van Gogh en Gauguin. Het atelier van het zuiden*, Zwolle 2002, p. 331.

10 Vincent van Gogh to Theo van Gogh and Jo Bonger, Auvers-sur-Oise, 10 July 1890.

11 *Ibid.*

12 *Naamlijst van de verpleegsters en dienstpersoneel (List of names of the nurses and staff) 1887–1924*, Erfgoed Leiden en Omstreken (ELO), Archieven Waalse Gemeente Leiden (Archives of the Walloon Community in Leiden), acc. 0535, inv. no. 401.

13 Vincent van Gogh to Willemien van Gogh, Auvers-sur-Oise, 5 June 1890.

14 Vincent van Gogh to Anna van Gogh-Carbentus
    and Willemien van Gogh, Auvers-sur-Oise,
    between 10 and 14 July 1890.
15 Lunsingh Scheurleer, Th.H., C. Willemijn Fock
    and A.J. van Dissel, *Het Rapenburg. Geschiedenis
    van een Leidse gracht*, Leiden 1989, vol. 4a, pp.
    147–48; Rijksdienst voor het Cultureel Erfgoed
    (Cultural Heritage Agency of the Netherlands).
16 Willemien van Gogh to Theo van Gogh, Leiden,
    [undated] June 1890.
17 Willemien van Gogh to Jo Bonger, Leiden,
    26 June 1890.
18 *Ibid.*
19 Paul-Ferdinand Gachet to Theo van Gogh,
    Auvers-sur-Oise, 27 July 1890, in Pickvance, R.,
    'A Great Artist is Dead', Zwolle 1992, pp. 26–27.
20 Pickvance, R., *'A Great Artist is Dead'*, Zwolle 1992,
    p. 27.
21 Stolwijk, C. and R. Thomson, *Theo van Gogh
    1857–1891*, Amsterdam/Zwolle 2000, p. 56, n.
    164; John Rewald, 'Theo van Gogh, Goupil and
    Impressionists', *Gazette des Beaux-Arts* 81 (1973)
    pp. 9, 72 76–77.
22 Anna van Gogh-Carbentus to Theo van Gogh,
    Leiden, 31 July 1890, in Pickvance, R., *'A Great
    Artist is Dead'*, Zwolle 1992, pp. 48–51; Beek, N.A.
    van, *De Aantekeningen van tante Mietje van Gogh*,
    The Hague 2010, p. 94.
23 Anna van Gogh-Carbentus to Jo Bonger, Leiden,
    31 July 1890.
24 Joan van Houten to Theo van Gogh, Leiden,
    31 July 1890, in Pickvance, R., *'A Great Artist is
    Dead'*, Zwolle 1992, pp. 45–47.
25 Anna van Gogh-Carbentus to Theo van Gogh,
    Leiden, 31 July 1890, in Pickvance, R., *'A Great
    Artist is Dead'*, Zwolle 1992, pp. 48–51.
26 Willemien van Gogh to Theo van Gogh, Leiden,
    31 July 1890.
27 Anna van Houten-van Gogh to Jo Bonger,
    Mastbos, 1 August 1890.
28 Lies was referring to Jan Aarsen (1805–1877). The
    family name also occurs as Aertsen or Aartsen.
29 Lies van Gogh to Theo van Gogh, Leiden,
    2 August 1890, in Pickvance, R., *'A Great Artist is
    Dead'*, Zwolle 1992, pp. 67–71.
30 *Ibid.*
31 Theo van Gogh to Lies van Gogh, Paris, 5 August
    1890, in Pickvance, R., *'A Great Artist is Dead'*,
    Zwolle 1992, pp. 72–73.
32 Naifeh, S. and G. White Smith, *Vincent van Gogh,
    De Biografie*, Amsterdam 2011, p. 972.
33 Émile Bernard to Gustave-Albert Aurier, Paris,
    31 July 1890, in Pickvance, R., *'A Great Artist is

Dead'*, Zwolle 1992, pp. 32–34.
34 *Ibid.*, pp. 32–38.
35 Anna van Gogh-Carbentus to Theo van Gogh,
    Breda, 29 December 1888.
36 Theo van Gogh to Anna van Gogh-Carbentus,
    Paris, 1 August 1890.
37 Cor van Gogh to Theo and Jo van Gogh-Bonger,
    Johannesburg, 8 October 1890.
38 Pickvance, R., *'A Great Artist is Dead'*, Zwolle 1992,
    pp. 74–79.
39 Paul Gauguin to Theo van Gogh, Paris,
    2 August 1890.
40 Anthon van Rappard to Anna van Gogh-
    Carbentus, Santpoort-Noord, date unknown, in
    Pickvance, R., *'A Great Artist is Dead'*, Zwolle 1992,
    pp. 102–3.
41 Isaac Lazarus Israëls to Theo van Gogh,
    Amsterdam, 17 August 1890, in Pickvance, R.,
    'A Great Artist is Dead', Zwolle 1992, p. 94.
42 Isaac de Haan Meijer to Theo van Gogh, around
    2 August 1890, in Pickvance, R., *'A Great Artist is
    Dead'*, Zwolle 1992, pp. 83–84.
43 Rabinow, R.A. (ed.), *Cézanne to Picasso: Ambroise
    Vollard, Patron of the Avant-Garde*, New York 2006,
    p. 374.
44 Naifeh, S. and G. White Smith, *Vincent van Gogh,
    De Biografie*, Amsterdam 2011, pp. 976–79; Stolwijk,
    C. and R. Thomson, *Theo van Gogh, 1857–1891.
    Kunsthandelaar, verzamelaar en broer van Vincent*,
    Amsterdam/Zwolle 1999, pp. 56–57; Beek, N.A.
    van, *De Aantekeningen van tante Mietje van Gogh*,
    The Hague 2010, p. 94.
45 Naifeh, S. and G. White Smith, *Vincent van Gogh,
    De Biografie*, Amsterdam 2011, p. 981; Stolwijk,
    C. and R. Thomson, *Theo van Gogh, 1857–1891.
    Kunsthandelaar, verzamelaar en broer van Vincent*,
    Amsterdam/Zwolle 1999, p. 189.
46 Beek, N.A. van, *De Aanteekeningen van Tante Mietje
    van Gogh*, The Hague 2010, pp. 95–96.
47 Weenink-Riem Vis, A., *Mijn oma Elisabeth Hubertina
    Van Gogh, (1859–1936)*, De Bilt 2003, pp. 31, 33;
    the marriage certificate of J.P. du Quesne van
    Bruchem and E.H. van Gogh, Leiden, 2 December
    1891: Erfgoed Leiden en Omstreken, marriage
    certificates 1891: acc. 0516, inv. no. 4887, deed 329.
48 Gustave-Albert Aurier, 'Les Isolés: Vincent van
    Gogh', *Le Mercure de France* (January 1890),
    pp. 24–29.
49 Wintgens Hötte, D. and A. de Jongh-
    Vermeulen, *Dageraad van de Moderne Kunst. Leiden
    en omgeving 1890–1940*, Zwolle/Leiden 1999, p. 13.
50 *Ibid.*, pp. 13–14, 19–24, 30–31, 60, 95–99;
    Vogelaar, C., *Floris Verster*, Leiden 2002, pp. 23–28;

Kools, F., *Vincent van Gogh. Als een boer van Zundert*, Zutphen 1990, p. 38.

51 Verster, C.W.H., 'Vincent van Gogh', *Leidsch Dagblad*, 26 April 1893; Wintgens Hötte, D. and A. de Jongh-Vermeulen, *Dageraad van de Moderne Kunst. Leiden en omgeving 1890-1940*, Zwolle/Leiden 1999, pp. 97-99.

52 Wintgens Hötte, D. and A. de Jongh-Vermeulen, *Dageraad van de Moderne Kunst. Leiden en omgeving 1890-1940*, Zwolle/Leiden 1999, pp. 95-97.

53 Emilie Knappert to Jo Bonger, Leiden, 9 February 1904; Wintgens Hötte, D. and A. de Jongh-Vermeulen, *Dageraad van de Moderne Kunst. Leiden en omgeving 1890-1940*, Zwolle/Leiden 1999, p. 116, n. 87.

54 Wintgens Hötte, D. and A. de Jongh-Vermeulen, *Dageraad van de Moderne Kunst. Leiden en omgeving 1890-1940*, Zwolle/Leiden 1999, p. 99.

55 Johan van Gogh, Wassenaar, pers. comm., 10 March 2016.

CHAPTER 14

1 In The Hague Anna van Gogh-Carbentus and Willemien van Gogh both drew up their testaments on 25 September 1894 with the notary Abraham Johannes Terlaak (1850-1918). Both Moe and Wil chose Joan van Houten to be the executor of their wills. Moe left an amount of money to Jo Bonger and to her youngest daughter. The contents of Wil's testament seem to be quite extensive. She left sums to her friends Line Kruysse, Emilie Knappert and Annette de Grauw, as well as to the district nursing project and the Dutch Protestant League's project to construct the 'Faith-Hope-Glory' building at 70 Oranjegracht in Leiden, and didn't leave out her family (Haags Gemeentearchief 0373-01-2816, 394 and 395). On 18 February 1899 Wil would revoke her will and draw up a new, simplified version, leaving the usufruct of her inheritance to her mother, later to be split among her surviving relatives. Again she chose Joan van Houten as the executor of her last will, at a compensation of Fl. 100. (Haags Gemeentearchief, 0373-01-2813-5, 1133).

2 Grever, M. and B. Waaldijk, *Feministische Openbaarheid. De nationale tentoonstelling van Vrouwenarbeid in 1898*, Amsterdam 1998, pp. 41, 288, n. 111.

3 Duyvendak, L., *Het Haags Damesleesmuseum 1894-1994*, The Hague 1994, pp. 31, 33.

4 *Onze Roeping* (Our Calling), the journal of the Algemeene Nederlandsche Vrouwenvereeniging

'Arbeid Adelt' (General Dutch Women's Society 'Labor Nobels'), was published between 1871 and 1873. Relleke, J., *Een bibliografische en analytische beschrijving van drie fikie-bevattende vrouwentijdschriften uit de negentiende eeuw: Onze Roeping (1870-1873), Lelie-en Rozeknoppen (1882-1887) en De Hollandsche Lelie (1887-1890)*, Amsterdam 1982, pp. 53; Jensen, L., '*Bij uitsluiting voor de vrouwelijke sekse geschikt': Vrouwentijdschriften en journalistes in Nederland in de achttiende en negentiende eeuw*, Amsterdam 2001, p. 186; Jensen, L., 'De Nederlandse vrouwenpers in een internationaal perspectief', *Nederlandse Letterkunde* 6 (2001), pp. 231-33.

5 Streng, T., *De roman in de negentiende eeuw*, Hilversum 2020, pp. 65-66, 113-16.

6 Bosch, M., *Een onwrikbaar geloof in rechtvaardigheid: Alletta Jacobs 1854-1929*, Amsterdam 2005.

7 Bel, J., 'Amazone in domineesland: Het hardnekkige streven van Betsy Perk', in Honings, R. and O. Praamstra, *Ellendige Levens*, Hilversum 2013, pp. 207, 210.

8 Grever, M. and B, Waaldijk, *Feministische Openbaarheid. De nationale tentoonstelling van Vrouwenarbeid in 1898*, Amsterdam 1998, pp. 10, 46.

9 Lies van Gogh to Theo van Gogh, Leeuwarden, 11 April 1875; Lies van Gogh to Jo Bonger, Villa Eikenhorst. Soesterberg, 21 October 1885.

10 Steen, A. van, 'De gehuwde vrouw moet maatschappelijk voelen: de tentoonstelling "de vrouw 1813-1913" en het maatschappelijk werk van leidse vrouwen', *Leids Jaarboekje* 1976, pp. 154, 181, n. 47; Eerdmans, B.D., 'In memoriam Dr. H. Oort', *Leids Jaarboekje* 1928, pp. xcii-xcv; Steen, A. van, 'Vol moed en Blakende van Ijver: Alletta Lorenz - Kaiser en de vrouwenbeweging in Leiden (1881-1912)', in *Jaarboek der sociale- en economische geschiedenis van Leiden en Omstreken* (23) 2011, p. 144.

11 Bomhoff-van Rhijn, M.L., 'Leidse jaren van Emilie C. Knappert', *Leids Jaarboekje* 1976, pp. 142-50.

12 Willemien van Gogh to Jo Bonger, Leiden, [undated] 1893.

13 Grever, M. and B. Waaldijk, *Feministische Openbaarheid. De nationale tentoonstelling van Vrouwenarbeid in 1898*, Amsterdam 1998, pp. 58-59.

14 *Ibid.*, p. 254.

15 Bomhoff-van Rhijn, M.L., 'Leidse jaren van Emilie C. Knappert', *Leids Jaarboekje* 1976, pp. 142-50.

16 *Ibid.*, pp. 142-44.

17 Grever, M. and B. Waaldijk, *Feministische Openbaarheid. De nationale tentoonstelling van Vrouwenarbeid in 1898*, Amsterdam 1998, p. 41;

Hofsink, G. and N. Overkamp, *Grafstenen krijgen een gezicht*, Ermelo 2011, p. 59.

18 Grever, M. and B. Waaldijk, *Feministische Openbaarheid. De nationale tentoonstelling van Vrouwenarbeid in 1898*, Amsterdam 1998, pp. 54, 271; Wezel, G. van, *Jan Toorop zang der tijden*, The Hague/Zwolle 2016, p. 126, ill. 214.

19 Grever, M. and B. Waaldijk, *Feministische Openbaarheid. De nationale tentoonstelling van Vrouwenarbeid in 1898*, Amsterdam 1998, pp. 274–75.

20 *Ibid.*, p. 273.

CHAPTER 15

1 Schoeman, C., *The Unknown Van Gogh. The Life of Cornelis van Gogh from the Netherlands to South Africa*, Cape Town 2015, pp. 69, 122–23.

2 *Ibid.*, p. 152.

3 *Ibid.*, p. 155.

4 *Ibid.*, p. 156.

5 Willemien van Gogh to Jo Bonger, The Hague, 22 April 1901.

6 Anna van Gogh-Carbentus to Jo Bonger, The Hague, on or about 25 April 1901.

7 Anna van Gogh-Carbentus to Jo Bonger, The Hague, 19 December 1901.

8 Anna van Gogh-Carbentus and Willemien van Gogh to Jo Bonger, The Hague, 9 May 1902. Willemien would visit Denmark at the beginning of July 1902.

9 Anna van Gogh-Carbentus and Willemien van Gogh to Jo Bonger, Leiden, 25 November 1890. Lies was not able to visit Theo in Utrecht; the same goes for Willemien.

10 Dr. Reering Brouwer, The Hague, 4 December 1902.

11 *Ibid.*; Hofsink, G. and N. Overkamp, *Grafstenen krijgen een gezicht*, Ermelo 2011, p. 140.

12 Dorus van Gogh to Theo van Gogh, Nuenen, 19 July 1884.

13 Willemien van Gogh to Jo Bonger, Breda, 10 February 1889.

14 Hofsink, G. and N. Overkamp, *Grafstenen krijgen een gezicht*, Ermelo 2011, pp. 7–9.

15 *Ibid.*

16 Vincent van Gogh to Theo van Gogh, Cuesmes, between 22 and 24 June 1880; Druick, D.W. and P. Kort Zegers, *Van Gogh en Gauguin. Het atelier van het zuiden*, Zwolle 2002, pp. 21, 356, n. 54; Vincent van Gogh to Theo van Gogh, Etten, 18 November 1881.

17 Hofsink, G. and N. Overkamp, *Grafstenen krijgen een gezicht*, Ermelo 2011, p. 140; Dr Reering

Brouwer, The Hague, 4 December 1902.

18 *Ibid.*

19 Veldwijk report, 1938.

20 *Ibid.*

21 Anna van Houten-van Gogh to Jo Bonger, Leiden, 30 January 1905.

22 Lies van Gogh to Jo Bonger, Baarn, 21 November 1905.

23 Obituary in *Leidsch Dagblad*, 30 April 1907.

24 Lies van Gogh to Jo Bonger, Baarn, 7 May 1907.

25 Lies van Gogh to Jo Bonger, Baarn, 26 June 1907.

26 Lies van Gogh to Jo Bonger, Baarn, 19 May 1908.

27 *Ibid.*

28 Anna van Houten-van Gogh to Jo Bonger, Dieren, 22 November 1909.

29 *Ibid.*

30 *Ibid.*

31 *Ibid.*

32 Anna van Houten-van Gogh to Jo Bonger, Dieren, 25 March 1910.

33 Lies van Gogh to Jo Bonger, Baarn, 4 April 1910.

34 Beek, N.A. van, *De Aanteekeningen van Tante Mietje van Gogh*, The Hague 2010, p. 96.

35 *Ibid.*, p. 98.

36 *Ibid.*, p. 100.

37 *Ibid.*, p. 101.

38 Weenink-Riem Vis, A., *Mijn oma Elisabeth Huberta van Gogh (1859–1936)*, De Bilt 2003, p. 33.

39 *Ibid.*

40 *Ibid.*, pp. 33–34.

41 J.H. de Bois to Lies van Gogh, Haarlem, 13 December 1917.

42 W.M. Mensing to Lies van Gogh, Amsterdam, 19 May 1926.

43 Weenink-Riem Vis, A., *Mijn oma Elisabeth Huberta van Gogh (1859–1936)*, De Bilt 2003, p. 37.

44 *Ibid.*, pp. 37–39.

45 *Ibid.*, p. 34.

46 *Ibid.*, p. 37.

47 Rose Wilhelmine (Mien) du Quesne to Jeannette du Quesne, Baarn, 19 November 1920.

48 Weenink-Riem Vis, A., *Mijn oma Elisabeth Huberta van Gogh (1859–1936)*, De Bilt 2003, p. 38.

49 Lies van Gogh to Jo Bonger, Baarn, 18 July 1910.

50 Lies van Gogh to Jo Bonger, Baarn, 20 May 1909 (Ascension Day).

51 Lies van Gogh to Jo Bonger, Baarn, 4 April 1910.

CHAPTER 16

1 Weenink-Riem Vis, A., *Mijn oma Elisabeth Huberta van Gogh (1859–1936)*, De Bilt 2003, p. 45; Literatuurmuseum The Hague, autobiographical account by Lies van Gogh at request of the

municipal archivist of The Hague, Dr Willem
Moll: G 00504 H1, 1932.

2 Literatuurmuseum The Hague, autobiographical
account by Lies van Gogh at request of the
municipal archivist of The Hague, Dr Willem
Moll: G 00504 H1, 1932.

3 Weenink-Riem Vis, A., *Mijn oma Elisabeth Huberta
van Gogh (1859–1936)*, De Bilt 2003, p. 45.

4 *Ibid.*, p. 47.

5 *Ibid.*

6 Literatuurmuseum The Hague, autobiographical
account by Lies van Gogh at request of the
municipal archivist of The Hague, Dr Willem
Moll: G 00504 H1, 1932.

7 Scharten, C., 'Naschrift bij De Stand onzer
hedendaagsche Dichtkunst', *De Gids*, Amsterdam
1909 (73), pp. 151, 155.

8 Lies van Gogh to Jo Bonger, Baarn, 20 May 1910
(Ascension Day).

9 Lies van Gogh to Rik Wouters, Baarn, 5 March
1915; Min, E., *Rik Wouters, een biografie*,
Amsterdam 1909, pp. 381–82; Hautekeete, S.
and S. Bedet, *Rik Wouters, de menselijke figuur*,
Mechelen 1999, pp. 26–28; Weenink-Riem Vis,
A., *Mijn oma Elisabeth Huberta van Gogh (1859–1936)*,
pp. 35–37.

10 Weenink-Riem Vis, A., *Mijn oma Elisabeth Huberta
van Gogh (1859–1936)*, De Bilt 2003, p. 49.

11 Lies van Gogh in: Literatuurmuseum The Hague,
autobiographical account by Lies van Gogh at
request of the municipal archivist of The Hague,
Dr Willem Moll: G 00504 H1, 1932; Weenink-
Riem Vis, A., *Mijn oma Elisabeth Huberta van Gogh
(1859–1936)*, De Bilt 2003, p. 46.

12 Scharten, C., 'De Stand onzer hedendaagsche
Dichtkunst', *De Gids*, Amsterdam 1909 (73), p. 155.

13 Literatuurmuseum The Hague, autobiographical
account by Lies van Gogh at request of the
municipal archivist of The Hague, Dr Willem
Moll: G 00504 H1, 1932.

14 Weenink-Riem Vis, A., *Mijn oma Elisabeth Huberta
van Gogh (1859–1936)*, De Bilt 2003, p. 54.

15 *Ibid.*, pp. 47, 49; Du Quesne-van Gogh, E.H.,
Personal Recollections of Vincent van Gogh, Boston/
New York 1913 (translated by Katherine S. Dreier;
foreword by Arthur B. Davies).

16 Weenink-Riem Vis, A., *Mijn oma Elisabeth Huberta
van Gogh (1859–1936)*, De Bilt 2003, pp. 47, 49.

17 Du Quesne-van Gogh, E.H., *Vincent van Gogh,
Herinneringen aan haar Broeder*, Baarn 1923.

18 Literatuurmuseum The Hague, autobiographical
account by Lies van Gogh at request of the
municipal archivist of The Hague, Dr Willem

Moll: G 00504 H1, 1932; Weenink-Riem Vis, A.,
Mijn oma Elisabeth Huberta van Gogh (1859–1936),
De Bilt 2003, p. 49.

19 Weenink-Riem Vis, A., *Mijn oma Elisabeth Huberta
van Gogh (1859–1936)*, De Bilt 2003, p. 49.

20 Lies van Gogh to J. Verwiel, Baarn, 26 October
1927.

21 Lies van Gogh in *Algemeen Handelschblad*,
5 May 1934.

22 Weenink-Riem Vis, A., *Mijn oma Elisabeth Huberta
van Gogh (1859–1936)*, De Bilt 2003, p. 49.

23 *Ibid.*, p. 48.

24 *Ibid.*, p. 45; see especially the illustration 'An
Important Book'.

25 *Ibid.*

26 Stokvis, B.J, 'Introduction', in E.H. Du Quesne-
van Gogh, *Vincent van Gogh, Memories of her Brother*,
Baarn 1923, pp. 8–10.

27 *Ibid.*

28 *Ibid.*, pp. 10–11.

29 Weenink-Riem Vis, A., *Mijn oma Elisabeth Huberta
van Gogh (1859–1936)*, De Bilt 2003, p. 50.

30 *Ibid.*, p. 54.

31 *Ibid.*

32 *Ibid.*

33 *Ibid.*, pp. 56–57.

34 *Ibid.*, p. 57.

35 *Ibid.*, p. 41.

36 Rose Wilhelmine (Mien) du Quesne to Jeannette
du Quesne, Amersfoort, 22 December 1930.

37 Weenink-Riem Vis, A., *Mijn oma Elisabeth Huberta
van Gogh (1859–1936)*, De Bilt 2003, p. 55.

38 *Ibid.*

39 *Ibid.*, pp. 55–56.

40 *Ibid.*, p. 55.

41 Nico du Quesne to Lies van Gogh, [unknown
location], 6 October 1931.

42 *Ibid.*

43 Du Quesne-van Gogh, E.H., 'Tentoonstelling
Vincent van Gogh Vondelstraat Amsterdam',
De Telegraaf ('Kunst en Letteren'), 13 September
1924.

44 Weenink-Riem Vis, A., *Mijn oma Elisabeth Huberta
van Gogh (1859–1936)*, De Bilt 2003, p. 43.

45 *Ibid.*

46 *Ibid.*; Ton de Brouwer made a book
commemorating the visit of Lies du Quesne-van
Gogh on the 40th anniversary of the death of her
brother Vincent.

47 Lies van Gogh to Saar de Jong-van Houten and
An Scholte-van Houten, Baarn, 11 June 1933.

48 Weenink-Riem Vis, A., *Mijn oma Elisabeth Huberta
van Gogh (1859–1936)*, De Bilt 2003, p. 56.

49 *Ibid.*
50 *Ibid.*, pp. 57–58.
51 'Ter aardebestelling mevr. Du Quesne-van Gogh', *Baarnsche Courant*, 5 December 1936.

CHAPTER 17
1 Beek, N.A. van, *De Aanteekeningen van Tante Mietje van Gogh*, The Hague 2010, p. 99.
2 Anna van Houten-van Gogh to Jo Bonger, Ginneken (near Breda), 1 August 1890; Beek, N.A. van, *De Aanteekeningen van Tante Mietje van Gogh*, The Hague 2010, p. 99.
3 Anna van Houten-van Gogh to Jo Bonger, Leiden, 15 April 1901.
4 *Ibid.*
5 Anna van Houten-van Gogh to Jo Bonger, Leiden, 4 October 1904.
6 *Ibid.*
7 Anna van Houten-van Gogh to Jo Bonger, Leiden, 3 December 1904.
8 Anna van Houten-van Gogh to Jo Bonger, Leiden, 30 January 1905.
9 Saar de Jong-van Houten to Jo Bonger, Helenaveen, 24 April 1907.
10 *Ibid.*
11 An Scholte-van Houten to Vincent Willem van Gogh, Weidum, 24 March 1926.
12 Calkoen, H.J., 'Notities rondom Vincent van Gogh', *Weekblad van de Nederlandse Protestantenbond*, 1963 (1).
13 Beek, N.A. van, *De Aanteekeningen van Tante Mietje van Gogh*, The Hague 2010, p. 120.
14 Calkoen, H.J., 'Notities rondom Vincent van Gogh', *Weekblad van de Nederlandse Protestantenbond*, 1963 (1).
15 H.J. Calkoen, Jr. lived on the same street as Anna and Joan: the Hoflaan in Dieren (no. 28). Anna and Joan lived at no. 36.
16 Calkoen, H.J., 'Notities rondom Vincent van Gogh', *Weekblad van de Nederlandse Protestantenbond*, 1963 (1).
17 *Ibid.*
18 *Ibid.*
19 *Ibid.*
20 *Ibid.*
21 The obituary of Anna Cornelia van Houten-van Gogh was published in the *Leidsch Dagblad* on Tuesday 23 September 1930.
22 G. Klazes Bijlsma to Vincent Willem van Gogh, Rustoord, 7 August 1941.
23 Weenink-Riem Vis, A., *Mijn oma Elisabeth Huberta van Gogh (1859–1936)*, De Bilt 2003, pp. 31, 38.
24 *Ibid.*, p. 39.

25 Lies van Gogh to Jeannette Kooiman-du Quesne, Baarn, late January 1936.
26 Weenink-Riem Vis, A., *Mijn oma Elisabeth Huberta van Gogh (1859–1936)*, De Bilt 2003, p. 30.
27 *Ibid.*
28 *Ibid.*, p. 39.
29 *Ibid.*, p. 32.
30 *Ibid.*, p. 30; Capit, L.J., 'De eredoctor en het zwarte schaap', *Weekblad Panorama*, Haarlem, 12 March 1966.
31 Capit, L.J., 'De eredoctor en het zwarte schaap', *Weekblad Panorama*, Haarlem, 12 March 1966.
32 Weenink-Riem Vis, A., *Mijn oma Elisabeth Huberta van Gogh (1859–1936)*, De Bilt 2003, p. 32.
33 Gimel, R., *Le Provencal*, Marseille, 10 February 1965.
34 Capit, L.J., 'De eredoctor en het zwarte schaap', *Weekblad Panorama*, Haarlem, 12 March 1966.
35 G. Klazes Bijlsma to Vincent Willem van Gogh, Rustoord, 7 August 1941.

EPILOGUE
1 Pickvance, R., *'A Great Artist is Dead'*, Zwolle/ Amsterdam 1992, pp. 132–33
2 Anna and Joan van Houten-van Gogh, Lies van Gogh and Willemien van Gogh to Theo van Gogh, in an undated letter, probably from Leiden in August 1890, in the hand of Joan van Houten.
3 Calkoen, H.J., *Vacantie-schetsboek van een schilder*, Delft 1963, p. 131.
4 Linde-Bijns, R. van der and O. Maurer, *Jakob Nieweg: in stille bewondering*, Amersfoort 2001, p. 14.
5 'Lieve Lize...Ik heet Jo' ('Dear Lies...my name is Jo'). Jo Bonger in her first letter to Lies van Gogh, Elburg, 13 October 1885.
6 Margaretha Meijboom to Willemien van Gogh, Assen, 27 September 1887.
7 Margaretha Meijboom to Willemien van Gogh, Assen, 14 November 1887.
8 Vincent van Gogh to Willemien van Gogh, Saint-Rémy-de-Provence, 21 October 1889.
9 Rose Wilhelmine (Mien) du Quesne to Jeannette du Quesne, 21 February 1917; Weenink-Riem Vis, A., *Mijn Oma Elisabeth Hubertina van Gogh 1859–1936*, De Bilt 2003, p. 37.
10 Weenink-Riem Vis, A., *Mijn oma Elisabeth Huberta van Gogh (1859–1936)*, De Bilt 2003, p. 56.
11 An Scholte-van Houten to Vincent Willem van Gogh, Schoondijke, 24 March 1926.
12 His eldest son, Theodoor, was executed by the German authorities on 8 March 1945 for his activities as a resistance fighter.

FURTHER READING

In researching the lives of the Van Gogh sisters, I have read as much literature as I could find about Vincent and the Van Gogh family – from large standard works to small self-published booklets – as well as about the wider cultural world in which they lived. A history of 19th-century literature, listing the most important authors and their themes and work, can be found at www.literaryhistory.com/19thC/Outline.htm; the same specifically for Dutch authors (and in Dutch) can be found at https://www.literatuurgeschiedenis.nl/19de/literatuurgeschiedenis/index.html. The Digital Library for Dutch Literature (www.dbnl.nl) is another useful source of 19th-century Dutch literature in particular, though its impressive collection represents all periods of Dutch language, literature and cultural history.

Besides the letters (for which see p. 242), the literature and my conversations with Van Gogh descendants, I have also visited almost all the towns and villages mentioned in the book, where the houses, churches and schools known to the sisters are often still standing. I received a lot of help from the friendly staff of local libraries, museums and archives. In such places I discovered dozens of files and clippings, photographs, drawings, baptism and marriage records, school records, tax statements and much more.

A list of the most relevant and accessible sources for English-speaking readers follows. The complete list of sources that I consulted in the writing of this book can be found on my own website, www.thevangoghsisters.com.

Aurier, G.-A., '"Les Isoles": Vincent van Gogh', *Le Mercure de France*, January 1890.

Bailey, M., *The Sunflowers Are Mine: The Story of Van Gogh's Masterpiece*, London 2013.

Bailey, M. and D. Silverman, *Van Gogh in England: Portrait of the Artist as a Young Man*, London 1992.

Beek, N.A. van, *De Aanteekingen van Tante Mietje van Gogh*, The Hague 2010.

Beek, N.A. van, *Het geslacht Carbentus*, The Hague 2011.

Beers, J. van, *Levensbeelden: Poezij...*, Amsterdam/Antwerp 1858.

Bell, J., *Van Gogh: A Power Seething*, Boston 2015.

Boekholt, P.Th.F.M. and E.P. de Booy, *Geschiedenis van de school in Nederland vanaf de middeleeuwen tot aan de huidige tijd*, Assen/Maastricht 1987.

Bomhoff-van Rhijn, M.L., 'Leidse jaren van Emilie C. Knappert', *Leids Jaarboekje* 1976 (68), pp. 142–50.

Bosch, M., *Een onwrikbaar geloof in rechtvaardigheid: Aletta Jacobs 1854–1929*, Amsterdam 2005.

Bruin, G., 'Van Gogh en de schetsboekjes voor Betsy Tersteeg', PhD thesis, University of Leiden 2014.

Calkoen, H.J., 'Notities rondom Van Gogh', *Weekblad van de Nederlandse Protestantenbond* 1963.

Calkoen, H.J., *Vacantie-Schetsboek van een Schilder*, Delft 1963.

Capit, L.J., 'De eredoctor en het zwarte schaap', *Weekblad Panorama*, 12 March 1966, pp. 17–19.

Crimpen, H. van *et al.*, *Brief Happiness: The Correspondence of Theo van Gogh and Jo Bonger*, Amsterdam/Zwolle 1999.

Denekamp, N., R. van Blerk, T. Meedendorp and L. Watkinson, *The Vincent van Gogh Atlas*, Amsterdam 2015.

Dirven, R. and K. Wouters, *Vincent van Gogh: het mysterie van de Bredase kisten. Verloren vondsten*, Breda 2003.

Du Quesne-van Gogh, E.H., *Bretonsche volksliederen: bloemlezing uit den bundel Barzaz Breiz*, Baarn 1906.

Du Quesne-van Gogh, E.H., *Gedichten*, Amersfoort 1908.

Du Quesne-van Gogh, E.H. *Latelingen*, Baarn 1928.

Du Quesne-van Gogh, E.H., *Proza*, Baarn 1929.

Du Quesne-van Gogh, E.H., *Tijlozen*, Bussum 1932.

Du Quesne-van Gogh, E.H., *Vincent van Gogh: Persoonlijk herinneringen aangaande een kunstenaar*, Baarn 1910 (new edition translated by K.S. Dreier, *Personal Reflections of Vincent van Gogh*, New York 2017).

Du Quesne-van Gogh, E.H., *Vincent van Gogh. Herinneringen aan haar Broeder*, Baarn 1923.

Du Quesne-van Gogh, E.H., *Volkslied en volksdicht: volksliederen uit verschillende landen met begeleidend proza*, Baarn 1908.

Duyvendak, L., *Het Haags Damesleesmuseum: 1894–1994*, The Hague 1994.

Druick, D.W. and P. Zegers, *Van Gogh en Gauguin. Het atelier van het zuiden*, Zwolle 2002.

Gogh, W.-J. van, 'Boeketten Maken', *De Hollandsche Lelie*, 14 September 1887, 1.

Gogh-Bonger, J. van, *Brieven aan zijn broeder*, Amsterdam 1924; published in English as *The Letters of Vincent van Gogh to his Brother*, London 1927.

Grever, M. and B. Waaldijk, *Feministische Openbaarheid: De Nationale Tentoonstelling van Vrouwenarbeid in 1898*, Amsterdam 1998.

Groenhart, K. and W.-J. Verlinden, *Hoe ik van Londen houd. Wandelen door het Londen van Vincent van Gogh*, Amsterdam 2013.

Hamoen, G. and J. van Dijk, *Maatschappij van welstand: 175 jaar steun aan kleine protestantse gemeenten*, Amersfoort 1997.

Hautekeete, S. and S. Bedet, *Rik Wouters: De menselijke figuur*, Gent 1999.

Heugten, S. van and F. Pabst, *'A Great Artist is Dead', Letters of Condolence on Vincent van Gogh's Death*, Zwolle 1992.

Heugten, S. van et al. *Vincent van Gogh: The Drawings*, 2 vols, Amsterdam 1996 and 1997.

Hoffman, W., 'De tantes: wederwaardigheden van een paar "van Goghjes"', *Noord-Brabant: tweemaandelijks magazine voor de provincie*, March/April 1987, pp. 61–64.

Hofsink, G. and N. Overkamp, *Grafstenen krijgen een gezicht: Stichting begraafplaatsen Ermelo-Veldwijk*, Ermelo 2011.

Homburg, C. et al., *Vincent van Gogh and the Painters of the Petit Boulevard*, New York/Frankfurt 2001.

Honings, R. and O. Praamstra, *Ellendige Levens*, Hilversum 2013.

Hulsker, J., *The Complete Van Gogh: Paintings, Drawings, Sketches*, New York 1984.

Jacobi, C. (ed.), *The EY Exhibition Van Gogh and Britain*, London 2019.

Janssen, H. and W. van Sinderen, *De Haagse School*, Zwolle 1997.

Koldehoff, S. and C. Stolwijk, *The Thannhauser Gallery: Marketing Van Gogh*, Brussels/Amsterdam 2017.

Kools, F., *Vincent van Gogh en zijn geboorteplaats. Als een boer van Zundert*, Zutphen 1990.

Kramer, W. 'De Hervormde Kerk te Helvoirt', *Bulletin van de Koninklijke Nederlandse Oudheidkundige Bond*, February 1976, pp. 19–34.

Kröger, J. (ed.), *Meijer de Haan: A Master Revealed*, Paris 2009.

Luijten, J. *Everything for Vincent: The life of Jo van Gogh-Bonger*, Amsterdam 2019.

Luijten, J., L. Jansen and N. Bakker, *Vincent van Gogh – The Letters: The Complete Illustrated and Annotated Edition*, 6 vols, London/Amsterdam 2009.

Lunsingh Scheurleer, Th.H., C. Willemijn Fock and A.J. van Dissel, *Het Rapenburg: Geschiedenis van een Leidse gracht*, vol. 4a, Leiden 1989.

Naifeh, S. and G. White Smith, *Vincent van Gogh, De biografie*, Amsterdam 2011; published in English as *Van Gogh: The Life*, New York 2011.

Nelemans, R. and R. Dirven, *De Zaaier: Het begin van een carrière – Vincent van Gogh in Etten*, Breda 2010.

Nelemans, R., *Van Gogh & Brabant*, Schiedam 2012.

Noo, H. de and W. Slingerland, *Helvoirt. De Protestantse Gemeente en de Oude Sint Nikolaaskerk*, Helvoirt-Haaren 2007.

Oosterwijk, B., 'Vincent van Gogh en Rotterdam', *Rotterdams Jaarboekje*, 1994 (2), pp. 329–89.

Overbruggen, P. van and J. Thielemans, *Van domineeshuis tot Van Goghhuis 1764–2014. 250 jaar pastorie Nuenen en haar bewoners*, Nuenen 2014.

Poppel, F. van, *Trouwen in Nederland. Een historisch-demografische studie van de 19e en vroeg 20e eeuw*, Wageningen 1992.

Rabinov, R.A. (ed.), *Cézanne to Picasso: Ambroise Vollard, Patron of the Avant-Garde*, New York 2006.

Rewald, J., 'Theo van Gogh, Goupil, and the impressionists', *Gazette des Beaux-Arts*, January/February 1973.

Rozemeyer, J.A. (ed.), *Van Gogh in Etten*, Etten-Leur 1990.

Scharten, C., 'Naschrift bij "De Stand onzer hedendaagsche Dichtkunst"', *De Gids*, 1909 (73).

Schoeman, C., *The Unknown Van Gogh: The Life of Cornelis van Gogh, from the Netherlands to South Africa*, Cape Town 2015.

Smulders, H., 'Van Gogh in Helvoirt', *De kleine Meijerij* (1990: 1).

Smulders, H. et al., *Helvertse schetsen: geïllustreerde beschrijvingen van historische en monumentale gebouwen*, Helvoirt 1985.

Stokvis, B.J., *Lijden zonder klagen. Het tragische levenslot van Hubertina van Gogh*, Baarn 1969.

Stolwijk, C. and R. Thomson, *Theo van Gogh 1857–1891*, Zwolle 1999.

Stolwijk, C. and H. Veenenbos, *The Account Book of Theo van Gogh and Jo van Gogh-Bonger*, Amsterdam 2002.

Stolwijk, C. et al., *Van Gogh: All works in the Kröller-Müller Museum*, Otterlo 2020.

Streng, T., *De roman in de negentiende eeuw*, Hilversum 2020.

Suh, A. (ed.), *Vincent van Gogh: A Self-Portrait in Art and Letters*, London 2011.

Thomson, B., *Gauguin*, London 1997.

Tilborgh, L. van, 'Letter from Willemien van Gogh', *Van Gogh Bulletin*, (1992–93: 3), p. 21.

Tilborgh, L., 'Vincent van Gogh or Willemina Vincent?' in G.P. Weisberg et al., *Van Gogh: New Findings, Van Gogh Studies, #4*, pp. 125–32.

Tilborgh, L. van and F. Pabst, 'Notes on a donation: the poetry albums for Elisabeth Huberta van Gogh', *Van Gogh Museum Journal*, 1995.

Toorians, L., 'Op zoek naar Lies van Gogh. Bretonse volksliederen in het Nederlands.' *Brabant Cultureel*, 4 April 1997, p. 19.

Uitert, E. van (ed.), *Van Gogh in Brabant. Schilderijen en tekeningen uit Etten en Nuenen*, Zwolle 1987.

Vogelaar, C., *Floris Verster*, Leiden 2003.

Vroom, U., *Stoomwasserij en kalkbranderij*, Bussum 1983.

Weenink-Riem Vis, A., *Mijn oma, Elisabeth Huberta van Gogh (1859–1936)*, De Bilt 2003.

Wezel, G. van, *Jan Toorop: Zang der tijden*, The Hague 2016.

Wintgens Hötte, D. and A. De Jongh-Vermeulen (eds), *Dageraad van de Moderne Kunst, Leiden en omgeving 1890–1940*, Zwolle 1998.

Zemel, C., *Van Gogh's Progress. Utopia, Modernity, and Late Nineteenth-Century Art*, Berkeley 1997.

ACKNOWLEDGMENTS

You don't write a book like *The Van Gogh Sisters* by yourself. The help and support I have had in researching and writing this book makes me want to put a number of people and institutions in the spotlight and thank them here, realizing I am not exhaustive in doing so.

First of all, my thanks go to the employees of Dutch publishing house Querido and Ambo|Anthos Publishers before them. But above all I would like to express my gratitude to the staff of Thames & Hudson in London: Roger Thorp, Jen Moore, Mohara Gill, Anabel Navarro, Karolina Prymaka and Poppy David. What a great team to work with! In addition, I would like to thank the management and employees of Sebes & Bisseling Literary Agency in Amsterdam, especially Willem Bisseling, who helped me with the editing. This certainly also applies to Sophie Verburgh. Finally, my thanks are due to Liz van Hoose for her editorial comment on an early draft of the manuscript.

I would also like to thank all those employees of archives, museums and institutes who always answered my questions and requests with great benevolence, and opened their collections for my research. I am thinking in particular of the Van Gogh Museum in Amsterdam, in the characters of Isolde Cael, Zbigniew Dowgwillo, Hans Luijten, Albertien Lykles-Livius and Anita Vriend, but above all Anita Homan, whose pace and efficiency are remarkable. But also requiring mention are: Archives Eemland, Amersfoort; Atria, Knowledge Institute for Women's History and Emancipation, Amsterdam; Brabant Collection, Tilburg University, Emy Thorissen; Brabant Historical Information Center, 's-Hertogenbosch, Annemarie van Geloven, Mariët Brugman; Breda City Archives; Damesleesmuseum, The Hague; City Archives Municipality of 's-Hertogenbosch; Dordrecht City Archives; Heritage Center Leiden and Environs; Koninklijke Bibliotheek, The Hague; Kröller-Müller Museum, Otterlo; Leeuwarden Regional Historic Center, Klaas Zandberg, Nykle Dijkstra; Literature Museum, The Hague; Municipal Archives, The Hague; Municipal Museum de Lakenhal, Leiden, Nicole Roepers; Noordbrabants Museum, 's-Hertogenbosch, Helewise Berger; Parkzicht Museum and library at Veldwijk, Ermelo; Regional Historic Center Eindhoven; Vincent van Gogh Foundation, Etten-Leur, Cor Kerstens; Vincent van GoghHuis, Zundert, Ron Dirven; Vincentre Nuenen, Simone van der Heiden and Peter van Overbruggen; and West-Brabant Regional Archives. I am also grateful to Wout Jan Balhuizen, who photographed a number of the documents that I unearthed.

There is of course also a personal side to writing a book. This applies to my own friends and family, but also to the Van Gogh family, especially to Johan van Gogh, who sadly passed away in 2019. He very kindly received me, listened to my findings and spoke from his own, vivid memory. I also thank Willem van Gogh.

The personal aspect of my research became clear to me at an early stage, when I was in contact with Nico van Beek. He had written two books about his family and sent me a copy of Aunt Mietje van Gogh's *Notes*, which were of great value in the course of the investigation. I am deeply indebted to the descendants of the Van Gogh sisters for the trust they have had in me and my book, and grateful for the pleasant form of contact I have enjoyed with so many of you. I sincerely hope that the book will also offer family members new insights into the history of their ancestors. From the hundreds of letters I have been privileged to read, I have of course tried to select the most important, most beautiful or most moving fragments and, in most instances, I quote them verbatim. I have on occasion paraphrased or summarized minor fragments, especially where the letters lack punctuation, use abbreviations known only to their family circle, or where the poor legibility of the handwriting means interpretation is necessary. I also had to omit many letters, or parts of them, that were outwith the scope of this book; nonetheless, I hope that through the quotes I have selected, I have been able to make the sisters' voices audible.

I would like to honour in particular two special people here. The first is a Helvoirt citizen from a more distant past. His name was Harrie Smulders (1916–1995), a regional historian whose work forms the basis of the chapter on Helvoirt. As a boy I used to sit at the dinner table at his house discussing Helvoirt's history, of which reverend Van Gogh and his family were an important part. My interest in this extraordinary family was aroused there, at that table, and it led me to the second person, Kristine Groenhart, who in 2012 approached me to co-author *How I Love London: Walking through Vincent van Gogh's London*. I am so grateful for that to her, and the book you are holding in your hands right now is a direct result of our partnership on that project.

All of this would have been written with less ease if my parents, Jan Hein Verlinden and Willemijn Verlinden-van Dijk, had not given my brother Floris and me such a wonderful childhood on the Molenstraat in that very same Helvoirt. My thanks for this can hardly be expressed in a paragraph on a page. I would also like to thank my godparents, Maartje van Wijmen and Vic van Dijk, for fostering the same feeling of continuity and kinship.

My beginning, however, comes at the very end. The inexhaustible support in my life and work, for over seventeen years now, is my husband and my most critical co-reader, Paul Sebes. Thank you for always being there for me.

SOURCES OF ILLUSTRATIONS

a = above; b = below; l = left; r = right

2 Private collection, Canada; 8 Private collection; 9 Van Gogh Museum, Amsterdam (Vincent van Gogh Foundation); 11l Collection Kröller-Müller Museum, Otterlo, The Netherlands. Photo The Picture Art Collection/Alamy Stock Photo; 11r, 16, 18 Van Gogh Museum, Amsterdam (Vincent van Gogh Foundation); 19 Private collection; 20 Van Gogh Museum, Amsterdam (Vincent van Gogh Foundation); 23 Van Gogh Museum, Amsterdam; 24 Collection Haags Gemeentearchief, The Hague; 30 Van Gogh Museum, Amsterdam; 31 Van Gogh Museum (Tralbaut archive); 34 Private collection; 37 Vincent van GoghHuis, Zundert; 38 Private collection; 40 Van Gogh Museum, Amsterdam (Vincent van Gogh Foundation); 41, 42 Private collection; 43 Van Gogh Museum, Amsterdam (Vincent van Gogh Foundation); 44 Brabants Historisch Informatiecentrum, 's-Hertogenbosch; 46 Private collection; 48 Van Gogh Museum, Amsterdam (Vincent van Gogh Foundation); 49 Collection Historisch Centrum Leeuwarden; 50 Private collection; 53, 55 Van Gogh Museum, Amsterdam (Vincent van Gogh Foundation); 59 Van Gogh Museum, Amsterdam, gift of H. Nieweg; 60 Private collection; 61 Heritage Image Partnership Ltd/Alamy Stock Photo; 63 Look and Learn/Bridgeman Images; 65 Courtesy of Welwyn & District History Society, UK; 71, 78, 79 Van Gogh Museum, Amsterdam (Vincent van Gogh Foundation); 81 Private collection; 83, 84, 85 Van Gogh Museum, Amsterdam (Vincent van Gogh Foundation); 93 Private collection; 94a Norton Simon Museum, Pasadena, USA; 94b Private collection; 98, 100 Van Gogh Museum, Amsterdam (Vincent van Gogh Foundation); 101 Private collection; 108 Collection Regionaal Historisch Centrum Eindhoven, RHCe; 114 National Portrait Gallery, London; 115 Van Gogh Museum, Amsterdam (Vincent van Gogh Foundation); 121 National Portrait Gallery, London; 122 Foto collection Historical College FNI, Culemborg; 125, 126, 127 Van Gogh Museum, Amsterdam (Vincent van Gogh Foundation); 128, 130 Private collection; 132 The Digital Library for Dutch Literature (DBNL); 133 From the booklet *In memory of Margaretha Meyboom*, published by her friends, 1928; 139 Van Gogh Museum, Amsterdam (Vincent van Gogh Foundation); 141 Private collection; 143 Bridgeman Images; 148 Private collection; 152, 153 Van Gogh Museum, Amsterdam (Vincent van Gogh Foundation); 161 The Pushkin State Museum of Fine Arts, Moscow; 173 Van Gogh Museum, Amsterdam (Vincent van Gogh Foundation); 175 Private collection; 176 Erfgoed Leiden en Omstreken; 178, 181, 183, 185, 187 Collection IAV-Atria, Amsterdam; 191 Van Gogh Museum Amsterdam (Vincent van Gogh Foundation); 195 Erfgoed Gelderland, the Netherlands; 196 Van Gogh Museum, Amsterdam (Vincent van Gogh Foundation); 198, 199, 200, 201, 202 Private collection; 205 Collectie Stad Antwerpen, Letterenhuis; 211 Van Gogh Museum, Amsterdam (gift of Engelbert L'Hoëst); 213, 214, 216, 217, 218, 219, 220, 221 Private collection; 222 Van Gogh Museum, Amsterdam (Vincent van Gogh Foundation); 223, 224, 225, 226, 228, 229, 230, 237, 238, 239a, 239bl Private collection; 239br Van Gogh Museum, Amsterdam (Vincent van Gogh Foundation); I Van Gogh Museum, Amsterdam (Vincent van Gogh Foundation); II Bibliothèque National de France, Paris; III, IV, V Van Gogh Museum, Amsterdam (Vincent van Gogh Foundation); VI The State Hermitage Museum, Saint Petersburg; VII, VIII Van Gogh Museum, Amsterdam (Vincent van Gogh Foundation); IX Het Noordbrabants Museum, 's-Hertogenbosch, acquired with the support of the Province of Noord-Brabant, Mondriaan Fonds, Vereniging Rembrandt (thanks in part to the Alida Fonds and the Jheronimus Fonds), and the bequest of H.M.J. van Oppenraaij. Photo Peter Cox; X, XI Van Gogh Museum, Amsterdam (Vincent van Gogh Foundation); XII Collection Mr and Mrs Frank, Gstaad, Switzerland; XIII Van Gogh Museum, Amsterdam (Vincent van Gogh Foundation); XIV Christie's Images/Bridgeman Images; XV Yale University Art Gallery, New Haven, CT; XVI Metropolitan Museum of Art New York, The Walter H. and Leonore Annenberg Collection, Gift of Walter H. and Leonore Annenberg, 1995, Bequest of Walter H. Annenberg, 2002; XVII Bridgeman Images; XVIII, XIX, XX Van Gogh Museum, Amsterdam (Vincent van Gogh Foundation); XXI Collection IAV-Atria, Amsterdam

INDEX

This publication has been made possible with financial support
from the Dutch Foundation for Literature.

First published in the United Kingdom in 2021 by
Thames & Hudson Ltd, 181A High Holborn, London wc1v 7qx

First published in the United States of America in 2021 by
Thames & Hudson Inc., 500 Fifth Avenue, New York, New York 10110

The Van Gogh Sisters © 2021 Thames & Hudson Ltd, London
Text © 2021 Willem-Jan Verlinden

Designed by Karolina Prymaka
Translated by Yvette Rosenberg and Brendan Monaghan

British Library Cataloguing-in-Publication Data
A catalogue record for this book is available from the British Library

Library of Congress Control Number 2020932677

ISBN   978-0-500-02360-0

Printed in China by Reliance Printing (Shenzhen) Co. Ltd

Be the first to know about our new releases,
exclusive content and author events by visiting
thamesandhudson.com
thamesandhudsonusa.com
thamesandhudson.com.au

N ederlands
 letterenfonds
dutch foundation
for literature